Adam Gopnik

The Table Comes First

Author of the beloved bestseller *Paris to the Moon,* Adam
Gopnik has been writing for *The New Yorker* since 1986.
He is a three-time winner of the National Magazine
Award for Essays and for Reviews and Criticism and of
the George Polk Award for Magazine Reporting. He lives
in New York City with his wife and their two children.

"Compelling. . . . Gopnik gets elbow deep in heady theory, culinary history, and his own passions. . . . He is a champion at making connections, wild and free-ranging. Among the allusions are revelations."
—*The Boston Globe*

"The perfect book for any intellectual foodie, a delicious book packed with so much to sink your teeth into." —Padma Lakshmi

"Entertaining. . . . Gopnik's long experience with France and fine dining yields some fine observations. . . . [Reading *The Table Comes First*,] you feel as if you're sitting across the table from an amusing friend recounting his adventures."
—*Minneapolis Star Tribune*

"Gopnik's discussions on the changing nature of tastes and how it defines what we believe to be 'good' and 'right' in food are a timely study on the divergent yet complementary trends in modern cooking." —*Pittsburgh Post-Gazette*

"Gopnik's writing about food is highly intellectual and profoundly witty, while also being warm and personal and rooted in common sense. He thinks hard about the routines of the table, and makes you think too." —John Lanchester, author of *The Debt to Pleasure*

"Those who share Gopnik's twin affections for food and reading will find plenty to savor in *The Table Comes First*. . . . He's an essayist in the grand tradition, throwing out pithy sentences that offer the reader plenty to argue about, and then blithely contradicting himself on the next page. It's easy to imagine how pleasant a table companion he must be."
—*The Columbus Dispatch*

The Table Comes First

FAMILY, FRANCE, AND THE MEANING OF FOOD

Adam Gopnik

VINTAGE BOOKS

A Division of Random House, Inc.

New York

FIRST VINTAGE BOOKS EDITION, AUGUST 2012

Portions of this work were previously published in
different form in *The New Yorker*.

The Library of Congress has cataloged the Knopf edition as follows:
Gopnik, Adam
The table comes first : family, France, and the meaning of food / Adam Gopnik.—
1st ed.
p. cm.
1. Food—Social aspects. 2. Dinners and dining. 3. Food habits—France. I. Title.
GT2850.G67 2011
394.1'20944—dc23
2011013564

Vintage ISBN: 978-0-307-47696-8

Book design by Maggie Hinders

www.vintagebooks.com

Printed in the United States of America
10   9   8   7   6

For Martha, Luke, and Olivia,

who set and share the nightly table . . .

and for Calvin Trillin, who set the standard

A cook a pure artist
Who moves everyman
At a deeper level than
Mozart, for the subject of the verb
To-hunger is never a name:
Dear Adam and Eve had different bottoms,
But the neotene who marches
Upright and can subtract reveals a belly
Like the serpent's with the same
Vulnerable look. Jew, Gentile or pigmy,
He must get his calories
Before he can consider her profile or
His own, attack you or play chess,
And take what there is however hard to get down:
Then surely those in whose creed
God is edible may call a fine
Omelette a Christian deed.

The sin of Gluttony
Is ranked among the Deadly
Seven, but in murder mysteries
One can be sure the gourmet
Didn't do it: children, brave warriors out of a job,
Can weigh pounds more than they should
And one can dislike having to kiss them yet,
Compared with the thin-lipped, they
Are seldom detestable. Some waiter grieves
For the worst dead bore to be a good
Trencherman, and no wonder chefs mature into
Choleric types, doomed to observe
Beauty peck at a master-dish, their one reward
To behold the mutually hostile
Mouth and eyes of a sinner married
At the first bite by a smile.

—W. H. AUDEN, "On Installing an American Kitchen in Lower Austria"

Contents

The Table Comes First

A Small Starter: Questions of Food

We have happy days, remember good dinners.
—CHARLES DARWIN

We eat to live? Yes, surely. But why then did the immortal
gods also come to the table, and twice a day?
—LÉON ABRIC

IN THE early morning—six-forty, precisely—of May 24, 1942,
a young professor of German, a resistant who had taken the
underground name of Jacques Decour (his real name was Daniel
Decourdemanche) and who taught before the war at the Lycée
Henri IV in Paris, wrote a letter to his parents:

> You know that for the past two months I have been expecting
> what is to happen to me this morning; so I have had the time to
> prepare myself for it; but since I have no religion, I have not given
> myself up to any meditation on death. Here are a few requests. I
> was able to send a word to the woman I love. If you see her—soon
> I hope—give her your affection. This is my dearest wish. I also
> wish that you could keep an eye on her parents who need help
> badly. Give them the things that are in my apartment and which
> belong to their daughter: The volume of the PLEIADE, THE FABLES
> DE LA FONTAINE, TRISTAN, LES QUATRE SAISONS, two water colors,
> the menu of the inn LES 4 PAVES DU ROY.
>
> All these last days I have thought a lot about the good meals
> that we should have together when I was free. You will eat them

without me, all the family together—but not sadly, please! I don't want your thoughts to dwell on the good times that we might have had but on those that we really have shared. During these two months of solitude without even anything to read I have run over in my mind all my travels, all my experiences, all the meals that I have eaten. I even composed the outline of the novel. I had an excellent meal with Sylvain on the 17th. I have often thought of it with pleasure, as well as of the New Year's supper with Pierre and Renée. Questions of food, you see, have taken on a great importance.

Three hours later, what was going to happen to Decour happened to him. He was shot by the Nazis in the courtyard of the prison. Yet there he was, in the last hours of his life, thinking about sending a menu from a little inn near Versailles to his girl-friend's parents. (They must have eaten there, once.) His last thoughts turned to his best-loved meals. Of course, he's nobly trying to ease the horror for his parents, but he's also trying to find something to hang on to. *Questions of food, you see, have taken on a great importance.*

Questions of food seem to have taken on a great importance for us now, too. An obsessive interest in food is not a rich man's indulgence, confined to catering schools and the marginal world of recipe books. Questions of food have become the proper pre-occupation of whole classes and cable networks. More people talk about food now—why they eat what they eat and what you ought to eat, too—than have ever done before. Our food has become our medicine, our source of macho adventure, and sometimes, it almost seems, our messianic material. Good food, or watching it get made, anyway, has become, in the age of Rachael Ray and Food Network, a popular sport, and even the many who still pre-fer fast food to fancy or fresh get to prefer it loudly.

But if our own obsession (and the obesity it fathers) keeps increasing, its spirit seems at odds with that of Jacques Decour's last thoughts. Not just the gravity, but the pathos of the feeling he evokes, and its humanity, seem very far from the questions we ask about food. We do feel a kinship to him beyond our pity at his end and our wonder at his courage. A kinship because his sense of food—of the rituals of the table, the memories of eating, even as the noise of our cross-talk and cable clatter increases—still shares in our own sense of what makes us human and what forms the core of our memories. For us, as for Jacques Decour, what makes a day into a happy day is often the presence of a good dinner. Though we don't always acknowledge it enough, we still live the truth Darwin saw: food is the sensual pleasure that passes most readily into a social value.

Yet our questions of food are very different from Decour's. We tend to argue about matters of taste, about the health of the planet, about the rights and wrongs of vegetarianism—all questions, finally, about *what* to eat. And we ask these questions expecting material answers: the *right* way to cook or eat. Decour's questions are posed in a different key, one we can only call humanist: a view that life is a whole—that we can live fully, and that we ought to, with our pleasures as much as with our principles. He is talking about what goes on around the table as much as what's on it. We can't help feeling amazed at the sense of his letter but also a kind of unease, even a certain guilt, in his presence. Our questions of food, even the most high-minded, seem so small compared with his.

Why *do* we care so much about our food? There's a sociological explanation (it's a signal of status), a psychological explanation (it takes the place of sex), and a puritanical explanation (it's the simplest sign of virtue). But all these, while worth pursuing, seem to be at one side of Decour's questions. Thinking about questions of food an hour before his execution, Decour wasn't thinking virtuous thoughts about his health, or even the planet's health. Thinking about meals he was thinking about something else, about that inn near Versailles, about Sylvain and Pierre and

Renée and about the parents who had raised and were now to lose him. Food represented for him the continuity of living, and what gave form to life.

Having made food a more fashionable object, we have ended by making eating a smaller subject. When "gastronomy" was on the margins of attention it seemed big because it was an unexpected way to get at *everything*—the nature of hunger; the meaning of appetite; the patterns and traces of desire; tradition, in the way that recipes are passed mother to son; and history, in the way that spices mix and, in mixing, mix peoples. You could envision through the modest lens of pleasure, as through a keyhole, a whole world; and the compression and odd shape of the keyhole made the picture more dramatic. Now the door is wide open, but somehow we see less, or notice less, anyway. Betrayed by its enlargement, food becomes less intimate the more intensely it is made to matter.

I love to eat. I love to eat simple food and I love to eat fancy food. I love to eat out and I love to eat at home. I love the Grand Véfour in Paris, where the banquettes are made of velvet and the food is filled with truffles, and I love the coffee shop down the street, where the eggs all come with greasy potatoes. I've loved to eat since I was little, when my mother, a terrific cook, would make all the dishes, large and small, near and far. I learned early on the simple path between eating well and feeling happy. And, as all eaters do, I also early on learned the short, sudden path between desire and disappointment: my first strong taste memory is of taking a deep bitter swig of vanilla extract in a dark closet into which I had sneaked the bottle, sure that something that smelled that good had to taste good, too. (It doesn't.) If all my pleasures are gathered around the table, all my disillusions taste bitter, like that vanilla.

Getting older, with children of my own, I was trained enough to cook for them—my wife's feminist mother had purposefully neglected her daughter's kitchen tuition. And, over the years, I wrote a lot about cooking and eating, as a writer is bound to dwell on the things he loves. But though I had written happily about what food tasted like and what it looked like and also about the odd personalities of the people who made the best food, I was left, decades on, wondering: what did it really mean? Why did we care? What was, so to speak, the *subject* of food? The attempts to make food "art" I found embarrassing, and the attempts to make it adventure I found absurd. I recognized sexual politics in that effort, the result of traditionally women's work now being done by men, including me. Men being men, they had to assert themselves by trying not to seem too obviously feminine, pretending that cooking was really just as macho as NASCAR, and so producing the taste for rattlesnake testicle ragout. And with the coming of Mr. Perfect, something more insidious happened: the sheer brunt and dailiness of women's real lives—the everyday dance women still must do for family life to go on—was subtly undermined by the cooking husband, or host. (Putting on an apron and making a sauce is the easiest of household chores, and a neat way to escape doing the others.)

In place of Decour's Big Questions, we had many small ones. Should we eat locally? Stop eating meat altogether, and if so, should we do it out of humanity or for our health? All questions worth answering—and yet, weren't they still to one side of what we really felt when we came home to share dinner and felt happy when we did? Certainly within the new rites there *were* intimations of a new order, and of a new table, of a larger meaning to our questions of food. I could see, for instance, that in the past twenty-five years, two big things had happened in the world of fancy food. One was the growth of the pure-food movement, best captured in the name "slow food," and which encompasses localism, seasonal cooking, farmers' markets, organic produce—a whole host of interlocked activities and styles that spoke to the old, the past, the lost, the sustainable, the recoverable, heritage breeds, and forgotten peasant wisdoms. The other was the growth of "techno-emotional" cooking, as its founder, or anyway its first pope, Ferran Adrià, likes to call it, more often referred to as "molecular gastronomy." Adrià and his apostles use gels and foams and aerations and freeze-dried powders, outré rearrangements and deconstructed plates: the gleeful appliqué of new technology to cooking. This doubleness suggested a kind of ongoing confrontation between two forces in life, the eternal-natural and the techno-inventive—a confrontation, so to speak, between Hestia, Queen of the Hearth and Home, and Willy Wonka, King of the magic mountain. (Hestia had nymphs and rustics on her side; Willy, an army of Oompa-Loompas.)

I wanted to imagine an apocalyptic final battle for the fate of food. But actually, though often opposed to each other in principle, the people who supported one didn't fight much with the people who practiced the other. What were they really after? What was really going on with these questions? What did it all *mean*? We shouldn't intellectualize food, because that makes it too remote from our sensory pleasures; but we ought to talk as intelligently as we can about it, because otherwise it makes our sensory pleasures too remote from our minds. The knowledge that our senses are part of our intelligence is what makes us human. We alone *know* our fun. The sweetness in our morning coffee is at once a feeling, an idea, and a memory. Eating is an intelligent act, or it's merely an animal one. And what makes it intelligent is the company of other mouths and minds. All animals eat. An animal that eats and thinks must think big about what it is eating not to be taken for an animal.

And so we turn back to the table. It was the eighth of July, 2005, and I was in the kitchen of the British chef Fergus Henderson at his whole-beast restaurant, St. John. The day before, bombs had exploded throughout London, as I was getting off the train from Paris, and the tragedy had made Henderson think more intently of the purpose of his craft.

"I don't understand how a young couple can begin life by buying a sofa or a television," he said indignantly to me. "Don't they know the table comes first?" *The table comes first.* The table comes first, before the meal and even before the kitchen where it's made. It precedes everything in remaining the one plausible hearth of family life, the raft to ride down the river of our existence even in the hardest times. The table also comes first in the sense that its drama—the people who gather at it, the conversation that flows across it, and the pain and romance that happen around it—is more essential to our real lives, and also to the real life of food in the world, than any number of arguments about where the zucchini came from, and how far it had to travel before it got here. If our questions of food matter, it is because they imply most of the big fights about who we are—our notions of clan and nation, identity and the individual. Civilization is mostly the story of how seeds, meats, and ways to cook them travel from place to place. The parts of that story are surely things that everyone should know, if only because they lead us to who we are. If our questions of food are to hold out the promise of self-knowledge that gastronomy once offered, we can't ask them outside of history.

And so, thinking about questions of food turned me back to the subject of France, the old home of the eaters we have become. All the spice routes passed through Paris. And if they no longer do as much as they once did, that is part of the story, too. You don't have to be too ardent a Francophile to see that thinking about the table and its rituals means thinking about France, about French history and French manners, just as you don't have to be an Anglophile to know that understanding liberalism and its rhetoric means thinking about England. Even if you eat nothing but Thai noodles and Turkish kebabs, Paris looms somewhere on the horizon of your imaginings, if only in an awareness of where the idea of eclectic eating in big cities began.

For to the other explanations—Freudian and puritanical—of our food mania, we might add a French explanation: it's a sign of civilization. Jacques Decour ended his letter this way: "It is eight o'clock. It is almost time to go. I have eaten and drunk my coffee. I think I have attended to everything." *I have attended to everything.* In the end, the last ritual Decour performed was to eat his last breakfast and drink his last cup of coffee and think that he had attended to it all.

All the other questions of food condense into a single question, Jacques Decour's question, the question of pleasure in a tragic world. "Come to the table, dinner's ready!" the hostess says, her face alight with nervous promise, and we trot dutifully to our places, expecting little, hoping for a lot—that, sitting there, we may not improve our lives but may achieve at least our ambiguities. The brightness of life, the double nature of desire, the longings of hunger and the likings of appetite, all the table's troubled truths . . . In the midst of life we are at dinner. Why? *Why* do we think of food at times like these? What do we think of food at times like these? *How can you think about food at a time like this?* It's an old question. The indignant puritan repeats it today. Reading his last letter, we might even ask it of Jacques Decour. To find out how he once could, why we still do, is the purpose of these pages.

PART I

Coming to the Table

THE TWO pillars of modern eating are the restaurant and the recipe book. The restaurant is the place where all eating out takes place; the recipe is the thing with which all home cooking starts. Both are modern. Until the nineteenth century, big books of recipes did not exist, and there was no place to go and eat in exchange for money that was like the places we go now.

The restaurant was once a place for men, a place where men ate, held court, cooked, boasted and swaggered, and wooed women. The recipe book was traditionally "feminine": the kitchen was the place where women cooked, supervised, gave orders, made brownies, to steady and domesticate men. In the myth-world of the nineteenth century, the restaurant existed to coax women into having sex; the recipe book to coax men into staying home.

These two poles are, blessedly, switching (moms now eat out as commonly as dads make supper), but the double pillars—less like pillars, perhaps, than like the two steeples of Chartres, parts of the same church but unlike each other—remain. To grasp the play of the table, and its politics, let us begin with those two supporting *R*'s, before proceeding to treat the rituals of taste, which they both support. Begin, then, at the moment when we go to the fancy place for dinner and sit down, nerves alight, or else the moment when we come home and smell what's cooking. Both are moments of arrival, of expectation, overseen by history. We have gone out for lunch or come home for dinner, and now we start....

1

Who Made the Restaurant?

A RESTAURANT is a place where you go to eat. You usually arrive in the early afternoon or the middle of the evening, and are taken to a table of your own in a room, usually on the ground floor of a city building in a space leased by a cook and made to look like a dining room. There are plush chairs and benches, and often mirrors. Someone, a professional go-between, often dressed in a parody of evening wear, whatever the hour, brings you a card that lists the things the cook is ready to cook, and how much it will cost to get him to cook them for you. You study this card—usually a list with decorations, sometimes bound in a leather pseudobook—and say what you'll have, and then the go-between goes into another room, the kitchen, which you can't see or hear or probably even smell. After a wait, the go-between brings the food you asked for. Very often, you will start with soup before having some grilled or roasted meat, followed by a sweet, almost always something made with sugar, a pudding or cake, rather than something naturally sweet, such as a plain piece of fruit. You are expected to have tea or coffee afterward, and then a bill is brought to your table. Prices are never mentioned out loud, and you pay whatever the card said you would. The place isn't a whorehouse or anything like it, but often you take someone there because you would like to have sex with them afterward, and sometimes you do, although, if you do, you go and do it somewhere else.

All the details, from soup to sex, of this setup, which by now seems as normal as eating itself, as obvious as breathing, can be found in more or less the same form from Sydney to San Francisco. And all of them—waiters, menus, tables, mirrors, closed kitchen, seduction, and silences, even the little table in the corner, *tout compris*—were thought up in Paris during a twenty-five year period right before the French Revolution and in the twenty or so years after. When you consider that eating is one of the few things that humans did even before they were people, it seems strange that restaurants should be so recent, but they are—as though the idea of having sex in beds had been discovered in Berlin during the winter of 1857, and then word got around.

There were places where you could go and pay for a meal before there were restaurants, of course: the tavern, the cookshop, the inn, the table d'hôte, the *traiteur*, or cook-caterer. The tavern as it evolved throughout Europe in the later part of the eighteenth century had many of the essential emotional traits of the modern restaurant. But the restaurant, with its special rituals and its particular look, began at one time and in one place.

The restaurant was known at once to be a modern and amazing thing. The great gastronome Jean Anthelme Brillat-Savarin marveled in 1825 that now "any man with three or four *pistoles* in his purse, can immediately, infallibly, and simply for the asking procure all the pleasures of which taste is susceptible." Yet how resilient, many-sided, adaptable, this new thing turned out to be, defying the rule that a picnic is made for one lawn and no other! If the restaurant is not the most original of modern instances and institutions, it is surely the most tenacious. It is the primal scene of modern life. Most modern urban people mark their lives by their moments in cafés and restaurants, just as ancient people marked their time on earth by visits to the local oracle, or medieval people by pilgrimages: we are courted, spurned, recruited, hired, fired, lured to a new job, or released from an old one at a table while a waiter hovers nearby. There are few marriages that did not begin at dinner at a table leased for the evening, and few divorces that did not first show signs of approaching doom in a sigh of resentment or an eye roll of exasperation in a similar setting. ("Can't you just make up your mind and stick with it?/ Why do you always overtip?" . . . The "forever" sentiments of anniversary dinners out not rarely sugar over the approaching "no-mores" of domestic life.)

I love restaurants. I love them even though, after many years as a reporter spent being fully disillusioned about their behind-the-scenes—having labored once or twice in their kitchens and befriended their owners—I am aware of how brutal the work is, how long the hours are, and how, aside from the ventures of a handful of those entrepreneurs essentially indifferent to the food they serve, how tiny is the hope of profit. *"Sale métier,"* the cooks and waiters alike mutter in Ludwig Bemelmans's memoirs of restaurant life in prewar Europe—"Filthy occupation"—and the muttering goes on still. Yet when I think of happy moments, I think of eating out.

Though they sometimes witness the ends of our love lives, restaurants have a ring of hope about them, a note of innocent celebration that makes them the right background for seduction. The man who asks the girl to dinner is not, after all, actually suggesting sex except by the airiest remote inference; he is pretending to be a better man than that: let's meet, talk, try. The restaurant offers the hope of happiness that gives greedy sex the look of lighthearted love, and, in the erotic sphere as much as the eating sphere, turns raw hunger into formal appetite. The restaurant offers not seduction but what precedes seduction, the false promise of pure motives.

I am, doubtless, prejudiced by particular experience. On my tenth birthday, I took the Moloznik boys from across the street to see a double feature of the first two James Bond films, this at a blissful time when the second run of movies in theaters was still a regular event, so that one had the pleasure of reseeing a good thing in the velvet padding of the cinema—not on the sofa, as we do now—with its thrilling moments in the dark: the trickle of sweet, forbidden Coke through a straw, and the chewy, burnt, semipainful edges of caramels. My parents were blackmailed into taking all three boys out to dinner at a Howard Johnson's on, as I recall, City Line Avenue in Philadelphia.

Howard Johnson's is gone now, reduced to a handful of sad motels. But in its day it had something grand about it. There was the electric sign outside, in green and orange, showing, in rapidly animated yet obviously distinct action—you could see the unlit armature of the next moment of movement waiting just beyond the neon figure that was lit, an endlessly repeating flip book of colored light—simple Simon and the Pieman enacting a brief drama of supplication and supply; one took eternally, the other fed over and over again, on the sign above City Line Avenue.

I sensed then that the sign, though meant as a come-on, was one of those strange, dense referents that used to be part of the pool of myths of ordinary people. Simon, as I recall, had the bent-kneed neediness of a Maxfield Parrish illustration, which, combined with the zigzagged lettering, made the sign, in retrospect, a kind of *Saturday Evening Post* cover come to life, or at least to electricity. (It was similar in spirit to, though far more pop in form than, the mural of Old King Cole in New York's St. Regis Hotel, a stylized comment on a nursery rhyme assumed to be known to everyone.) The sign's whimsical high voltage— the elaborate fable electrically enacted simply to signal "Eat!"— was conducted into the HoJo's interior as well, where the color scheme of blue and orange seeped even onto the margins of the many-paged menu. Its dishes were familiar from the highway to

New York: the rubbery fried clams, the 3-D burger, the mint-chip ice cream, minted with green food coloring. The burger that I had that evening had the delectable aroma, now vanished from the world, of the griddles of my childhood, something buttery, and of the soda fountain. The possibility of choice, the splendor of existence, was all present.

It was not the deliciousness of the food—my mother made better burgers—but the overcharge of optimism that made the meal matter. Its excellence involved the removal of the obvious signs of labor, which even then I took to be a benevolent fiction, for the better food at home was benign good fortune but effortful. You had to have my mom to eat really well, but anyone could come here and share. It was a moment of transformation, lift-off, of anonymity transmuted into intimacy without the obligation of gratitude: you told the menu-bearing woman at the cash register "Four for dinner," and suddenly, inexplicably, you were in a booth, and there was dinner for four! This sense of being in the unimaginable right place with exactly the right company in the most welcoming of rooms attended by the most considerate of servers—whistling while they worked and candidly eyeing the reward—was a blessing felt there and sought ever since.

As museums cross, or so Updike tells us, with the mystique of women, restaurants cross in memory with the optimism of childhood, with birthdays, promises, quiet, and the guilty desires of childhood, too: special treatment, special favors. The Cardinal, who never arrives, who sweeps you up into his carriage saying, "Child, you please me," becomes the maître d' who says, "Ah, sir, we're so glad to see you!" Some note of gaiety, of excess, of potential, lingers even at the most pedestrian lunch counter. (I have never looked at the Edward Hopper study of loneliness without thinking happily about how cozy the combination of diner chili and lemon meringue pie must be that late at night.)

Years went by—and here one must imagine calendar pages blowing and stock shots of jets crossing the Atlantic—and I found myself in Paris, just at a moment when the Grand Véfour had changed hands from Raymond Olivier's to the great cook Guy Martin's. Jet-lagged in the golden light of the Palais Royal, I recognized instantly the same sweet charge, the sibling resemblance to City Line Avenue and the Howard Johnson's of my tenth birthday. The enameled nymphs and goddesses, the mirrors, the red velvet couches—it was, for all the Palais Royal sophistication, this *resemblance* that made it moving: the experience of overcharge, of more than was necessary, of décor and joy, and sobriety of eating. Both were places of possibility, the illusion of potentials: we shall be blessed, and know that we are.

Even purely "social" restaurants, where dramas of snobbery play out, can be turned to such pleasure. In my misspent editorial youth, I used to take two gifted, hard-drinking writers, Mordecai Richler and Wilfrid Sheed, to lunch once a month at the Four Seasons in the Seagram's building. While Tina Brown and Helen Gurley Brown dined on water and lettuce, my two authors would let themselves go on shrimp with chipotle sausage, linguine *alle vongole,* crab cakes . . . and a bottle of red wine and a bottle of white (and too many Cognacs at the end; it was the last decade of hard-drinking writerliness, the last gasps of literary alcoholism that Sheed wrote about movingly and bravely in his *In Love with Daylight*). While Anna and Helen and the rest sipped and barely munched, the maître d' would wheel out a kind of chocolate bombe, for the express and sole purpose of having them squeal with indignant denial of interest. But the writers would demand a piece, and then another, with whipped cream (or "crème fraîche," as the arc had bent again toward France).

The restaurant, whether in its most abstract, ritzy form or at its most elemental, can always be diverted back toward a primal magic, a mood of mischief, stolen pleasures, a retreat from the world, a boat on the ocean—years later, having ice cream aboard a cruise ship in a storm, I would find that sense of stolen kisses, of clandestine joy, instantaneously renewed. That is what the restaurant promises, and how its prosaic purpose—cooked food exchanged for money—passes into the poetic, which explains why when the young man, from Balzac to Scott Fitzgerald, comes to the city, the first thing he seeks out is the place to eat that he has read about.

Who invented the restaurant? How did it begin? How did it happen that the long history of paying for food in a setting so singular became such a resilient institution—so resilient that a single restaurant, like Gundel in Budapest, could survive wars and revolutions, communists and the new economy, only to end much as it began? How did restaurants happen, and why did they happen first, or best, in Paris?

Until recently, most cooking history was pop history, filled with canned "Eureka!" moments and arch legend-making. ("The great chef Dunand found himself after the battle with nothing but crayfish, chicken, some eggs, and a couple of tomatoes. What, he wondered, could he make from such a motley assortment of ingredients? A moment's thought, a minute's chopping, and an hour later, on the Emperor's table, chicken Marengo was born," etc.) The birth of the restaurant had its myth-made tang, too. The old, potent, and long-standing story was that it was the French Revolution that had made the restaurant: After the revolution, the cooks of the French aristocrats were out of work, since they no longer had any mouths to feed. With nowhere to go but the streets, they opened cafés and started selling in public what before you could get only in private. Willy-nilly, the modern restaurant came into existence. A little later, a few high chefs, the great pastry architect Antonin Carême among them, made up a "grammar" of French cooking; that is, they wrote down recipes. Together, the dining room on the street and the recipe book in the kitchen made a new place. The aristocrats lost their heads; their cooks lost their jobs and found a new way to make a living in a democratic world.

A clutch of scholars, many of them, interestingly, women, have in the past decade or so proved the expelled-from-Eden myth all wrong. (Priscilla Parkhurst Ferguson, Rebecca Spang, and Amy Trubek have all figured in this work, and so has the British historian Giles Macdonogh.) The invention of the restaurant, it turns out, predates the revolution by at least twenty years, and chefs being out of work had nothing to do with it. (The nobles' cooks were more like head butlers than like chefs in any case, and most stayed loyal to their old bosses after the fighting started.) The old story goes that the essential ways of cooking and practice already existed behind château doors but were democratized when chefs entered the ungilded world. But in truth the cooking they did wasn't anything like the new cooking of the restaurants. Carême, though a great figure in his way, as a writer and provider, belongs more truly to the history of catering.

So then why did it happen? The birth was philosophical, before it was circumstantial; men's minds changed before their palates. It was a threefold affair. There were intellectual causes for the spread of the restaurant (reasons of the mind), commercial causes (reasons of merchandising), and sentimental causes (reasons of morality). All of them, of course, were, as real reasons must be, intertwined and interlarded. The reasons of the mind have to do with a new cult of health and simplicity; the reasons of merchandising have to do with a new site of commerce, the Palais Royal, and the birth of the modern street store there; the reasons of morality have to do with a breakdown of a neat caste hierarchy already long under way before the revolution—the neat thing about the restaurant was that anyone with a sou to pay can buy his meal. Along with the new social model came a new belief that appetite, the animal part of man, could be refined and civilized but need not in the end be remade. Brillat-Savarin thought that the purpose of dining well was to turn mere needs into desires, animal appetite into educated taste. But he didn't think that appetites ought to be "purified" or "reformed." There is no Year Zero at the table. The pig persists in spite of every effort to give him wings.

The restaurant, it turns out, was a thing to eat before it was a place to go. *"Restaurant,"* appearing around 1750, was the new name for bouillon, a chicken or beef broth. At that time, if you wanted to eat out in Paris you had to go to a table d'hôte. This was a big public table where you took what was being served, a little like a tavern or an eating house in London. As you ate, you were expected to talk and joke and kid around with the other people at the table, including the host. (You can still eat in a modernized, à la carte version of this style at a few places in Paris: Polidor, the *crémerie* on the Rue Monsieur-le-Prince, has a menu, but it has large common tables, one or two daily plats, and individual napkin drawers.) This could be fun, but if the guy next to you at the table d'hôte was drunk and beery you were stuck, and if you were in the mood for chicken and only veal roast was being served you were stuck, too. If you were a woman, you couldn't go at all.

People who didn't like the tables d'hôte because of the company started to say that they didn't like them because they made you sick when you ate there. This was doubtless not true, or not true often, but it didn't matter. Health scares usually are haloed by habit. Every panic has its profit-seeker, though, and someone was around to exploit this one; in the same spirit in which egg-white omelets and frozen-yogurt stands appeared in New York a couple of decades ago, places appeared in Paris offering healthy broth cooked in clean kettles—restaurants.

The soup gave its name to the shop. The restaurant started offering a whole range of health food, in an entirely new type of place. The hero of this invention, if not quite singular enough to deserve the name of inventor, was an amazing character named Mathurin Roze de Chantoiseau. Chantoiseau was a philosophical entrepreneur of the kind who seem to have filled Paris right before the revolution, and might even have prevented it had they been given enough room to act. He started off as a financier, with a hard-to-follow but interesting scheme to float the calamitous French national debt, essentially by letting merchants of luxury goods print their own money. When nobody went for it, he put together the first almanac of artisans, inventors, and luxury merchants—the first real guidebook to the good life—and shrewdly listed himself as the first "restaurateur."

It was Chantoiseau's establishment, on the Rue Saint-Honoré, that turned the restaurant from a place where you went to get well into a place where you went to have a good time. Chantoiseau's restaurant and the others like it that soon clustered around the Palais Royal became places where you could go when you wanted to and eat what you wanted to eat, choosing from a limited but reasonably long list of dishes, sit at your own table with your own friends, and tell yourself you were doing it for your health. Doctors even let women go to restaurants. This was, perhaps, the single greatest revolution the restaurant wrought: under the pretext of health, women could come alone to an open social theater.

One by one, all the other things we associate with restaurants—menus, uniformed waiters, mirrored walls—were established, all with an eye to creating a public place that felt like home, and if not your home then the home of somebody richer, with better servants. "Some twenty years after they were first established, restaurants no longer specialized in providing delicately healthful soups to a genteelly weak-chested clientele but in catering to individual tastes. While the *traiteur* fed large groups, the restaurateur offered single servings and small, intimate tables," the historian Rebecca Spang writes. As Diderot noted, writing of Roze's restaurant, 'Everybody eats alone there. . . .'" The restaurateur invited his guest to sit at his or her own table, to consult his or her own needs and desires, to concentrate on that most fleeting sense: taste.

The restaurant soon sprouted a larger halo of virtue. New restaurants were made under the influence of or, at least, alert to the talk of Jean-Jacques Rousseau's cult of nature, of sincerity and simplicity, which, ironically, affected aristocrats as much as radicals—so that its greatest monuments are the Petit Trianon for Marie Antoinette (who was handed her head) and the Cult of the Supreme Being, the religion invented by Robespierre (who handed it to her). In his *New Heloise,* Rousseau sentimentally imagines a peasant harvest of the wine grapes. "You cannot conceive with what zeal, with what gaiety, it all is done; we sing, we laugh all day, and work has never gone better. All live in the greatest familiarity, everyone equal and no one overlooked. . . . One eats with appetite the peasant soup, a little raw and rude, but good, healthy and filled with fine vegetables!"

So it was that on a smaller, edible scale, the new cooking of the restaurant, far from offering fancy dishes you couldn't have at home, offered plain food that you couldn't forage for yourself, raw and rude but good and healthy. Jean François Vacossin, the second restaurateur in France, promised "Breton porridge, orange-flower-flavored rice creams, semolina, fresh eggs . . . fruits in season, preserves from the most famous manufacturers, fresh butter and cream cheese." This nouvelle cuisine, as it was called, was hard to define, but everybody agreed that the food was simpler than the old food, was good for you, and was eaten only by the best people—as nouvelle cuisine always is. In a document dated to 1739, the "Letter of an English Pastry maker to a new French cook"—the Englishman(!) already summons the French cook back to primal simplicity. We greedy eaters are always being summoned back to primal simplicity, as women in vogue are always being called back to classic fashion. (No one recalls that five years ago the shorter skirt was classic, too.)

Voltaire—not surprisingly, given the Rousseauian rhetoric of the restaurant—thought the whole thing was nuts, and said so. His diatribe against the new cooking, which some academics have insisted on interpreting as an allegorical protest against Communion, now appears to have been actually a diatribe against the new cooking. "I swear that my stomach cannot bear the new cooking. I cannot bear sweetbreads swimming in a salty sauce nor a hash composed of turkey, hare and rabbit, that dreams of being mistaken for a single meat. I don't like either pigeon in the frog style"—that is, flattened and deboned. "When it comes to cooks, I wouldn't know how to bear the essence of ham, nor the excess of morels, mushrooms, peppers and muscade, with which they cover meats healthy in themselves."

It might seem odd that what was meant to be romantically "simple" appeared to a jaundiced Enlightenment eye as needlessly complex—the morels and mushrooms doubtless were defended as striking that healthy country note—until one recalls that this is a standard event in the history of cookery: one need only remember the complaints about small fussy things centered in large empty plates to see that the same thing happened with the last burst of "new cooking," back in the 1970s. What looks like nature renewed to the new cook's eye always tastes like contrivance in the old diner's mouth.

There are no "Eureka!" moments in cooking. The real pattern of change that brought about the restaurant revolution looks less neatly segmented than the myths. The difference between Russian and French service; the communal habit of a *coup de milieu;* the mixing of fish and meats; the division of the meal into three courses; the sequencing of wine—far from being attached to a single moment of discovery and a clear sequence of customs, each of these new things arrives, and fades, and reappears, and, in the way of the world, becomes the norm before it is ever the oddity. Some things that seem traditional are very new. The order of wines, sparkling to white to red to brown, and the idea that wines should match the dishes, is a twentieth-century invention. Some that seem to be modern (the division of the meal into three courses—small treat, meat, and sweet—for instance) date to the sixteenth century. (The evolutionary basis of the sweet as coda is argued to be part of our ape heritage; they end with bananas, too.)

For a new thing to take, it needs a new soil, a new kind of city, a new place for it to happen. The restaurant, whether as a health bar, or as an outgrowth of the café, may have had no special moment of creation, but it did have its primal savannah. It turns out that, with eerie exactitude, we can localize the field of invention of the restaurant to one small place, still with us: it all happened in and around the Palais Royal.

Every tourist in Paris knows the Palais Royal as it is today: its great formal garden girded by long allées of plane trees, where neatly dressed functionaries crisscross en route to and from the Ministry of Culture, as in the great Cartier-Bresson photograph—with the placid arcades on all four sides filled by strange antique shops that sell old clothes and French medals. (Now newly invaded, sadly, by chic fashion boutiques.) Colette lived there, and photographs of her mad hair and wise face at her window are part of the Palais's legend.

But its note of elegant retreat and quiet mystery is a new one. The Palais Royal of the late eighteenth century was the shopping center of the Lumières, the first modern mall. The private property of Philippe, the duc d'Orléans, who was "the first prince of the blood," one of the richest men in Europe, he was an enlightened aristocrat who invented radical chic, in the end paying for it with his life. Known by the slightly used-car-salesman moniker of Philippe Egalité—Equality Phil—he was the prince of the hopeful prerevolutionary period when radical political philosophy took its inspiration from an idea of "English" free-market enterprise: the monopoly in bits and pieces of trade held by aristocrats was one of the complaints against them. It was very much as part of his egalitarianism, not as a piece of hypocrisy against it, that Philippe decided to rent the four great arcades of his palace to merchants: to modistes, tailor shops, bookstores, but above all to new places to eat and drink. Under Philippe's protection, the Palais Royal became a petri dish of edible ideas, mutating and multiplying and then being devoured.

Although Chantoiseau's first true restaurant was just around the corner on the Rue St.-Honoré, it was in the Palais Royal that the café and the restaurant flourished, and then, cross-fertilized by strange twistings of hunger and commerce, evolved into the thing we know now. All of the first great generation of restaurants—Véry, Méot, Beauvilliers, which were perhaps the most famous, if not the best, of the new places—found a home there. It is hard, walking through the Palais Royal today, to re-create what it must have been like in 1780: the noise, of course, and the sense of bustle, and the constant clandestine conspiracies and argument. We would have been shocked by their dirt, and delighted by their debate.

The revolution, far from sparking this change, actually damp- ened it briefly. Even as restaurants prospered in the Palais, the Jacobins of the Terror became suspicious of them—not because they were linked to the old kind of ostentation but because they were linked to the wrong kind of simplicity, had a tang of Petit Trianon fresh-butter-and-cheese nouvelle wholesomeness about them. The revolution, in its most radical moments, encouraged "grands couverts," instead—the tables d'hôte of the Reign of Terror, where people sat at long tables, sharing the food and tell- ing each other loudly what a good time we are having, Citizen, never mind the produce! Philippe himself, who had patronized the early restaurant, paid with his life during the Terror, as a victim of the Jacobins who regarded his revolutionary fervor as mere ambition. "Champagne is the poison of the people," Robes- pierre announced, turning down an invitation to dinner. Blood was the people's liquor.

Yet, though the revolution did not create the restaurant, in the end it could not stop its growth. The revolution was the lightning that struck the primal soup already in place and helped a new form of life to emerge. "If the French revolution had a detrimen- tal effect on almost all the arts," the gastronome Alexandre Gri- mod de La Reynière would write, and no fan of the revolutionary politics, he, "that was not the case with cooking; far from having suffered as a result, it has the Revolution to thank for its rapid progress and motive force." The fifty years between 1780 and the revolution of 1830, when the world that we think of now as Parisian came into being—the soft-power civilization whose authority the great gastronome and liberal Brillat-Savarin tried to trace when he published *The Physiology of Taste* in 1825—were when it all happened, and it nearly all happened in the Palais Royal, "this lewd hanger, brazenly tweeting with some mad gaiety," as Balzac called it. By 1805, there were fifteen restaurants and twenty cafés under the arcades; the most famous of the cafés, the Café de Foy, occupied no fewer than seven full arcade arches. The Foy was at number 59, the Beaujolais Theater at number 13, the Café Corazza at 12, and at number 80 was the Café Chartres, which persists to this day, largely unchanged, as the Grand Véfour. My intimations of origins were not false; the sun-flooded room with the dainty enameled nymphs really was the savannah from which Restaurant Man emerged.

Though Beauvilliers was the most famous of the first-generation restaurants, Véry, run by two brothers of that name, was perhaps the first "three-star" restaurant recognized as supreme—the undisputed top temple, first in a line that would pass through Maxim's and end in its classic form at the Tour d'Argent. Though the Véry brothers' first place was in the Palais Royal, they soon had an offshoot in the Tuileries, lodged in a specially designed, self-contained neoclassical temple on the Terrace des Feuillants. (Alain Dutournier's contemporary Carré des Feuillants, off the Rue de Rivoli, is named in its honor.)

Theater lovers put themselves to sleep at night imagining the performances from the past that they would love to have seen: Richard Burbage, say, in the original *Hamlet,* or David Garrick in the eighteenth-century production. People who love to eat lull themselves thinking about the places where they wish they could have eaten. What would be the five restaurants that a greedy eater would most want to have dined at, but that no longer exist even in ghost form? Maybe the Café Foyot in the nineteenth century, when *côtes de veau Foyot* had just been invented; Prosper de Montagne, the first of the luxury bistros of the 1920s; or Pyramide in its heyday in the 1950s, with Fernand Point at the stove; or maybe Michel Guérard's original Pot-au-Feu in the 1970s. (A list to which now will be added, as it closes, Ferran Adrià's elBulli, in Catalonia.) But certainly Véry in its little temple should be very high on the list of restaurants to dream of.

And, just as the theater lover hesitates, worrying what Garrick or Burbage would have really been like in *Hamlet*—embarrassingly broad? surprisingly subtle?—greedy eaters worry whether they would have relished or been bemused by a Véry meal. What would we have eaten there? The menus that survive from its contemporaries (I know of none from Véry itself) alternate between dishes that one might make tonight—beef braised in Madeira, garnished with vegetables; grain-fed chicken with crayfish butter—and others that seem to belong to a weird remote past: a sauté of lark filets; filet of partridge in aspic with almond milk and rusks. Doubtless this duality is what we would register at a David Garrick performance, too: if we could go back to any past, we would surely be struck by how *past* it seems, its best fruits inevitably seeming dried, as seeds of the present we know now. An eighteenth-century Shakespeare performance would surely swing between recognizably sublime moments and weirdly remote rhetorical flourishes; even watching films of early-twentieth-century acting we rock uneasily between Madeira-braised beef and sautéed lark. So, surely, dinner at Véry. We would have been struck, for one thing, by how odd their drinking habits were, with sweet wines offered throughout the meal—sherries and ports. The familiar wet progression—starting with champagne, and then a bottle of white wine, on to red wine, then liqueurs and brandies, ending with a sweet wine—is a late invention, and largely English.

Though something like familiar "French cuisine" would have

been found, life in the lewd hanger was, above all, mixed up. And it was the mixing-up in the kitchens, as much as the screwing in the apartments above, that made it lewd. The restaurants at the Palais Royal were, as often as not, what we would now call "ethnic," not narrowly "French." The cuisine of the Palais Royal was open. Things poured in. "Wines have been imported from all over the world," Brillat-Savarin tells us proudly—not a boast that a French food writer would be inclined to make two centuries later—and "French cookery has annexed dishes of foreign extraction, such as curry and the beefsteak and relishes, such as caviar and soy."

At least two of the most famous and admired restaurants in the Palais Royal were proudly "Provençal": Les Trois Frères Provençaux—actually run by three brothers from Provence (Maneille, Trouin, and Simon)—and the Boeuf à la Mode, founded by two brothers from Marseille. Both flourished at a time when Provence was as exotic as the Maghreb is now, when familiar dishes such as braised beef and bouillabaisse were what *tagines* and couscous seem today. That Provence could have contributed to the lewd hanger's cosmopolitanism, achieved by *métissage,* strange mixing, shows you how sedate a world the Palais restaurants were shaking up. That braised beef with poached vegetables, still the best of company dishes, should ever have been considered "à la mode," much less exotic! The secret to its dazzle, then as now, was to add a calf's foot in the braising liquid, to make it gelatinous. (I remember the odd pride with which my favorite Parisian butcher would include the foot, somehow so white and forlorn, with the roast when you told him what you wanted to make.)

The cosmopolitan current did not flow from Provence alone; when Brillat-Savarin said that a Paris meal could be a cosmopolitan whole, he meant that everything was there. Everyone talked about how many kinds of food you could find—the cuisine of the provinces, of course, Béarn, and the southwest and Burgundy, which kept some of their character as little countries right up to the coming of the railroads and the highways. But still more the cooking and goods of Africa, and America and Asia. "French cooking" was a composite disguised as a whole, an airborne and seaborne thing recast as a shoot from the soil.

Another change that the new restaurants imposed in the 1790s was the abandonment of French or banquet service for what the French themselves called Russian service, which is just what we today think gives order to a meal: instead of a lot of dishes placed nobly on a table with servants to serve them—Carême's idea of dinner—dishes would come one after another, in an order chosen by the host and his chef. The loss in architectural splendor and arrangement of the kind Carême made great was compensated for by a gain in freedom: once every diner was brought his own dish, soon every diner could *choose* his own dish.

The passage from French to Russian service turns out, the historian Jean-Louis Flandrin reports, to be a lot more complex than it seems. It took place over time, and, indeed, probably seemed less marked when you experienced it than when you read about it. It is sometimes said that, in the grand French service, the diner's place at the table determined what he ate: if you were seated down by the beets, beets is all you got. (I have been to New York dinner parties where, seated down among the lesser notables, this was true: you ate what was nearest, and what was nearest was a sign of who you really were.) But in the novels and histories from the period that is not the way people eat at all; what later historians overlook is the superabundance of footmen, ready to help you get the bits you wanted from the other end. One of the hardest things for modern people to keep in mind is the difference between a servant-scarce and a servant-rich environment. Whether the service at the table was Russian service or French service, it was servant service. "It makes a servantless New Yorker sore, to think that Mozart had to bare his head," Auden wrote once. "But Mozart never had to make his bed." Servants are to history what dark matter is to the universe: the omnipresent thing that affects everything but that no one quite sees. But surely the change to Russian service was driven, just a little, by fear of footmen, too. "The presence of valets at table is the greatest scourge that can be inflicted on a meal. Their eyes avidly devouring all the dishes, their ears mopping all the opinions, and their tongues always ready to denounce their masters," the lawyer-turned-bon-vivant Grimod wrote. Even if the threat of betrayal was made melodramatic, the problem was probably really there.

It took time to turn this mixed-up menu into a single ordered enterprise. If the story of the transition from French to Russian service is cloudy, the idea of "French cooking" is truly foggy. Though the idea of "French cuisine" as a systematic enterprise with a single starting point and a neat underlying grammar would spread out to take over the world, French restaurant cooking in 1810 was really a jumble of country food, health food, city food, old chefs from fancy families, and cheap food for hungry people. Only in reading about it later did anyone think of it as old, fixed, and neat as a pin.

Is this not the way big change often happens in all the arts? A composite, hybrid, open-ended, and eclectic thing, is soon treated as though it were a closed grammar, systematic and finished, only to be revealed later to have been a splendid mess all along. (Jackson Pollock's spatters and pourings only latterly assume the utter precision and harmony we are directed to observe in them; the chaos one beholds on first glance is not entirely or even mostly an illusion. It was part of the intention.) It is the job of artists, including cooks and painters, to make whatever they can of whatever matter lies at hand. Then it is the job of critics to pretend that what looks like chaos is really closed order. (Clement Greenberg, the American art critic, had to take Pollock's spatters and pourings, applied intuitively, and make them look like a logical culmination of everything that had ever happened in painting.) And then it falls to scholars later on to show that what looks closed was really just as chaotic as it first seemed: that American painting, or French cooking, is a mix of sixteen different things and eighteen different impulses, and anyway, was not the same in 1808 as it was in 1819. (This gives generations of critics and scholars work and keeps us off the streets, leaving the next generation of cooks and artists to do *their* work in relative peace.)

Yet the story of the birth of the French restaurant cannot be well told without the twin story of its Sancho Panza, the French café. The history of the café and the restaurant are no less intertwined than the history of the bed and the table; both entanglements represent a passage subtle and not always easily traced, then or now. In the best study of that history, *From Taverns to Bistros: The History of Cafés,* a French scholar named Luc Bihl-Willette identifies at least six distinct features that separated the restaurant from the café, though some seem more metaphysical than concrete.

It does seem sure that the modern café was born by government decree. One of the first laws made by the National Assembly after the revolution was one passed in 1789 that simply made it legal to sell coffee and wine and spirits in the same place—for the first time a drinking shop, where alcohol was sold, could be a place where other things to ingest were sold as well. We have been conditioned by Edmund Burke and his followers to think of the French Revolution as only a scary, top-heavy Utopian folly, and forget that it had its libertarian aspects, too. For the moderate Girondins, economic liberty was a crucial part of revolutionary liberty; Adam Smith was a new god France should worship. Monopoly was the enemy. Where, before the revolution, the selling and serving of food was bound around by archaic rites and privileges—only certain guilds could make breads; others pastries; still others sell tea and coffee; these aristocrats had the monopoly on salt, those on molasses—the revolution deregulated all that, and allowed, with modest momentousness, the neighborhood café, and, soon, the ordinary restaurant, to sell spirits and caffeine at the same place and time.

This helped the restaurant to become what it was and is. First, of course, by encouraging the entrepreneur, but also by mixing up the goods, and particularly by mixing up the two liquids of coffee and wine. For modern restaurant cooking is first and foremost a boat that, as in a Saul Steinberg drawing, steams its way downriver from the thousand dreamy islands of alcohol to the wide beckoning current of caffeine, from the stress-busting drink to the reawakening demitasse. A modern French meal not including both (even if the caffeine sometimes takes the degenerate form of tea, and the alcohol of spirits) is impossible to imagine. Dinner with water is dinner for prisoners. A modern meal is a drama unfolding between the Opening Drink and the Concluding Coffee, with the several acts passing between the libations.

And, without strong coffee and red wine, it isn't possible to have good restaurants. Though it is hard to tell the restaurant from the café in following the restaurant's semi-occult history, a case can be made that the café was the more original of the two inventions, or at least the more singular: around 1900, there were thirty thousand cafés in Paris, and fewer than six thousand in London—and it is hard to know how many of those in London were true cafés, and how many mere tea shops. On the other hand, when it came to the "drinking shops," early bars, there was one for each one thousand potential drinkers in London, eleven to one thousand in Paris. The café was a civilizing institution, whose name guaranteed, or suggested, a genuine ward against alcoholism. The grand café of the Paris boulevards, like the proper restaurant, was always a source of wonder to English people, as it was to Americans.

Yet though joined at the hip, the temperamental difference between the two was real. The restaurant belongs to its cook. You come to eat, and though, as Brillat-Savarin saw, anyone can eat there, still you come to eat. Four pistoles are not nothing. The café, though, belongs to its habitués, and pleasure can be rented for the price of a coffee. We do not all feel equally at home within it; the newcomer to the quartier gets uneasy looks from the chess players at their usual table. But at the ritzy restaurant the awkwardness of the nouveau riche who has money in his pocket though not yet the rules of conduct graven in his heart is part of the comedy (and pathos) of urban modernity. (In Chaplin's early masterpiece *The Immigrant*, Charlie as a recently arrived Jew knows *some* of the rules of the new American grand café— that you applaud when the music ends—but not others that don't apply back where he comes from: for instance, that you should not ever, under any circumstances, eat with your knife.)

That the double presence of coffee and wine is necessary to "force" the restaurant, as the seeded underbrush is necessary to force the trees, is made plain when you see what happens in places—Ireland and England—where you drink your drink in one place and take your coffee in another: it's a recipe for alcoholism, bad coffee, and a weak restaurant culture. (It was only after the proliferation of the espresso bar and the wine bar that London cooking began, thirty years ago, to become first rate.)

French cooking was made not merely in the space between caffeine and alcohol but in the simultaneous presence of both, thus blending, in sequence, the two drugs by which modern people shape their lives. Good food takes place in the head space between them. Most modern people use these drugs in some guise at one dose or another, but some of the primacy of Paris as a restaurant town surely has to do with its first having perfected the proportions and the form of each one. Modern life is regulated by these drugs, morning to night—one speeding us up, and one slowing us down. (The rock-and-roll-age equivalents, cocaine and pot, do the same work for another generation—do it more hysterically, but do the same work.) The British variants, tea and whisky or beer, are separated, by tradition and perhaps by necessity, in space and time: the four o'clock tearoom and the ten o'clock pub. (In the American diner, the two shaping drugs are caffeine and sugar—a cup of joe and a piece of pie.)

The decree of 1789 not only provided the French restaurant meal its fluids; it gave it its form. It was then that the system of alcohol began—fortified wines began to be drunk at the end of meals rather than right through. The wine began to be rated, blossoming into the greatest triumph of the French genius for systematization, the classification of Bordeaux in 1855. None of this happened quickly. The evidence for the introduction of the *trou normand,* the shot of spirits in between courses, for instance, is very shaky until our own time. But everyone noted that it was a new thing in France to drink sweetened coffee at night, at the end of meals, as a stimulant and digestif.

Alcohol, as Malcolm Gladwell has reminded us, is above all a *myopic* drug: it forces the imbiber's attention ever more narrowly upon what's in front of him. It closes us off and isolates us, that's its odd charm. (And its special danger. You can see only the boy or girl in front of you—but not the truck bearing down on the side road.) A little glass of wine, and all there is in the world is the date and the table—or often, in lonely moments, the bar and the bartender—but the world and its stresses flee for a moment into a vague blur of the background.

Caffeine, on the other hand, is a far-sighted drug. Several sips of café noir and the sipper feels charged up, the corners of the café gleam, and we look around the room, ready to take on the world again. We read while we drink coffee, romance while we drink wine. Coffee, one might say, is a flow drink, wine a focus drink. Focused, we can let our attention wander; feeling in the flow, we can happily try to focus once again. By a familiar mental or merely chemical trick, we dose ourselves with one drug to get our brains to produce the opposite effect: our tongues burn intolerably as we eat capsaicin, which is the hotness in hot peppers, and so the brain overproduces its own opiates, to compensate. The pleasure of spicy food is a trick we play on our inner junkie. Wine, though clinically a depressant, forces us to feel happy for no reason; as we sink, we search for pleasure. Coffee, though a stimulant that should propel us out of our seat, lets us concentrate more fiercely on the task at hand. (Good writers have often been drunks, but none has written well while drunk; the drinking is an escape from the pressing pain of concentration—awareness—fueled by coffee through the working day.) Wine takes us from the world, and coffee restores us to it again. In between, we eat.

A restaurant meal, in 1789 as now, is really a short sonata in head fuels. Without the drinks, we could hardly find our hungers. Wine "depresses" and narrows the buzzing room until we feel happily alone, on our own little island. Without it, a restaurant can feel as unbearably crowded as a subway car. After the meal (then as now richer in a restaurant than at our own home, and more lulling in its fullness and richness), coffee reawakens us to the world—the room's walls press outward again. If there is a tiny bit of salt in the coffee—an old French trick—the enhancement is even greater. The walls recede, the door opens, and the night beckons us on.

The café and restaurant have their interplay in history, but they also had one that went on every night. In Henry Murger's mid-century *Scènes de la Vie de Bohème*—the novel that gave us *La Bohème,* and which is also the best memorial of ordinary food life in early-nineteenth-century France—the "Bohemians," artists and writers, all go out to dinner after the hero, Rodolphe, suddenly comes into money. Significantly, they go to one of those "exotic" Provençal restaurants, this one on the Rue Dauphine, "well known for its aioli and for the literary tastes of its waiters," but eat there only moderately, since they have plans for a late supper, too. Only after their restaurant dinner do they go to their pet café, the Café Momus, where "from that day the establishment became uninhabitable for the rest of the patrons." There, they have coffee and liqueurs. The restaurant belongs to food, and to its waiters; the café to caffeine, and to its patrons. The two together, like scrub oak and driftwood in a beach resort, make the landscape of the modern food town.

Brillat-Savarin saw this—that coffee, once a breakfast drink alone, had, in the era of the restaurant, come into general use "after dinner as an exhilarating tonic." Grimod, too, recognized the essential alliance of the two elements. "It would now be unthinkable to invite guests to the simplest of meals were there not two or three liquors flanking the coffee pot," he said. In the café first, and in the restaurant later, the marriage of the two true fuels was made, and modern life began.

Beyond all this—beyond even the life of the lewd hanger, the marriage of the two modern drugs, the merging of faraway cooking styles into one idea of "French food," beyond the spirits flanking the coffeepot and the advent of the Opening Drink and the Concluding Coffee—there was a world of writing and thought in Paris then that made the new thing, the restaurant, happen. Priscilla Parkhurst Ferguson, in a path-making article on the invention of gastronomy in nineteenth-century France, borrows the French sociologist Pierre Bourdieu's idea of a social "field" as the unit of social life to explain why Paris became the place where dining first happened.

This idea of a social "field" seems opaque until one sees that it is not really far from what we already call in common speech "a scene." There is, for instance, a fine French bakery in the little American seaside town where I am writing this, started there by a couple of émigré Frenchmen, but there is no food *scene.* The shop will live and die, thrive or fail, together with the two Frenchmen who planted it. A bakery in New York, on the other hand, will be replaced by another, perhaps a better one. Or we might say, "There are a couple of good rep cinemas in Philadelphia, but there's really no movie scene," meaning a crowd of critics, commentators, loyal fans. There can be good basketball players in a city and no basketball "culture," no scene, and a good jazz scene in places that few jazz players actually come from. A field is really just the fancy name for a scene. The scene most often conjures up the object of its desires. In London in the 1970s, for instance, good writing about food happened before the food did: a scene emerged before there was a subject. There were places to eat all throughout Europe at the end of the eighteenth century. There had to be. But there was a restaurant scene in Paris alone.

One thing that makes culinary history, the story of how people used to make and eat food, different from other kinds of stories about the past is that it has as its object something that still goes on every day for everyone—eating is the great democratic equalizer, like breathing, more even than sex is—and at the same time it also goes on particularly, in weird or expensive ways, for a handful of people. It is as if in the history of culture everyone in every city in every age were painting three pictures a day: separating common history from "art history" would then become very hard. They were eating just as often, cooking and spicing their meals just as precisely to the tastes of the people about to eat, in Bulgaria in 1790 as they were in Paris. But in Paris, and only in Paris, was there yet a real food scene—a mass of critics, diners, chefs, and above all writers who were talking and writing about food in new ways. They didn't eat *more* in Paris. They couldn't. But they did talk about it more than they did in other places, and then wrote about the things they said.

This may seem to make more of the role of writers than one should. *What do you mean . . . they wrote their food?* But it happens all the time. Studying the growth of American baseball at the beginning of the twentieth century, the great sabermetrician Bill James once pointed out that you can't really separate what

Christy Mathewson and Ty Cobb were doing from what Grant-land Rice and Ring Lardner were publishing. The growth of the sports page made the growth of sports possible; the baseball writers made what we think of as baseball. We sense that the two are different and we should, since what the cook or the first baseman does is harder than what critics and columnists do. But you need both to get high-order accomplishment. It was the scene that gave birth to the restaurant, as much as the restaurant that gave birth to the scene. It takes a scene to make a world.

What made the food scene spring up in Paris? What made the writers critique food instead of love or life or pure reason? Older histories, as we've seen, tend to put the "creative" moment a little too late, and say that chefs were pushed out from the aristocratic houses as the mouths they fed were lost along with the heads around them, and, desperate to make a living, they opened restaurants. But no one, however desperate, starts a business without perceiving an unmet demand; a place to sell food for money would never have opened if the interest wasn't there to start.

Historians now tend to put their finger on a few linked causes for the new "field." First, and most important, though easy to forget, was the end of famine in France. We take the fact of plenty now so much for granted that the press of scarcity can strike us as charming, or even, at times, enviable: how they must have enjoyed having strawberries only in season, a steak once a month. And if they missed a season or couldn't get a steak, all the more relish when they finally had it! In truth, starvation was, through the eighteenth century and well into the nineteenth, a constant fear, a yearly specter in Europe. As Ferguson writes, "Cyclical famines had ravaged the continent for centuries." New methods of farming; new means of distribution, instanced by the growth of central city markets; and, above all, the end of the feudal order, with its monopolies of grain and other goods, resulted (in most places, at most times, for most people) in, at last, enough to eat throughout Europe. The first need for those who want to reflect on the meaning of lunch is the certainty of having dinner. Though there were periods of hunger through the revolution, they were only periods. There were still famines, during the Terror, but people thought of them as discrete crises because they didn't happen all the time. Bad and cruel things still happened, but France, at least, was now a country of relative plenty.

Scarcity creates sanctions; abundance encourages altruism. When your plate is empty, you are inclined to see eaters as sinners; when your plate is full, gluttony looks fine. In a Catholic country like France, the new plenty helped promote a more relaxed idea of pleasure. The second change, linked to the end of famine, was that enjoying food for its own sake came to be regarded not as an instance of gluttony but a virtue of its own. So the sudden release from the bonds of guilt creates an exhalation of pleasure. "Luxury" suddenly looks like life. Voltaire wrote a poem about this change called "The Man of the World," in which he tries to show that everything once called superfluous can be seen as truly needed. Once we accept more than subsistence living, which needs are on the money, which over the top? The pace of freedom quickened, so that by the time that Eugène Sue's novel *The Seven Deadly Sins* appeared, in 1848, he could argue that the "sins" are not deadly at all, that they are in truth blessings—and gourmandise one of the best among them. All the people in Sue's imaginary family are in the food business—butcher, baker, fishmonger, food importer—and they all come together in the end to celebrate the good things that come from a life devoted to what would have once been called gluttony. From seeing the table as the enemy of virtue to pressing the glutton button at will—few alterations in human consciousness have been larger, or taken place over less time. It was a world changing its mind, as much as cooks changing places, that made Paris the capital of food, and caused the invention of the thing that we call French cooking.

There was still another distinction in the Parisian instance, this one built into the fact of food. Citing classical models had long been the best way to affirm the importance of a new thing. But everyone could sense that the way that Romans and Greeks ate, at least as recorded in their literature, was no way anyone wanted to eat now. The food of the ancient Romans—swans stuffed with live larks, and then refunded in a vomitorium—already seemed too odd to imitate.

While Carême looks back to classical architectural models for his grand *pièces montées,* his ideas about the food itself are empirical, practical, and inductive—thought from the bottom up rather than imposed from a noble past. His cookbook begins with the pot-au-feu—the simple braised beef that is still one of the best good things in the French kitchen—which he recognizes as the source of stocks, and he treats it to a chemical analysis. What remained of "Roman" spices—that heady, intoxicating play of ginger and pepper and cinnamon—was banished, too, and replaced by "no high spiced sauces, no dark brown gravies . . . every meat presented its own natural aroma, every vegetable its own shade of verdure." Whatever eating was to be, we were going to have to make it up. The scene was probably more open for innovation in cooking than in almost any other field. There are times in the history of culture when the "minor" arts lead the major; the Dutch designer Rietveld's chairs were "abstract" studies in primary colors before Mondrian learned from him and made it art. Cooking was the first of the modern arts to do entirely without classical sanction and the first to claim it modeled itself on nature alone—and, to a reasonable degree, it actually did so. At Carême's table you could eat chicken with chervil even before, at Corot's easel, you could see Italy as it was.

Morals change, then meals; desires drive our diets. Of all the new jobs that the new scene made, the most potent was that of the chronicler of changing desires, the pro food writer—the "gastronomic journalist." The emergence of journalists, with their natural affinity for eating, was one of the events of the day. Journalists, Grimod de La Reynière tells us, are all big eaters and drinkers: "recognizable by their apoplectic throats, their bushy mustaches, and their puffy bibulous visages."

It was Brillat-Savarin, the wandering French food lover and exile of the mixed-up Napoleonic and post-Napoleonic period, long resident in the newborn United States, who wrote the first great book about taste and why it matters, that famous 1825 *Physiology of Taste*. Brillat-Savarin's book was, or seemed to be, one of the first rule books, the first attempts to put "gastronomy"—the word he made famous—on a semiscientific basis: to make the serious study of cooking and eating one more of the Enlightenment's subjects, to be pinned in an encyclopedia. Yet though his tone was mock-scientific, his purpose was humane—he was an expatriate essayist, poor guy—and his theme was simple. For Brillat-Savarin, gastronomy is the great adventure of desire. Its subject is simple: the table is the place where a need becomes a want. Something we have to do—eat—becomes something we care to do—dine—and then something we care to do becomes something we try to do with grace. Eating together is the civilizing act. We take urges, and tame them into tastes.

Brillat-Savarin wasn't really writing an encyclopedia of sensations; he was writing a book on the reach of pleasures. We chew with our molars, but eat with our minds. "The pleasure of the table is a reflected sensation, originating in various facts, places, things and persons [taking in] all the modifications of society which extreme sociability has introduced among us: love, friendship, business, speculation, power, ambition, and intrigue, all enhance conviviality." His allied subject was sex, which also began with a gasp and was tamed into a game. "I observe with pride, that gourmandise and coquettery, the two great modifications which society has effected in our imperious wants, are both of French origin," he wrote. Flirtation, like good cooking, was the way impulse submitted to social discipline—manners.

Brillat-Savarin became an exile because he had been a political radical: he was a member of the revolutionary National Assembly, a Jacobin, not a lovable old duffer with a few sweet epigrams about food, but a leading voice for liberty. Yet his passion was for the politics of pleasure as Voltaire had proposed them, not the politics of purity as Robespierre and the radicals perverted them. Eating was, for Brillat-Savarin, what fighting wasn't: mixed, mongrelized, common, and all to the good. What sped him into exile was a horror at the Utopian politics of Robespierre, the man who liked only soft and simple food, and who thought that champagne was the poison of the people's liberty. The sansculottes came for him, and wrote a death warrant.

Brillat-Savarin fled France, penniless, in 1792, and it was then that his wanderings took him to America, where he lived and taught French and the violin to American girls in Boston and Philadelphia and New York. He played first violin in a park orchestra. (And loved the good matter, if not the then-inadequate finish, of our East Coast plenty: oysters, shad roe, and scallops.) He went back to France in 1797, with the Terror past, to work as a judge and legal theorist, but the epiphany for Brillat-Savarin as an eater occurred in 1816 when, with France as defeated as any country could be, English and German victors poured into Paris and were converted (and fleeced) by the cultural force of French food and flirtation. He realized—and this was not the last time people would see this in France; the same would follow the even more bitter defeat of the Franco-Prussian War—that the soft power of food and free love (or love for hire) could be more powerful than the steel power of armies.

To understand why gourmands could be more potent than generals became his purpose. His *Physiology of Taste* is not a study of an old man's pleasures; it is a plea for the systematic study of that soft power. Brillat-Savarin's idea that *besoins*—needs, wants—become demands and desires was made political through the civilizing act of the table. His program for soft power was based in what he called "social gourmandise"—what we might now call altruistic greed, or, better, unselfish gluttony. Brillat-Savarin's ideal eater was not the gourmet—the fussbudget with a napkin—but the gourmand, the greedy guy with a date. "Gourmand," though a word everyone knows, is a hard word to translate. Literally a glutton—but "glutton" in English has overtones of loutishness that the French word doesn't have. To be gourmand is not just to be greedy for whatever it is they put in front of you but alive with appetite for the special thing you want. To be a gourmand is not to be a gourmet; you're not finicky. But it is to want the good things in life. It can also be, as Brillat-Savarin recognizes, a perversity: something we have to do cut off from its proper place, and made into a fetish, a wanting. We can't care too much about dining, but we *can* care too much about food. The sin isn't loving the flesh; it's losing our minds in loving the flesh. A moment of mindful appreciation comes between the observation and the act. Eating well is purely animal if it doesn't become a way to think about appetite itself.

Brillat-Savarin was not just a good eater; he was, in every sense, a liberal eater. It was Brillat-Savarin who inspired the first century of food writing in French and English both. (M.F.K. Fisher's translation of Brillat-Savarin is one of the monuments of the movement.) The tone of food writing remained most often his tone of mock-epic appreciation and semisatirical systemization, systematic but self-mocking, too. His approach—eating for pleasure and writing about what the food was like while meditating on its place in a big picture of life—is still the one that draws us closest to the real meaning of our appetites.

If Brillat-Savarin was the first philosopher of eating as a humanistic act, he was also, as Alexandre Dumas the elder remarked a little disparagingly, "a man of theory," who hovered above and around the table and never, as Dumas scoffed, offered an actual recipe. His great rival and bookend, Grimod La Reynière, as he was known—I've already had to quote from him at length, as any fan or student of the period must—was a man born to pen and paper, who sat right at it.

Born in November of 1758, Grimod de La Reynière was the son of a kind of borderline aristocrat, a tax collector whose license to tax on behalf of the King was usually turned into a habit of stealing on behalf of himself. Grimod had a hideous birth defect; both of his arms were missing hands, and ended, like the lobster-boy's in a sideshow, in strange fleshy pincers. His shame-filled parents, at a time when birth defects were still seen as signs from God, put about the bizarre story that the boy had been dropped in a pigpen, and that the swine had devoured his hands. (The effect of this lie on a boy who grew up with a special—vengeful?—love for bacon is hard to know for sure, but it's easy to imagine morbidly.)

Grimod in any case soon had prosthetic hands and the deformity, as deformity so often does, had only a passing effect on his life: he liked to tease people by putting his wooden hands on a hot stove, leading his friends to do the same, thinking that it wasn't. Like Brillat-Savarin, he had a bad revolution. (Though perhaps only bad people had good ones.) Starting out as a kind of libertine democrat—"I was a Republican when there was some glory in being one," he said later, mostly truthfully—just before the revolution he had been, ironically, sent into exile by his rich and well-connected uncle, Malsherbes, as punishment for a series of sophomoric literary scandals. This meant that Grimod sat out most of the revolution in the little southern town of Béziers, where he ate well—"rabbits fed on scented herbs, quails as fat as chickens, aubergines, heaven-sent melons, muscat grapes, and Roquefort cheese fit for a non-dethroned King"—he said, with a wince of irony, and found his vocation writing about it. As word of the bloodletting spread to him—his own uncle was one of Robespierre's prime victims—food also became a retreat from reality: "I would die of despair if I were not rescued by my good appetite," he wrote back. Eating was then, as it is now, self-medication, a therapy of the panicked.

It was after the end of the Terror and his return to Paris that he became both a passionate reactionary—"Never did fanaticism produce a thousandth part of the evils which incredulity causes today," he said—and the inventor of the first regular food journalist's magazine, the *Almanach des Gourmands,* which first appeared in 1803. The magazine, though a bit chaotic, included blind tastings, articles on foods, and a restaurant guide. Grimod himself was a star, with his picture—overweight, sweaty looking, and a little undignified—in the first issue.

He was a greedy guy, who used his new fame to sponsor eating clubs, where the best of the new restaurants would send free food in exchange for a certificate of approval to put in their windows, and where he could invite the starlets of the day to dine with him. (Though he had a way with those wooden hands he seems, unsurprisingly, to have boasted of his skill at cunnilingus.) The idea of the French journalist as a man in search of free meals and free company and free *chatte,* too—which Balzac mocks, and which persists into our own day, when the Parisian food critic who pays the bill is a rare bird indeed—was already part of Grimod's persona, and his self-invention.

What distinguishes Grimod de La Reynière from the artisanal sound of all prior food writing, even Brillat-Savarin's, is his taste for aphorism, for summing up a sensual moment in abstract mots. The writer searches for a pregnant phrase to sum up a pleasure just past. Grimod is a first-rate epigram-maker, and still apt today. There is, for instance, his line that "the three things to avoid at the table are 'a little wine which I bought from the grocer,' a dinner 'just among a few friends,' and amateur musicians." Or he can be neatly compact, as when he writes, "A gourmand should respect his teeth as an author his talent." (It need be noted that it was only in the Second Empire, when a Philadelphia dentist visited France and befriended the Empress, that anything like decent dentistry came to Paris.)

Yet there is a tongue-in-cheek, self-mocking tone to his work, and to French food writing of the period generally, which academics often miss. We have often heard these days about the difference between sincerity (saying what you truly think) and authenticity (being who you really are). There is as big a difference, though, between being sincere and being in earnest. Both Brillat-Savarin and Grimod de La Reynière are entirely sincere in their passion for eating, as they are in their small discriminations, their appetite for order and system. They love food. They really do. But they are never completely in earnest, always kidding about their subject even as they celebrate it, and Grimod's aphorisms are always to be taken as an instance of the mock-heroic. (With the understanding that mock-heroic is different from the ironic: the ironic says, "I don't really mean this"; the mock-heroic says, "I mean what I say, but I know that saying so has its absurd aspects.")

Brillat-Savarin and Grimod don't entirely mean what they write, but then they sort of do. When de La Reynière says that "lunch is the meal of friendship, dinner of etiquette, and tea of children; supper alone belongs to love," he is both summing up the new pecking order of meals (under which, for instance, there really were two kinds of *déjeuners*—one a true lunch, the other, *petit déjeuner*, a "little lunch," or breakfast, a separate meal of chocolate or coffee and bread) and using the Enlightenment turn of mind, with its love of oversimple summary and a neat schedule of emotions, against itself, to mock its own proprieties. It's a joke, but not just a joke. Grimod is smiling, but he's not kidding. Or when he writes that "all the other people of Europe theorize and argue; only the Frenchman knows how to talk," he is in part paying a patriotic compliment to his own people, but also recognizing, as Brillat-Savarin had before him, that the table was the one place where French superiority could still assert itself. It's a loser's boast. Even Brillat-Savarin's most famous mot, "Tell me what you eat, and I will tell you who you are," is a jest as much as a judgment, not meant to be taken entirely seriously— a prejudice dressed up as an absolute.

"Playful" is an ugly word in English, since it suggests the opposite of true play: tyrannical teachers, brutish coaches, sadistic bosses, all like to think of themselves as "playful." So one pauses before saying that the writing of Brillat-Savarin and Grimod is "playful." But "ludic," an older and odder word, suits the gastronomes well; they are aware of the absurd aspects of their enterprise even as they undertake it. When Brillat-Savarin writes of his "Dynamometer," which registers where on the social ladder you belong according to how you choose to eat, or ranks gourmands according to many classes—from the first level, at which you eat truffled turkey, to the fourth, where presumably it's pot-au-feu right down the line—using "gastronomic tests," there's a smile on his prose. He's kidding around about the French mania for systematization, while taking part in it at the same time. (This tone has its American equivalent later in the nineteenth century; when Melville and Twain write about the confidence man as the most representative and greatest American figure, they really mean it and they don't. As con men in America, so cooks in France; they really are admired, but admiring them is also a way of making fun of the people, generals and statesmen, whom you are supposed to admire more.)

This double-talk, kidding the new powers by praising the lower arts, is present in most of Grimod de La Reynière's best lines about food. When he writes, for instance, that "the cook looks death in the eye more often than the soldier," he means it—to be a cook is to see a lot of carnage and to know how to evaluate it, to know when to hang the carcass and when to slice it up at once—but he is also suggesting that the soldier's courage is hardly more useful than the cook's. Or when he writes beautifully that "the pig is the encyclopedic animal"—meaning that it includes everything from lowly feet to all-purpose bacon and tender filet—he is both offering a lovely summary *and* joking about those other "encyclopedic animals" the high-minded *philosophes* attend. *There's* your encyclopedia, on four trotters. We miss something essential about the birth of food writing if we miss this tone of sober counter-Enlightenment clowning, its tongue-in-cheek parody of the age's pieties, a new tone sobered by experience and made lighter by life. There is a noisy form of quietism in Grimod, a lip-smacking form of life doubting. Nothing works out the way you think it will; you might as well eat. This note of bitter, brilliant, defeated glamour exudes from his work.

For where Brillat-Savarin's liberalism is central to his idea of good eating, Grimod's reactionary politics is key to the passion of his *gourmandise.* When Grimod writes that a gourmand's first duty "is to sample everything and have an aversion to nothing," he is proposing a kind of table-based extension of Voltaire's great comment, upon being asked to return a second time to a male bordello, "Once a philosopher, twice a pervert." But we can recognize the chastened wisdom of the postrevolutionary period, too. Loss, defeat—first the moral defeat of hope in the Terror, then the practical defeat of the French by the Germans and English—are the *emotional* keys to the growth of the food scene in Paris. The thought that we have our greatest triumphs at the table implies that we have been defeated on the field. No successful militaristic nation has ever cared too much about eating. Robespierre and Napoléon, who brought disorder, fear, and eventual defeat to France, were both ascetics. Thinking too hard, trying too hard, can lead to terror and war; thinking alternately with eating is a saner plan. We can organize and systematize all we like about eating—but in the end the animal will return. Whatever we say about food today, we will be hungry again tomorrow.

The Paris food scene, the first "culinary field," is in this way partly an extension of "the habit of cultural explanation," an incursion of intellect into an area previously thought to be the simple province of Nature. But the food writers never forget that natural appetite persists in the face of all systems. Brillat-Savarin, the disillusioned liberal, remains a man of the Enlightenment, bringing order to the table; Grimod, the reactionary, is very much a man of the counter-Enlightenment, seeking in abiding pleasures salvation from all those scary absolutes. But both know better than to plan a perfect meal.

Brillat-Savarin and Grimod divide between them the empire of food; they are the two working philosophers of taste who invented its literary form, and almost all food writing since has taken as its mask either Brillat's warm ironic smile or Grimod's brilliant epigrammatic grimace. Yet they have much in common, too. The soft snap and crackle of long-braised rueful wisdom in the work of Brillat-Savarin and Grimod is very different from the racket of arriviste learning. The table's intuitions always trump its new rules. Food writing was born in the wake of the revolution and the Terror, and one hears in its corridors and back hallways the sigh of those who stayed alive, returned from exile and panic, and are now grateful for the smallest of pleasures. It's an animal truth—the pig's truth at Christmas, the turkey's the day after Thanksgiving—and more welcome for that: the wisdom of those who survive is that survival is itself a kind of wisdom.

This tone, and this kind of food writing, seems uniformly easy to like. Still, we should also see that while Brillat-Savarin's writing on food is reformist and optimistic, Grimod's, for all its genius, is a counsel of defeatism and despair, and was seen that way at the time: the *Almanach des Gourmands* soon had a rejoinder published by an angry liberal: *The Almanach of Starvation*. In Grimod's celebration of eating, there are the first intimations of the cordoning off of the French palate—the emergence of the *idéologie française,* the myth of a *douce* France, safeguarded from outside influence and living on its own bounty and beauty, that would do so much harm to the Republic. Not by accident does Grimod's brilliant grimacing take the very same tone as that of Robert Courtine, the famous twentieth-century food critic who took over Grimod's pen name, La Reynière, and wrote for decades in *Le Monde* with the same wincing high style. Only after his death did the eminent newspaper discover, or reveal, that Courtine had been a virulent anti-Semite and an extreme right-wing Vichyiste. The turn to the table can be made as often in bitterness as in benevolence.

Indeed, among the real La Reynière's circle, a reactionary countermyth soon sprang up, romanticizing French food. Instead of being the work of *métissage*, mixed-up influences and urban crossbreedings, French cooking was said to be quite simply the cooking of the noble French peasant and the simple French provinces brought to the tables of the city. This attempt to make the cooking that had grown up in Paris look as though it had always been stewing in the same pious pot would have its bad effect on French cuisine.

The culinary historians who have written the new history of the restaurant are mostly what might be called "sizzlists." They think the atmosphere, the sizzle, around the steak is more important to its aura than the steak itself. Most of the new culinary historians practice "niche" history, and, like the best of such books, theirs are rich in weird data, unsung heroes, and bizarre true stories about the making of familiar things. They also practice what you might call the new secret-code school of history—history that claims that some familiar thing, like a pair of pants, which is supposed to do one thing (say, cover your legs) is really there to do another (say, show off the insecure double nature of bourgeois masculinity).

The trouble with this kind of reading—and one of the more obvious banalities of seeing everything as a social construction, the ultimate postmodern vice—is that it vastly underestimates the difficulty of *doing* things, as opposed to thinking about them. It implies that ideas are hard, while pants (or soup) are easy. In fact, it is as hard to make good chicken soup as it is to make a reason that it is good for you, and the technical history of cooking is, after all, not a tourist trap for historians but a necessary subject.

The historian Amy Trubek has pointed out, rightly, that one of the most momentous changes that the restaurant brought to French cooking was simply the invention of stock. While the drinkable *restaurants* became restaurants in our sense, they also became stocks, and the use of stocks, as Trubek points out, is what distinguishes French cooking from all other kinds. You could simmer some bones and vegetables in a pot full of water, cook it down and reserve the liquid. Add something else and finally you would have a dish that tasted both like the stuff you simmered and the something else you bathed in it. (This is different from putting a sauce on pasta, or adding chutney to a curry, where the idea is that the main thing and the sauce are nothing alike.) This way of enriching and layering flavors seems obvious once you think of it, and, once it was thought of, the range of fine shadings became so vast that by the 1820s, French cooking had built its whole "grammar" upon this way of relating each thing on the plate to every other.

Grammars are easier to teach than accents, as every Berlitz instructor knows, and because French cooking had a grammar, within fifty years it was the only kind of cooking rich people wanted. The restaurant was, among other things, the potential originator of sauces, and it was sauces that became the glory of the new cooking. Whether for the goose or the gander the sauce was the thing even more than the thing being sauced.

With the end of the revolution, and the restoration of the monarchy, the restaurant got a new life, as the bourgeois palace par excellence. It moved for good from the complicated, "semi-public" space, the Palais Royal world, of before the revolution to the "semiprivate" space that it has been since. The restaurant in later nineteenth-century Paris was a place that only seemed to offer a public experience; in fact, you were having a private, anonymous experience. You were out and about, in society, yes, but without being social. So it is that restaurants became, in Rebecca Spang's words, "places of daydream and fantasy."

Should we believe that there is no substance in cooking beyond the economy of signs passed for a price? When we sit down to that dinner on those red velvet banquettes, are we taking part in the overture of pleasure, or are we just paying to play out a fantasy: a brief impersonation of power, in a rented theater of false possibilities? There is an impulse among historians, who like narrow, punitive moralities, to divide the new republic of eating in two, and imagine the café as the good popular institution that the working classes found for themselves, while the restaurant is the bourgeoisie's spiderweb where working-class girls go to be seduced and working-class boys go to wait on tables. It is part of the cynicism of such historians to say that the bourgeoisie merely replaced the old aristocracy as masters of the table. The merchant with his three chins took the place of the count with his three mistresses (and pet dogs waiting to be fed). The locale changed, but the relation between shearer and shorn didn't.

But this is to understate the degree to which the restaurant, no less than the café, really was a popular invention. Republicans and reactionaries alike found what they needed in the restaurant. Brillat-Savarin and La Reynière—a singed victim of the revolution's excess—are both categorical about this: the free market in food meant that for the first time someone could get rich by cooking good food for many people, who had the choice to go eat elsewhere. Choice was limited by money, of course, but there was, for the first time in history, choice. Brillat-Savarin writes in wonder about the sudden democratic spread of restaurants meant chiefly for the poor, and of how they raised the possibilities of eating as pleasure even for the impoverished.

This larger argument about the meaning of the café and the restaurant reflects one of the few academic-seeming arguments that all thinking people ought to care about: the one between the mid-twentieth-century French philosopher Michel Foucault and his disciples and the still-living German philosopher Jürgen Habermas and his, about the real meaning of the eighteenth-century Enlightenment. Was the Enlightenment really that, a progression toward a more humane and just world, as Habermas would have it? Or was it just an effort to answer with absolutes questions that could only be settled for a moment, a con game designed to empower a new class by pretending that they had special access to certain new knowledge, as Foucault insists?

Do the café and the restaurant represent a class prison—or are they revolutionary cells with coffee on the boil? Many of the new historians of cooking come down very hard on the restaurant as a typical lair of bourgeois trickery. The Enlightenment promises freedom and everywhere is forging chains; the essence of the restaurant racket is that the diners are shut off from the hot and messy kitchen, where the real work, and exploitation, goes on. *Sale métier,* indeed. The restaurant acts as though it is all-welcoming and anyone can come in, and then hands you the check that far from everyone can pay—consider it a form of "culinary imperialism." But if "imperialism" has any meaning at all, it is surely that the imperialized are getting something they don't want; in the restaurant they get something they *do* want, so much so that they are willing to pay people they don't much like for it. The spread of French cooking is not an example of cultural imperialism. It is an example of culture.

Jürgen Habermas's view seems to come down on the side of the new republic of eating. Habermas has famously argued that the rise of cafés and clubs and the like in the Enlightenment helped create "social capital"—what's sometimes called civil society—by fostering the practice of arguing in small groups over tables. Where the Foucauldians suggest that the real purpose of the restaurant was to distract you from social life by lulling you into an effete reverie about taste—man was born to eat with his fellows, and everywhere you see him dining alone—Habermas sees it more hopefully: even if you were only arguing about pleasures, you were developing the habit of argument, exchange. Meal by meal and game by game and cup of coffee by cup of coffee, people got the knack of thinking for themselves.

At the ideal Habermasian table, it seems, everyone would argue about what to have, and there would be a vote on it, and everyone would emerge a better citizen. (I have eaten with Germans like that.) The political scientist Robert Putnam has become famous in America for making a similar point: social capital is made up of bowling leagues and glee clubs and 4-H groups, and what's lost when these groups are lost can't be made up by the semiprivate realm of fast-food joints or video arcades.

Surely a wiser point, though—one neither too German in its earnestness nor too unreal in its gloom—is that we build as much social capital, civic good, from semiprivate places as we do from public ones. There are many collegial institutions—the bowling league, the gardening club, the scout troop, the block party—that are obviously virtuous, and then there are some, like the restaurant, that may not be quite so wholesome but are benevolent all the same, in that they extend the blessings of freedom to letting you order what you choose. After all, the other exemplary nineteenth-century public place where you could go whenever you liked but couldn't talk to the person beside you was a library. Our sense of liberty begins not with the freedom to argue but with the freedom not to have to argue—to do what we like, whenever we like to do it, without having to make an articulate case one way or another. This is why teenagers, despite their privileges, feel so un-free. They are stuck in Habermasian society, always obliged to make the case for their pleasures.

Loneliness is not the "price" of liberty but part of the profit we take from it. The restaurant's moral glory, like that of the library and the department store—another nineteenth-century bourgeois invention—is its semiprivate state, for semi-ness is the special half-tint of bourgeois societies. The bowling league has been replaced not by solitary bowling but, more decisively, by the gym, another classic semiprivate place: on the bike you read your newspaper as you pedal in a long row of solitudes.

In the same way, at the restaurant on Third Avenue now as at the Palais Royal then, our joys intersect with those of others only at odd angles. My tenth birthday, though it passed so gloriously in the Howard Johnson's, passed unmarked by anyone but my three friends, my parents, and me and left only a memory. My first lunch in the Palais Royal was another lunch service among ten thousand at the Grand Véfour, and no one else who was there will think of it again at all.

That is not our sadness, except in the sense that all that passes makes us sad. It is also part of what makes a thing good. Happiness may come at us face-to-face, but joy always comes at us at an angle. We are used to the arrival; for a man it's when your wife, the perfect girl, comes back from powdering her nose, and you first catch sight of her out of the corner of your eye. The pleasures of the restaurant are occluded, sudden, haphazard in this way. You're eating at this table, and you listen to that one. You're watching one woman, or man, and spy from the corner of your eye another. The taste of your dinner mingles, or used to, with the aroma of your neighbor's cigar. Places of hope, restaurants and cafés are also places of reassuring mystery, and the mystery reassures because, in reminding us of lives and appetites beyond our own, they remind us of worlds we have yet to enter.

As with most interesting inventions of bourgeois culture, restaurant-going is cushioned on the surface, angular and dramatic just beneath. It is a study in tensions and role-playing. To visit Le Grand Véfour, the one restaurant that remains intact and has been in business continuously since Roze de Chantoiseau's day, is to instantly take part in a drama that has gone on so long because its point is so unsettled. The maître d' is both servant, having to wait, and master, being empowered to choose and offer. The customer is both aristocrat for an hour and anxious suitor. Even the closed kitchen, while it distances the work, increases the mystique. If the dimwitted diner doesn't know what goes on back there, it is still the case that the ultimate compliment to the savvy diner is to be invited into the kitchen. We eat out to find out who we are, and part of who we are is who we pretend to be, and whom we elect to pay for our pretense.

The roles we play are part of the people we are. All democratic society may or may not begin in small communities, but all civility depends on little lies. The restaurant is our classroom for what Dr. Johnson called "fictitious benevolence," and teaches its first lesson: as important as finding people you have things in common with is learning to live in pleasure alongside people with whom you don't. This may be why, though there's a new "new cooking" every few years, the institution of the restaurant has shown itself so resilient, so durable, so amazingly the same across time and tears. The waiter now introduces himself by name, and he may have changed his tux for an Agnès B. collarless shirt, but he still comes and goes and rarely mentions money. We might gag on what was served at Chantoiseau's restaurant, we might not be able to find our idea of a good meal at Véry's little temple, but, seeing the pantomime of waiters and menus and mirrors and erotic murmur, we would know at once just where we were. Home, Robert Frost wrote, is the place where, when you have to go there, they have to take you in. A restaurant is a place where, when you go there, they not only have to take you in but have to act as though they were glad to see you. In cities of strangers, this pretense can be very dear.

2

What's the Recipe?

A MAN AND A WOMAN lie in bed at night in the short hour between kid sleep and parent sleep, turning down page corners as they read. She is leafing through a fashion magazine, he through a cookbook. Why they read these things mystifies even the readers. The closet and the cupboard are both about as full as they're going to get, and though we can credit the magazine reader with at least wanting to know what is in fashion when she sees it, what can the recipe reader possibly be reading for? The shelf of cookbooks long ago overflowed, so that the sad relations and failed hopes (*Monet's Table, A Drizzle of Honey: The Lives and Recipes of Spain's Secret Jews*) now are stacked horizontally, high up. The things he knows how to make that are actually in demand are as fixed as any cocktail-lounge pianist's set list, and for a clientele of children every bit as devoted to the old favorites as the barflies around that piano: make Parmesan-crusted chicken—the "Feelings" of food—every night and they would be delighted. Though a dinner party looms, and with it the possibility of a new thing made and added to the repertoire, the truth is that, on the night, the amateur cook falls back, like the amateur actor, on the set recitation. It's going to be lamb *tagine* or the roasted chicken thing with preserved lemons, and there's no helping it. . . . Yet the new cookbooks continue to show up in bed, and the corners still go down.

Vicarious pleasure? More like deferred frustration. Anyone who cooks knows that it is in following recipes that one first learns about the anticlimax of the actual, the perpetual disappointment of the thing achieved. I learned it as I learned to bake. When I was in my early teens, the sick yearning for sweets that adolescents suffer often drove me, in afternoons taken off from school, to bake, which, miraculously, meant just doing what the books said and hoping to get the promised yield. I followed the recipes as closely as I could: dense Boston cream pie, Rigó Jansci slices, Sacher torte with apricot jam between the layers. The potential miracle of the cookbook was immediately apparent: you start with a feeling of greed, find a list of rules, assemble a bunch of ingredients, and then you have something to be greedy about. In cooking you begin with the ache and end with the object, where in most of the life of the appetites—courtship, marriage—you start with the object and end with the ache.

Yet, if the first thing a cadet cook learns is that words can become tastes, the second is that a space exists between what the rules promise and what the cook gets. It is partly that the steps between—the melted chocolate's gleam, the chastened, improved look of the egg yolks mixed with sugar—are often more satisfying than the finished cake. But the trouble also lies in the same good words that got you going. How do you know when a thing "just begins to boil"? How can you be sure that the milk has scalded but not burned? Or touch something too hot to touch, or tell firm peaks from stiff peaks? Define "chopped"? In those days I was illicitly baking in the afternoons, I was learning main-course cooking at night without recipes from my mother, a scientist by day, who had long been off-book, as they say in the theater. She would show, not tell: how you softened the onions, made them golden, browned them. This practice got you deeper than the words ever could.

Handed-down wisdom and worked-up information remain the

double piers of a cook's life. The recipe book always contains two things: news of how something is made, and assurance that there's a way to make it, with the implicit faith that if I know how it is done I can show you how to do it. The premise of the recipe book is that these two things are naturally balanced; the secret of the recipe book is that they're not. The space between learning the facts about how something is done and learning how actually to do it always turns out to be large, at times immense. What kids make depends on what moms—or, now, dads—know: skills, implicit knowledge, inherited craft, buried assumptions, finger know-how that no recipe can sum up. The recipe is a blueprint but also a red herring, a way to do something and a false summing up of a living process that can be handed on only by demonstration, a knack posing as a knowledge. We say, "What's the recipe?" when we mean "How exactly do you do it?" And though we want the answer to be "Like this!" the honest answer is "Be me!" "What's the recipe?" you ask the weary pro chef, and he gives you a weary-pro-chef look, since the recipe is the totality of the activity, the real work. The recipe is to spend your life cooking.

What is this thing, the recipe? Where did it come from, and how does it work? As the cookbooks keep coming, and we continue to turn down their pages—*The Asian Grandmothers Cookbook, The Adaptable Feast,* the ones with disingenuously plain names, like *How to Roast a Lamb: New Greek Classic Cooking* (a good one, in fact, by Michael Psilakis), and the ones with elaborately nostalgic premises, like *Dining on the B & O: Recipes and Sidelights from a Bygone Age*—we begin to ask, What? Why? Patterns emerge. Changes over time. Once-familiar things depart from their pages silently, like Minerva's owls. "Yield," for instance, a word that appeared at the top of every recipe in every cookbook that my mother owned—"Yield: six portions," or twelve, or twenty—is gone. Maybe it seemed too cold, too technical. In any case, the recipe no longer yields; it merely serves. "Makes six servings" or "Serves four to six as an appetizer" is all you get.

Other good things go. Clarified butter (melted butter with the milk solids skimmed and strained) has vanished—Graham Kerr, the Galloping Gourmet, once used it like holy water—while emulsified butter (melted butter with a little water whisked in), thanks to Thomas Keller's sponsorship, plays an ever-larger role. The cult of the cooking vessel—the wok, the *tagine,* the Dutch oven, the smoker, the hibachi, the Tibetan kiln, or the Inuit ice oven, or whatever—seems to be over. Paula Wolfert may have a book devoted to clay-pot cooking, but it feels too ambitious in advance; we have tried too many other modish pots, and know that, like Elvis's and Michael Jackson's chimps, after their hour is done they will live out their years forgotten and alone; they'll end up on the floor of the closet, alongside the fondue forks and the spice grinder and the George Foreman grill. Even the imagery of cooking has changed. Sometime in the past decade or so, the actual eating line was breached. Now the cooking magazines and the cookbooks are filled with half-devoured dishes and cut-open vegetables. Michael Psilakis's fine Greek cookbook devotes an entire page to a downbeat still-life of torn-off artichoke leaves lying in a pile; the point is not to entice the eater but to ennoble the effort.

With their own torn leaves and unyielding pages, the newer cookbooks show two overt passions: one is for simplicity, the other is for salt. The chef's cookbook from the fancy place has been superseded by the chef's cookbook from the fancy place without the fancy-place food. David Waltuck, of the ever-to-be-mourned Chanterelle, started this trend with his *Staff Meals from Chanterelle,* and now we have Thomas Keller's *Ad Hoc at Home,* and, from Mark Peel, of the Los Angeles hot spot Campanile, *New Classic Family Dinners.* ("Every single recipe was tested in Peel's own home kitchen—where he has only one strainer, just like the rest of us, and no kitchen staff to clean up after him.") Simplicity's appeal as a religion is inherent. But the trend is in part also a reaction to the cult of complexity of the Ferran Adrià school of molecular cooks, with their cucumber foam and powdered octopus. Reformations make counterreformations as surely as right makes left; every time someone whitewashes a church in Germany, someone else paints angels on a ceiling in Rome.

But simplicity remains the most complicated of all concepts. In one month we may stumble over six simple recipes for a ragout or Bolognese—plain spaghetti sauce, as it used to be known, when there was only one kind—with chicken livers or without, diced chuck roast or hamburger, white wine or red. Yet all movements in cooking believe themselves to be movements toward greater simplicity. (Even the molecular gastronomes believe that they are truly elemental, breaking things down to the atomic level.)

Simplicity is the style, but salt is the ornamental element—the idea of tasting flights of salt being a self-satirizing notion that Swift himself couldn't have come up with. The insistence on the many kinds of salt—not merely sea salt and table salt but hand-harvested *fleur de sel*, Himalayan red salt, and Hawaiian pink salt—is everywhere, and touching, because, honestly, it all tastes like salt. And now everyone brines. Brining, the habit of dunking meat in salty water for a bath of a day or so, seems to have first reappeared out of the koshering past in *Cook's Illustrated*, sometime in the early nineties, as a way of dealing with the dry flesh of the modern turkey, and then spread like ocean water in a tsunami, until now both Keller and Peel are keen to brine everything: pork roasts, chicken breasts, shrimp, duck.

Although brining is defended with elaborate claims to tenderness, what it really does is make food taste salty; we're doing what our peasant ancestors did, making meat into ham. All primates like the taste of salt; that's a feature, not a bug. Salted food demands a salty sweet. I read that in Spain recently one connoisseur had "a chocolate ganache coated in bread floating in a small pool of olive oil with fleur de sel sprinkled on it," while we can now make pecan-and-salt caramel-cheesecake chocolate mousse with olive oil, and flaky-salt sticky peanut cookie bars for ourselves.

The salt fetish has, I think, a deeper and more psychological cause, too: we want to bond with the pro cooks. Most of what a pro cook has to his advantage comes down to the same advantages that Caribbean sugarcane planters used to have: high heat and lots of willing slaves. (The slaves seem happy, anyway, until they escape and write that testimonal, or start that cooking blog.) But the pro cook also tends to salt a lot more than feels right to an amateur home cook; both the late Bernard Loiseau and the Boston cook Barbara Lynch have confessed that hyperseasoning, and, in particular, high salting, is a big part of what makes pro cooks' food taste like pro cooks' food. The poor home cook, with no hope of an eight-hundred-degree brick oven, and lucky if he can indenture a ten-year-old into peeling carrots, can still salt hard—and so salt, its varieties and use, becomes a luxury replacement, a sign of seriousness even when you don't have the real tools of seriousness at hand.

The desire to bond with the restaurant recipe book is a form of its own now. No one really believes, or believes deeply, that it is possible to cook at home in the way that we eat at restaurants. When we buy Thomas Keller's *French Laundry Cookbook*—though I will admit that his short ribs are a steady thing—on the whole we grasp not only that you can't do it, but that there is something gauche in even trying. It is a form of pretense, with a gauzy mask over your own features. You're not Thomas Keller or Gordon Ramsay, or whoever else. So what's the use? To read them is to grasp not a dish you'll make, but a new sequence of possibility: we read a long recipe and take from it a single feature—a new way of reducing onions, the idea of mixing cubed potatoes with the green beans, a gesture rather than a gestalt—just as the woman in bed beside you reading *Elle*, though she will never buy anything she sees, finds new matches, current cuts, ways of rearranging. We read epics, and end with a single spice. One elegant idea—*beurre monté,* say (butter whipped with water)—sustains a hundred pages of perusing.

What the restaurant cookbook never delivers is a way to replicate the restaurant experience. Like the "home version" of the game show presented to departing contestants on the game shows of my childhood—*The Match Game,* or *Hollywood Squares*—the home version of a restaurant cannot even vaguely approximate the applauded version, whose whole point, after all, was that it was not taking place at home. Even Gene Rayburn and Paul Lynde had their unique quiddity, their aura of celebrity not reproducible by your sister, or even by your ambiguous uncle. There is no true home version of *Password,* and there is no way to put Balthazar between hard covers, *The Balthazar Cookbook* notwithstanding. The home games' made-up celebrities—Harry Holsum; Stella Starlit; Slick Nick; Susie Slurp; Tim Type; Alice Actress—were mocking you, in effect, for imagining that you could reproduce the thrill of the show at home. When it comes to Thomas Keller or Ferran Adrià, we are all Susie Slurp, each one a Harry Holsum.

Yet the urge to meld identities with the pros is tied to a desire to get something out of a cookbook besides another recipe. For beneath these conscious enthusiasms lies a deep new uncertainty that complicates the traditional relationship between the recipe book and its reader. In this, the Great Age of Disaggregation, all the old forms are being smashed apart and looted like piñatas at a birthday party. The cookbook isn't spared. The Internet has broken what once seemed like the natural membrane of recipes, just as it has ruptured the newspaper's old containment of news stories. You can find pretty much any recipe you want online now. If you need a recipe for mustard-shallot sauce or *boeuf à la mode,* you enter a few search terms, and there it is.

So the old question "What's the recipe for?" gives way to "What's the cookbook for?," and this existential crisis has moved the cookbook, like everything else these days, toward the memoir, the confessional, the recipe as self-revelation. Barbara Lynch's preface to her *Stir* sounds like the opening lines of *Goodfellas:* "We were poor, fiercely Irish, and extremely loyal. . . . The older boys I knew grew up to be policemen, politicians, and criminals (often a mix of the three). . . . If I ever had thoughts at all as to what I might be when I grew up, they were modest ones. I might have pictured myself running a bar (in Southie) or maybe opening a sub shop (in Southie). But having a restaurant of my own on Beacon Hill? No way. In fact, if a fortune-teller had told me at fourteen what good things were in store for me, I would have laughed in her face and told her where she could shove such bullshit. . . . I marvel that any of us made it out of there without winding up in jail or the morgue." Michael Psilakis, in *How to Roast a Lamb,* includes his own childhood traumas: "As I sat on top of the lamb, watching it struggle to free itself, as if in slow motion my father came up behind me, reached down over my right shoulder with a hunting knife, grabbed the lamb's head and ears, and, in one swift motion, slit the lamb's throat. . . . Blood shot out of the lamb like water from a high-pressure hose." You never had a moment like that with Julia Child or Joseph Wechsberg.

The pull toward storytelling is perhaps more than a reaction to the crisis in book publishing or even to our personality-driven culture. It may well be a clue to the origins of the form. Recipes, like cave paintings, are seen only in their maturity, when they astonish us by their confident finish. Less perfect earlier versions are wiped away like the early drafts scrawled on the cave wall. We see a mystical liturgical whole and miss the background of trial and error. For centuries, cooks must have passed down "receipts" to other cooks. They appeared in the seventeenth and eighteenth centuries in a compressed language—very much like the "fake books" that jazz musicians compiled raggedly over the first half of the last century, with chords and melodies scribbled in—just enough to tell someone already expert how to do the tricky turns.

The true cookbook—the kind this lonesome bedtime page-turner hungers for today—only appeared very late, in the nineteenth century. Like so many things that seem part of a semieternal order of eating—the soup starter, the white wines before red—the recipe book is younger than the novel, more dewy-eyed than the end of slavery. In its first blush the cookbook was not for the professional but for the home cook, and it was less a matter of self-help than business management. Modern cookbooks were meant not to teach women how to cook but to teach women how to teach other women how to cook. Part of the apparatus of the domestic chatelaine, cookbooks like Mrs. Beeton's famous tome of the 1860s allowed one to instruct the female servants, unlettered girls, in the preparation of standard dishes. Taking charge of all things domestic certainly bound women to the home, but there was something emancipating about it. The cooking woman was also a managing woman, a woman who ran things, not a doll but a doer.

"Men are now so well served out of doors,—at their clubs, well ordered taverns and dining houses, that in order to compete with the attractions of these places, a mistress must be thoroughly acquainted with the theory and practice of cookery," one cookbook author wrote. The erotic message—the mistress needs to compete—is buried but implicit. It was the same message that was still being impressed on women as late as the early sixties—please him at home and he won't go wandering. (Think of the Burt Bacharach and Hal David song "Wives and Lovers"; by the end of the decade the same great team had composed "I Say a Little Prayer" in a very different spirit.) By then, too, the middle-class woman had a more robust role model and manual than Mrs. Beeton: Julia Child was calling cooking an art and calling women to mastery of it, in a world once again mostly without servants.

sert, but a Port Salut cheese, and a single tangerine, the whole thing washed down with a good bottle of Burgundy.

Yet all of this is couched not, as a man's writing might be, as detached "Epicurean" revelry but, as even an aesthetic woman's must be, as spurs to shopping and cooking. Her greed is productive. Her recipes are makeable, but they are also offered as prose poems (even those of us allergic to the prose poem can like these)—for example, on turbot au gratin:

> In Turbot gratin, the ecstatic possibilities are by no means limited. In a chaste silver dish, make a pretty wall of potatoes, which have been beaten to flour, enlivened with pepper and salt, enriched with butter and cream—cream thick and fresh and adorable— seasoned with Parmesan cheese and left on the stove for ten minutes, no more nor less; then let the wall enclose pieces of turbot, already cooked and in pieces, of melted butter and of cream, with a fair covering of breadcrumbs; and rely upon a quick [i.e., broiler hot] oven to complete the masterpiece.

Elizabeth Pennell had extremely, almost scarily, good taste: she loved Burgundy, Cognac, strong coffee; she wanted simple food that wasn't too simple—roasted spring chicken, a ragout of mushrooms—and subscribed to the enduring truth that "the secret of good cooking lies in the discreet and sympathetic treatment of the onion." "And after," she adds, "if you still hanker for the roast beef of old England, then go and gorge yourself at the nearest restaurant." She wants you to accompany this with a good Beaune, and then with coffee, "a mix of Mocha and Mysore." "Forgo feminine liqueurs, but rely on cognac," the "immortal liquid," and then "lean back and smoke in silence, unless speech, exchanged with the one kind spirit, may be golden and perfect as the dinner."

The Pennells must have had a very good sex life.

Elizabeth Pennell was brave and eerily modern. She recom-

mended salad as a meal, while deploring the "salad cream" that
was still an alarming feature of British meals just a generation
ago. She loved Italian food, long before her postwar heir Elizabeth David, and put it on the same level as the French. Pasta
she especially adored—she calls it, generically, "macaroni," and
introduces her readers to the delights of spaghetti, the "smaller
daintier variety" of macaroni—in exactly the tones that a contemporary writer would introduce them to *traghetti* or *chitarra* or
some other obscure and newly trendy noodle. (She has the sense
to insist that the best way to eat it is cooked al dente and served
with grated Parmesan and butter.)

I feel about Pennell as A. J. Liebling felt about Pierce Egan, his
favorite chronicler of early-nineteenth-century prizefighting: that
here at last is a friend at court, a source of wisdom, an ally. One of
the hard-to-tell truths about even the best food writing before our
time is that we often have to learn to read past the food, which we
don't quite "get," on our way to the hunger, which we do. Almost
all descriptions of dinners past reveal something weird and
Martian in the choices—you bounce along happily enough with
Brillat-Savarin or even La Reynière eating truffled turkey, and
then suddenly you have long inscrutable stretches of boiled
lamb and larks on brochettes and sweet Sauternes served with
boiled salmon in anchovy cream. But there is nothing on Pennell's menus that is not delicious, like the menus themselves.
Where, reading old recipe books, you usually say, "Huh?" as
often as "Ummm," with Pennell it's all just right. Her ideal dinner is indeed ideal: onion soup soubise (with cream), tournedos
with wild mushrooms, and a winter root salad—carrots and cauliflower with a vinaigrette—followed by a single ripe tangerine,
all served with a good Beaune, very strong coffee (that preferred
Mocha and Mysore blend), and a glass of Chartreuse after.

Reading Pennell's recipes makes you think of what you'd want
your last meal to be. Mine is probably roast chicken with lemon,
cubed potatoes, cooked with a white wine reduction of the *jus*

from the chicken—this poses a danger since the cubed potatoes will absorb the juices, so I might do a gratin instead—and then mustard cream sauce, broccoli purée with crème fraîche, carrot circles with cumin and orange. An apricot soufflé for dessert, and for wine a rosé champagne to start, then a great Burgundy—a Vosne-Romanée or a Vougeot or Volnay—concluding with a glass of Calvados. Alternative menu: Filet of beef with béarnaise sauce and plenty of shallots and wild mushrooms; *pommes souf-flées;* green beans with more shallots; and a tarte tatin and a glass of Calvados to end. Chocolate *pot-au-crème* for dessert. A stronger wine to drink, like a California Syrah. Or, not to be too finicky: a well-brined pork chop—you can keep the filet, which is too vapid—with gray shallots and white wine mustard sauce, and roasted carrots and brussels sprouts with balsamic vinegar and bacon, and a tarte tatin with (again) a glass of Calvados for dessert (some things are not negotiable). But as I order these perfect suppers, I remember that the best meal our family ever shared was in fact a milk-fed leg of lamb, a gigot, from the Pyrenees, with a Beaune wine, and a purée of potatoes and green beans, I think; the sauce was a magical, improvised combination of a garlic cream and the white wine reduction from the lamb drippings that I've never quite been able to re-create. (And what was dessert that night? I think we had French strawberries, and then took the children out for ice cream.)

Yes, I digress. Elizabeth Pennell is the rare kind of food writer who makes you digress, turn from analytic scrutiny to ardent fantasy.

Pennell's recipes are all usable still, and her advice on seasonal dining is the best before Richard Olney. (She likes only light desserts, and insists on steak with shallots and chicken with mushrooms. I spent a weekend cooking from her diary, and it was all good, and the sequence of dishes impeccable.) A defining and presciently original aspect of all her work: she assumes that the reader is the cook, and also the shopper. The "Ladies, bless 'em" tone of much wine and food writing of the period is alien to her; that cozy clubby sound of George Saintsbury, for instance, for whom good wine and food is an extension of the college high table into private life is not hers. She writes of markets and stoves as one who knows, not as one who urges someone else on, and she assumes, with a minimum of melodrama, that woman is equal to man as a subject of the sensual life—so much that it still startles to read her easy use of "she" in this connection. She breezily assumes sexual equality, and her proof of it is the common pleasure men and women take from eating and drinking: "Love may grow bitter before cheese loses its savour," she counsels. "Therefore the wise, who value the pleasures of the table above tender dalliance, put their faith in strong limburger or fragrant Brie rather than in empty kisses. If only this lesson of wisdom could be mastered by all men and women, how much less cruel life might be!"

However new her sentiments, she is still writing in the form of the cookbook, reproducing, in her own English aesthetic, Chelsea-and-Whistler way, the mock-epic microcosmic sound of the first great generation of food writers, of Brillat-Savarin and Grimod. I have called their tone the tone of accepted defeat, the deep wisdom of loss, and Pennell, though writing from the triumphant seat of Victorian Britain, duly partakes of this tone, though she adapts it for the same reason that moves all English (and American) food writers until our own day: the assumption is that the good food is all over there, across the Channel, and that we over *here* can get to it only on holiday and in memory. Her cookbooks are an anthology of evocations: breakfasts by the Loire, supper in Naples, a bouillabaisse from Marseille, or a dish of simple pasta from outside Rome. "In a dish of macaroni lies all of Italy for the woman with eyes to see or a heart to feel . . . olive clad slopes and lonely stone palms; the gleam of sunlit rivers winding with reeds and the slim tall poplars; the friendly wayside *trattoria* and the pleasant refrain of the beaming *cameriere*, '*Subito, Signora, ecco!*'—a refrain ceaseless as the buzzing of the bees among the clover." Thinking of "the creamy subtle little Suisse cheese" recalls "a vision of Paris, radiant in Maytime, the long avenues and boulevards all white and pink with blossoming horse chestnuts, the air heavy laden with the fragrance of flowers; a vision of the accustomed corner in the old restaurant looking out towards the Seine and of the paternal waiter holding the fresh Suisse on a dainty green leaf. Life holds few such thrilling interludes." (Proust's famous use of food to evoke memory is perhaps the least original thing in that most original of writers: it was a commonplace of the fin-de-siècle aesthete. The genius of Proust was to substitute time for place: he didn't eat his crushed strawberries, as Elizabeth Pennell and every other aesthete did, to recall his time in Paris. Already there, he used them to recall his lost youth spent nowhere else. It is the homeboy's advantage.) She laments the philistine North she calls her home, even as her heart inclines toward the Elysian fields. Her advocacy of strong drink and stronger coffee, in a nation of tea-drinkers, is amazing, and she writes, all too accurately, that "over the barbarous depths into which the soul of the inspiriting berry has been dragged in unhappy Albion, it is kinder to draw a veil." (It would be another half century at least before Ian Fleming could, in *Goldfinger*, have James Bond, another Francophile gourmand, but a man with a license to kill, denounce tea with similar disdain, as a "cup of mud.")

As every Canadian knows, there are no springs so sweet as those that come a week too soon, and then fade back into winter. The delight in sharing recipes that Pennell's writing stirs was ended by a frost of educational necessities; the budding possibilities of the personal cookbook were nipped by the need to teach. The form would break in two: food writing, the cookbook improper, an offshoot essentially of travel literature, as in M.F.K. Fisher, preserved some of Elizabeth's tone: meanwhile, the cookbook proper evolved into something big and impressive, and took on the coloring of the books of authority. The standard kitchen bible, the book you turn to most often, has evolved from dictionary to encyclopedia, from anthology to grammar—a discernible progression if you compare the classics of the past century: Escoffier's culinary dictionary, Julia Child's *Mastering the Art of French Cooking*, Julee Rosso and Sheila Lukins's *The New Basics*, and Mark Bittman's recently revised *How to Cook Everything*.

Escoffier was pure dictionary: quick reminders to clarify a point or make a variation eloquent. He lists every recipe for tournedos and the medley of variations. His entries are summaries, aide-mémoires for cooks who know how to make a thing already and need only be reminded what's in it. (Is a béarnaise sauce tarragon leaves and stems, or just leaves?) This was the way all cooks cooked once. (In the old, railroad B & O cookbook, one finds this recipe for short ribs: "Put short ribs in a saucepan with one quart of nice stock, with one onion cut fine, steam until nice and tender. Place in roasting pan and put in oven until they are nice and brown." That's it. Everything else is commentary.)

In *Mastering the Art of French Cooking,* as in Waverley Root's *The Food of France,* which came out at around the same time, the age of elliptical assumption is over, and the turn is toward the encyclopedic: here's everything—all ye know on earth and all ye need to know—on a particular kind of cooking, which you can master by reading this book. Things are explained, but as in an encyclopedia, not a dictionary. The abundance and depth of information are scaled to the importance of each particular thing. Julia gives you not every recipe for tournedos, but only the recipes that count. Marcella Hazan would, later on, do the same kind of thing for Italian food. In this way cooking became not a sequence or catalogue of discrete moves that you used as you liked; it was a discipline with its own wholeness, a wholeness you mastered.

You wouldn't have wanted to bother mastering the art of French cooking unless you believed that it *was* an art uniquely worth mastering. When people did "master" it, they realized that it wasn't—that no one style of cooking is really adequate to the variety of our appetites. So the cookbook as anthology arrived, open to many sources, from American Thanksgiving dinner and Jewish brisket through Italian pasta and French Stroganoff—most successfully in the *New Basics* cookbook, which was the standard for the just-previous generation. The anthology cookbooks assumed curiosity about styles and a certainty about methods. In *The New Basics,* the tone is chatty, informal, taking for granted that the readers—still women, mostly—know the old basics: what should be in the kitchen, what kinds of appliances to use, how to handle a knife.

It was the dawn of a new answer to the question "What's a cookbook for?" The anthology cookbooks left behind the now stodgy-seeming encyclopedia and led toward what might be called grammatical grounding: the idea that what the cookbook should supply is the rules, the deep structure—a fixed, underlying technical grammar that enables you to use all the recipes you find, in this book or in others. This grammatical turn is clear in the popular "Best Recipe" series of *Cook's Illustrated,* and in *The Cook's Bible* of its editor, Christopher Kimball, in which recipes begin with a long disquisition on various approaches, ending with the best (and so brining was born), as well as in Michael Ruhlman's *The Elements of Cooking,* with the allusion to Strunk and White's usage guide, and, most of all, in Bittman's indispensable new classic *How to Cook Everything,* which, though claiming "minimalism" of style, is maximalist in purpose—not a collection of recipes for all occasions but a set of techniques for all time.

The cookbooks of the confessional turn suggest that we are all in this together; cookbooks of the grammatical turn assume that you don't know how to do the simple things, but that the simple things, once mastered, will enable you to do it all. Bittman assumes that you have no *idea* how to chop an onion or boil a potato, much less how chopping differs from slicing or dicing.

Each basic step is tenderly detailed. How to Boil Water: "Put water in a pot (usually to about two-thirds full), and turn the heat to high." How to Slice with a Knife: "You still press down, just with a little more precision, and cut into thick or thin slices of fairly uniform size." To sauté: "Put a large skillet on the stove and add the butter or oil. Turn the heat to medium-high. When the butter bubbles or the oil shimmers, add the food you want to sauté." Measuring dry ingredients, you are told to "scoop them up or use a spoon to put them in the cup." And that "much of cooking is about heat."

This all feels masculine in tone—not too many pretty side drawings, a car manual's systematic progression from recipe to recipe—and seems written with an eye to male readers who are either starting to cook for friends or are just married and learning that if you don't cook she's not about to. The old *New Basics*, one recalls nostalgically, was exclamatory and feminine. "The celebra-tion continues," reads a blurb, and inside the authors "indulge" and "savor" and "delight"; a warm chicken salad is "perfection when dressed in even more lemon," another chicken salad is "lush and abundant." The authors' perpetual "we" ("We like all our holidays accompanied with a bit of the bubbly"), though meant, in part, to suggest a merry partnership, was generous and inclu-sive, a "we" that honest-to-God extended to all of their readers.

Bittman never gushes but always gathers up: he has seven ways to vary a chicken kebab; eighteen ideas for pizza toppings; and, best of all, an "infinite number of ways to customize" mashed potatoes. He is cautious, and even skeptical; while Rosso and Lukins "love" and "crave" their filet of beef, to all of animal flesh Bittman allows no more than "Meat is filling and requires little work to prepare. It's relatively inexpensive and an excellent source of many nutrients. And most people like it." Most people like it! Rosso and Lukins would have tossed out any recipe, much less an entire food group, of which no more than that could be said. Lamb is a thing they "fall in love with again every season of the year," and of pork they know that it is "divinely succulent." Bittman thinks that most people like it. His tone is that of Ed Harris in *Apollo 13:* Let's work the problem, people. Want to thicken a sauce? Well, try Plan A: cook it down. Copy that, Houston. Plan A ineffective? Try Plan B: add roux. This progressive pattern appeals to men. The implication, slightly illusory, is that there's a neat set of steps from each point to the next, as in a Bill Walsh pass pattern: each pattern on the tree proceeds logically and the quarterback just has to look a little farther upfield.

Grammars teach foreign tongues, and the advantage of Bittman's approach is that it can teach you how to cook. But is working through a grammar book really a way to learn cooking, let alone to speak French? Doesn't it miss the social context—the dialogue of generations, the commonality of the family recipe—that makes cooking something more than just assembling calories and nutrients? It's as if someone wrote a book called *How to Play Catch.* ("Open your glove so that it faces the person throwing you the ball. As the ball arrives, squeeze the glove shut.") What it would tell you is not that we have figured out how to play catch but that we must now live in a culture without dads. In a world denuded of living examples, we end up with the guy who insists on making Malaysian shrimp one night and penne *all'amatriciana* the next; it isn't about anything except having learned how it's done. Your grandmother's pound cake may have been like concrete, but it was about a whole history and view of life; it got that tough for a reason.

The metaphor of the cookbook was long the pet metaphor of the conservative political philosopher Michael Oakeshott in his assault on the futility of thinking that something learned by rote was as good as something learned by ritual. Oakeshott's much repeated point was that one could no more learn how to make good government from a set of rules than one could learn how to bake a cake by reading recipe books. The cookbook, like a national constitution, was only the residue of a practice. Even the most grammatical of cookbooks dies without living cooks to illuminate its principles. Unsupported by your mom, the cookbook is the model of empty knowledge.

That's true, and yet the real surprise of the cookbook, as of the constitution, is that it sometimes yields something better in the space between what's promised and what's made. You can follow the recipe for something exotic—green curry or paella—and though what you end up with would shock the natives, it may be just as good as or even better than the thing intended. Before I learned that green curries were soupy, I made them creamy, which actually is nicer. In politics, too, where the unwritten British constitution has been turned into a recipe—like the constitutions of Canada and Australia—the condensation of practices into rules can make for a rainfall of better practices; the Canadian constitution, for instance, wanting to keep the bicameral vibe of a House of Lords without having a landed gentry, turned it into a senate of distinguished citizens by appointment, an idea that might rebound toward the mother country as a model for the new House of Lords. Between the rule and the meal intervenes the ritual, and the ritual of the recipe is like the ritual of the law; the reason the judge sits high up, in a robe, is not that it makes a difference to the case but that it makes a difference to the clients. The recipe is, in this way, our richest instance of the force and the power of abstract rules. All messages change as they're re-sent, but messages not sent never get received. Life is like green curry.

However we prefer our cookbooks—as grammar or encyclopedia, as storehouses of craft or illusions of knowledge—one can't read them in bed for many years without feeling that there is a conspiracy between readers and writers to obscure the ultimate point. A kind of primal scene of eating hovers over every cookbook, just as a primal scene of sex lurks behind every love story. In cooking, the primal scene, or substance, is salt, sugar, and fat held in maximum solution with starch; add protein as necessary, and finish with caffeine (coffee or chocolate) as desired. That's what, suitably disguised in some decent dimension of dress-up, we always end up making. We make béarnaise sauce by whisking a stick of melted butter into a couple of eggs, and, now that we no longer make béarnaise sauce, we make salsa verde by beating a cup of olive oil into a fistful of anchovies. The herbs change; the hope does not.

Mark Peel, in his Campanile cookbook, comes near to giving the game away: "We chefs all lie about our mashed potatoes," he admits. "We don't tell you we've used 1½ pounds of cream and butter with 1¾ pounds of potatoes. You don't need to know." (Joël Robuchon, the king of his generation of French cooks, first became famous for a purée that had an even higher proportion of butter beaten into starch.) After reading hundreds of cookbooks, you may have the feeling that every recipe, every cookbook, is an attempt to get you to attain this ideal sugar-salt-saturated-fat state without having to face it head-on, just as every love poem is an attempt to maneuver a girl or a boy into bed by talking as fast, and as eloquently, as possible about something else. "Shall I compare thee to a summer's day? / Thou art more lovely and more temperate" is the poetic equivalent of simmering the garlic with ginger and Sauternes before you put the cream in; the end is the cream, but you carefully simmer the garlic.

Yet, though the end of the poem may be to get the dish in bed, its entertainment lies in how many steps it takes to get there. Though the end is salt, sugar, and fat in high solution, the entertainment lies in how we get there, too. It is not as if anyone thinks the story would be improved if Jane Austen described Darcy and Elizabeth actually screwing—not because these things violate the conventions but because they are so obviously the point that it is embarrassing to see them spelled out. We elide them not because we don't want to know but because we know already. Salt, sweet, fat, and starch, caffeine, alcohol—we juggle these simple things in endless rounds, just as we juggle our limbs and other simple things night after night (if we're lucky) out of a conviction that while the substance of the exertion sustains life, it is the variety that keeps life interesting. The truth that variety is the spice of life carries within it the implicit recognition that monotony is the daily meal.

All appetites have their illusions, which are part of their pleasure. That's why the husband turns those pages in bed. The truth is that we don't passively peruse the pictures and leap to the results; we actively read the lines and internally act out the jobs. The woman who reads the fashion magazines isn't passively imagining the state of having; she's actively imagining the act of shopping. (And distantly imagining the act of wearing.) She turns down pages not because she wants merely to look again but because, for that moment, she really intends to buy that—for a decisive imagined moment she *did* buy it, even if she knows she never will. Reading recipe books is an active practice, too, even if all the action takes place in your mind. We reanimate our passions by imagining the possibilities, and the act of wanting ends up mattering more than the fact of getting. It's not the false hope that a dish will turn out right that makes us go on with our reading but our contented resignation to the knowledge that it won't ever, quite.

The desire to go on desiring, the wanting to want, is what makes you turn the pages—all the while aware that the next Boston cream pie, the sweet-salty-fatty-starchy thing you will turn out tomorrow, will be neither more nor less unsatisfying than last night's was. When you start to cook, as when you begin to live, you think that the point is to improve the technique until you end up with something perfect, and that the reason you haven't been able to break the cycle of desire and disillusion is that you haven't yet mastered the rules. Then you grow up, and you learn that that's the game.

3

E-MAIL TO ELIZABETH PENNELL:
Anchovies, Bacon, Lamb

Dear Elizabeth Pennell:

Or Liz, if I may. The thrill of coming across someone in another
time whose take on the world resembles your own—not in the
big things, which are common enough to be shared, but in the
small ones—is *enormous*. We all expect people in the past to love
their children, seek a better world—but we are stunned when
they prefer a Volnay to Château Pétrus, or roast chicken to veal
saddle. We expect nineteenth-century people to be noble, but
not to be *nice*, exactly—we sometimes expect them to fight for
women's rights and envision the democratic age, but we also
expect them to like saddle of veal and old port.

So, coming upon you and your work while reading about recipes gives me the sense of a friend at court: greedy, Francophile
(but with enough Italy in you to make you introduce pasta to
your readers), and aesthetic. And then, more selfishly, you gave
me a form. I had wanted to write recipes for this book—what is
the point of writing a book about food if you cannot put in the
ways to make the food you like best?—but realized that it was an
inappropriate idea. A *wildly* inappropriate idea, actually. Quite
apart from the question of compromising the dignity of the

essayist, full of wise saw and modern instance, by perkily telling you how to make rice pudding, there was the obvious truth that any recipes I have, apart from one, are not really *my* recipes, but other people's that I happen to like or cook a lot.

Yes, of course, everybody's recipe is someone else's recipe, with the exception of those few rare new things that someone really did invent. (I've invented one, sort of.) But there is a recipe that has, so to speak, through suffering become yours, unlike those that you have simply copied out of a book. We recognize the concept of sweat equity in recipe writing: if you have labored nightly over a stove in a restaurant kitchen cooking the thing, then you can write it down, even if its origins lie ultimately not in your own mind but in someone else's cooking. But if you have merely written down what someone else wrote down first, having cooked it in the meanwhile, it isn't yours. In *your* beautiful book, though, you offered both the method and the object. The method, which you invented, of turning every recipe into a little story, a bit of narrative, shows that recipes need not be neat tables of chemical interactions but short stories of mixed emotions: what I did that day, and why I did it.

And then I liked the idea of our conversation, however much it might be a *dialogue des morts*. You were the woman who, in the nineteenth century, without a vote or often a voice, save for a small one in the *Pall Mall Gazette,* had the nerve to call herself not a housewife or a domestic philosopher but a Greedy Woman—not cooking for her children or organizing her household but eating for the thrill of it. I loved that. And here was I, another writer in a weekly magazine, doing the reverse in a way, eating for pleasure but also cooking for a family . . . a kind of dialogue of amateurs, with the understanding that your announcing yourself as an eater first of all was as weird then—"subversive" would be the academic word, but the wrong one—as my announcing myself a cook first of all is now. The man in an apron is as typical, and yet as awkward, as wistfully *underexpressed,* an invention at the beginning of the twenty-first century as the woman with a napkin tucked under her chin was at the end of the nineteenth. I eat from greed! was your brave announcement. I cook from need! is my far less nervy but equally awkward one. The man in the apron, the woman with the napkin—you see them everywhere but they rarely speak for themselves. So let me write to you, and if the exchange of recipes is notional, or imaginary, well, recipes from the dead are the sum total of what civilization *is.*

Did they have "secret ingredients" in your day? When I was a child, secret ingredients were everywhere. Colonel Sanders had a secret recipe; the recipe for Coke and Pepsi were murmured over; one had orange zest and one had lemon. (Or so they said: I grabbed only the most surreptitious sips and clandestine snacking of either, with *my* mother. Save, now that I think of it, for a brief, six-month phase when my family lived in your town, London, where we got KFC chicken on several occasions. My mother's rules of engagement were somehow suspended in a place which, in those days, had only dank Maltese burgers and murky vindaloos for takeout.)

But even beyond that, there were cooking secrets. People, chefs, on television, the Galloping Gourmet for one, winked, hard, at the camera, when people asked about them. I recall reading a piece in *Time* magazine when I was about eight, about a man who made omelets at parties. Chic people in New York had this guy in a tux over to make omelets—with sour cream, as I recall. It was a big thing. And when asked—I know that memory plays tricks, but I recall this with indecent clarity—he said that his secret ingredient was Tabasco sauce, and he added more the later it got and the drunker the guests got. I think the word "drunk" wasn't in there, but that was the sense. The excitement I felt then, at the idea of someday landing at such a party, where, holding your drink and smirking in your dinner jacket, you would nonchalantly order an omelet, as James Bond him-self might order an omelet! "One. With sour cream. Oh—and double the Tabasco. Your . . . secret ingredient? Poured by hand, please." (I wrote a spy novel of my own in that period, called "To Be or Not To Be," my first extended work—come to think of it, I haven't written anything as continuously extended since—in which, varying the shaken-not-stirred martini formula, I gave the rather Bond-like hero a notable weakness for cream doughnuts.)

My God, the perpetual miracle of modernity! Mostly as a joke, I just now Googled "*Time* magazine man who makes omelets at parties"—and there he is! Rudolph Stanish was his name, and just as I thought—though I was a little older than I recalled—there was a *Time* piece about him, and a memorial Web page as well. According to the Web page,

> he had worked as a chef for Mrs. Twombly (Cornelius Vanderbilt's sister), and Joseph Donon, who trained with the famous French chef Escoffier. He also accompanied wealthy families to Europe as their chef, making twenty-six crossings, and broadening his skills with each trip. In the 1960s, Stanish became head chef of the Goldman Sachs lunchroom in New York City, and the "personal supper chef" for the Paul Mellon family. He became renowned for the personalized omelets he served at his employers' late night parties. In 1968, a *Time Magazine* article on his expertise propelled his fame as "The Omelet King." Stanish designed an omelet pan that was produced by Club Aluminum, and published a popular booklet of his omelet recipes. He had the honor of preparing the Inaugural breakfast for John F. Kennedy. Much in demand for his legendary omelet parties he traveled extensively to execute many celebrity entertainments. He continued to perform his omelet skills at many charity benefits until his death in 2008.

And there it is, dug in a micro-moment out of the *Time* archives. Except for dessert omelets, he adds one special ingredient: Tabasco sauce. "The later the night and the more the drinking, says Stanish, the more Tabasco." So the word "drunk" was not there, but the word "drinking" was!

I should confess, right here, as I am about to offer recipes in the guise, or at least the form, of letters to you, that I have no business doing this, in addition to the no-business-doing-it reasons outlined above, because there are certain standard, anyone-can-do-it things that I cannot do. These include:

1 A decent salad dressing.
2 A good crème anglaise (they never thicken enough; I think I am too frightened of turning up the heat high enough).
3 Anything to do with a "salt crust." Every book I have tells you how to form a paste of water and salt and build it over the fish or duck and then crack the baked crust and, for some reason, whatever is inside comes out succulent. I have tried, and I have failed, building little white igloos that collapse inward like sad snowmen, oversalting beyond all hope.
4 Omelets.

So, King Omelet II I am unlikely to become. I could be Mr. Scrambled Eggs, actually, since I do have a perfect recipe for those. I got it from Gérard Boyer, the great chef at Les Crayères, up in the champagne country in France. It was my friend the art historian Kirk Varnedoe's fiftieth birthday—he hadn't yet fallen ill, as he would a year later, with colon cancer, though I know now that the cancer was already eating its way silently inside him—and we all went to Reims to celebrate. "Lunch and a cathedral" used to be our motto; we did the cathedral first, usually, though it fit the rhythm less well. We did Chartres, Rouen, Amiens, and then Reims, most beautiful of all, with its lacy façade and smiling angels . . . then at lunch, the one thing we saw on the menu for my son, Luke, all of eighteen months old, was scrambled eggs and caviar, and we asked, as courteously as we could, if he might have just the scrambled eggs. Of course, the waiter said. And he brought back, twenty minutes later, a plate of scrambled eggs so creamy and bright yellow and gleaming that Luke devoured them in three minutes, the first plate of grown-up food that he had ever eaten—and perhaps to this day has ever eaten—without caution and doubt inflecting his bites. My wife, Martha, almost wept for joy, since at that point—despite his being a robust baby, *costaud,* as the French say—she was still chasing him from room to room with a jar of puréed *coings,* which he sort of liked, even though she did not know what *coings* were. (They're quinces.)

When Boyer came to make his rounds, as chefs once did, at the end of lunch, I told Luke that that was the cook who had made his eggs, and he rose in his high chair and applauded. I asked Boyer how he had made the eggs and he told me, and I have made them ever since. All you do is place a big noisette of butter in a pan—Boyer did them in a bain-marie, a double boiler, but I have found this not necessary if you work carefully on a low heat—and let the butter dissolve, and then mix in three well-beaten eggs. You stir and stir, relentlessly but lightly, until they begin to form into curds, custardy curds, not fluffy American ones, and then, at just the right moment, when they are still just too wet to eat, you put another noisette of butter on top to polish and veneer them. Then you sprinkle gray sea salt, if you have it—that was Boyer's grave, noncaviar touch—and any salt you have if you don't. With brioche toast, they're wonderful. From that day to this it is Luke's default dish, the one thing he will eat when he's tired or out late or worn out by life. "Can you make me French eggs, Dad?" he says, and I do.

So . . . I might become the Scrambler in the Rye. But I do, nonetheless, *have* a secret ingredient, or two of them, and they are anchovies and bacon. Garlic, Tabasco, Asian fish sauce, white truffle oil—all have their place as semisecret additives. But I find that I can add anchovies and bacon to pretty much anything, and it tastes better. Though not both at once, of course. Anchovies blended with garlic in a cooked-down tomato sauce; anchovies added to a paella. Bacon or bacon chunks, *lardons* in French, added to *boeuf bourguignon* or pot-au-feu or any kind of pot roast, actually, turns it from a faded thing into a bright and homey and countryish one.

"All you're really doing is adding salt!" an unknown voice says, apropos the two ingredients. The salt thing again. Has it occurred to you, Elizabeth, as it has to me, that this "all you're really doing" is the constant plaint against the chef, the one thing people say to cooks and greedy people that they won't say to anyone else? "All you're *really* doing is beating in fat," they say when you blend in the melted butter. "All you're *really* doing is adding fat to starch," they say when you do *pommes frites,* which is true, but so what?

"All you're actually doing is putting a pungent protein on a neutral starch," and that's true, too, of almost everything. In fact, that is the human meal, the one true meal. A neutral starch (pasta or rice or pizza dough), a pungent protein (curry or a tomato reduction or fish scraps in fermented sauce), and that is what perhaps six billion of the earth's seven will eat tonight! A pungent protein piled upon a neutral starch; a neutral starch awaiting its pungent protein, male and female, which is which? (And yet all that can be said about anything that we do is that it's "all you're really doing." All you're really doing is explaining what that passage means, Dr. Johnson! All you're really doing is putting sticky colors on a canvas, Mr. Titian! All you're really doing is seeing that every line has the same sound at the end, Mr. Pope! Everything we do is all we're really doing—all tasks in the end are simple, repetitive, easily broken into parts, and all we're really doing is all that can be done.)

Bacon is chic again, alas, and this makes me reluctant to

write more about it. Face bacon, side bacon, even tail bacon, I suppose—the bits and pieces of smoked pig have become cool. "Alas," because I have always loved bacon, and think that bacon is better as a guilty pleasure than as a fetishized fashion. Anchovies, though, seem to have resisted becoming fashionable. What could ever be more clearly the opposite of any idea of chic than an anchovy? So let it be said only that they come in two kinds—the gray greasy ones in the bottle and the lovely flat white ones you get at an Italian deli. I've always liked leg of lamb better than any other cut of meat, and so the idea of putting the three together was irresistible: bacon and anchovies on the lamb. There are ancient recipes in France for making little slits in the gigot, and then inserting the anchovies before you roast it, and I've tried them. But they salt the exterior without giving the punch and surprise that you want.

So I decided instead to just plop them on the lamb and see what happens. It turns out that they make a wonderful goo, and you pour off the fat, and pour in some white wine—I used flat champagne, since there was some left over—and cook it down, and it was great, the bacon crumbled over the lamb and the sauce pungent with the anchovies. Served with a simple buttery purée and buttered green beans with ginger, which should have been better. (I have only one killer vegetable side in my repertoire, a Brussels sprouts thing—and you know what, it has bacon in it. Oh, well.)

So here, in Pennell form, is my recipe for leg of lamb with bacon and anchovies, the Salt-Lover's Delight: You take a good grass-fed leg of lamb, about four or five pounds, and liberally salt it. Then you put it in a roasting pan that won't burn too much, and put garlic cloves and olive oil in the pan. Then you roast it for half an hour to forty minutes in a very hot oven—around 400°; though if you go up to 425° it will brown nicely, even if the garlic may scorch. Then, pull out the pan and lay four or five rashers of very thick-cut bacon right across the top of the gigot, and a nice handful of prepared white anchovies on top of the bacon. You can do it the other way round, and it's just as good, maybe better: anchovies first, bacon on top. I haven't tried this with the canned or jarred anchovies, and am sure that they won't be as good as the white ones, since they never are—but since the anchovies melt anyway, I bet it won't matter, much.

Then roast the lamb again at 400° or slightly less, depending on your oven, for another fifteen to twenty minutes, until the bacon is nicely browned and the anchovies have started to fall off and dissolve. Then take the leg out and make sure it's done as you like it—lamb is difficult, because it tends to stay bloody and mildly unappealing even to lovers of rare meat in the middle while the outer parts are well done; there's nothing to be done about this: it's lamb and you live with it. (*Cook's Illustrated* has a fussy, promising thing where you turn the lamb over and about with paper towels in the middle and trim and cut it in half, and if you can do all this and want to, more power to you. I just slice some well-done bits, some pinker bits, and give the semiraw stuff in the middle to the dog.)

Meanwhile, put the lamb on a plate and pour off all the fat from the pan; there'll be burned bits of garlic and lamb there, but that's okay. Pour in, oh, a cup of white wine or flat champagne, whatever you have—wine in the sauce all comes out more or less the same—and scrape and cook down; it should be a *jus*, not a thickened sauce. So cook it down to make the flavor intense, but not to thicken it too much. Then slice the lamb, crumble some of the bacon on it—put a whole rasher on, if you like—along with some of the burned anchovies, and pour lots of the pungent wine and drippings on it. Lots. Serve with a purée of potatoes without too much complexity, just potatoes, cream, and butter and salt (but for once not too much, since the meat will satisfy the salt-hunger). And green beans with sweetly caramelized shallots, better than gingered ones, I think. See if it isn't the best gigot you've ever had, with the gamy lamb and the salt-bitter anchovies and sweetish pork and smoke of the bacon and the good winy-salty juice on it. Good food. No more than that. Can we ask for more? Did you? When a secret ingredient is laid out flat on the dish and then transported to the top of the finished food, is it still a secret?

All best,
A.G.

PART II

Choosing at the Table

AFTER WE ARRIVE, at the restaurant or at home, we have to choose what we want to eat. At the restaurant, it's simple: we scan the menu and decide. But at home we choose first, shopping and deciding. And at that dangerous place, the friend's house, we have to pray that they have chosen, and chosen well. (And we pray, too, that they will have finished cooking before we arrive, so that the horrible hour in the kitchen, as they fuss and mix, is one that we are spared. Even with a glass of wine in hand, it is hard to watch another cook—and when they have the food still in plastic wrap . . . it's too much.)

Fish or chicken? Red meat or none? Vegetables boiled or braised? And what to drink, and how much should we care? If arriving is a story of hope, offered and deferred, choosing is always comparative. Behind every choice we make is another choice rejected. What shall it be? And when shall we get it?

4

How Does Taste Happen?

DE GUSTIBUS non disputandum est: There's no disputing taste. This is surely one of the most familiar Latin tags or mottos left to us, one of only maybe two that we still know and grasp. We hear it and we think we recognize its truth; it enjoins a shrug of acceptance in place of a futile argument: you like it your way and I like it mine. . . . You may say potato and I may say potahto, but if you like tomatoes and I like potatoes? Nothing to do but walk away.

But of course, the next thing that strikes us is that taste is all we *do* dispute. We dispute our taste in music. Who do you like better, Bob Dylan or Joni Mitchell? You do? You can't! Why? Every bookstore assumed—or assumes—disputes about taste. Those music lovers do *nothing* except dispute: Which do you prefer, the Beatles or the Stones? Blur or Oasis? Dixieland or bebop? To tell a fifteen-year-old boy or girl that it's all just a question of taste is *infuriating,* not helpful. Of course it's a question of taste—the question is, whose taste is right?

This distance between the pat certainty of the slogan and its obvious untruth reminds me of something my grandfather once said. He arrived in what he always called "this country" from the Old Country when he was twelve, and his English was accentless but still spoken at the slight puzzled remove of the second-language speaker. As a very old man he once confided to me that there was a single phrase in English that he could not understand: "What do they mean when they say that you can't have your cake and eat it, too?" he asked me, bewildered. What else were you supposed to do with your cake? Having it and eating it were parts of one description, a single act. There is nothing else to do with your cake. Like the claim about cake, the claim about taste seems like a falsehood parading as a fatuity.

When it comes to food, taste disputes can be intense, even wild. Meat-eaters against vegans, the locavore against the supermarket patron, or even just those who like the pallid look and squishy finish of meat boiled in vacuum bags against those who live in cast-iron pans. But when it comes to the kind of taste that people who care about taste care most about, the disputes are both more immediate and more peculiar. For we mean by "taste" both small taste—the flavor of what we put in our mouths—and big taste, the way we decorate our walls and clothing and lives. There is mouth taste, how it feels when you eat it—is it salty or sweet or bitter or buttery or somewhere in between, with all the fine gradations of lime and lemon and vinegar that mark out the general category of "sour." But then there is what we might call "moral taste"—the place of the food we eat within an epoch's style or our own self-image.

We could simply call these two "flavor" and "fashion," and that wouldn't be all wrong. But "flavor" and "fashion" miss the depth of the commitment that we make to our food tastes. In religious matters, we see this all the time. The Orthodox Jew likes the flavor of brisket during the Seder, but his liking it is something more than fashion. It is a moral taste—in his eyes, eating brisket is an ethical position. But this is just as true of seemingly smaller affections. I like the mouth taste of Dan Barber's food, but my liking to eat at his restaurant at the Stone Barns organic farm is something more than fashion. It is a moral taste, in the sense that I'm proud to be seen there, and like to pretend to participate in the project of sustainable produce and heritage breeds.

Of course, "moral taste" of this kind is in our era highly moralized: we think we're helping the planet by eating at Dan Barber's. But in every epoch, mouth taste leads to moral taste—the two are linked, and it is those links that drive our diets. My parents, mere college professors, in their youth went to Paris every year and ate at the new palaces of nouvelle cuisine, at Michel Guérard's or Alain Dutournier's old Au Trou Gascon. It was in the days before eating became so intensely "ethicalized," and so questions of where the lamb was born and how much the duck suffered to give up its liver were very secondary. I doubt that anyone even asked them. But the choice of France, and French cooking, involved many other self-defining positions. It was a moral taste, as it had been for every American gourmand from Fisher to Liebling. It meant choosing to make much of food as a humane activity, which in turn meant choosing Paris over Prussia, pleasure over austerity, extravagant expenditure in the interest of materialism over middle-class thrift, the indulgence of appetite over the suppression of hunger. It was tied to attitudes about sex, travel, God, life . . . in all those ways, the mouth taste for Dutournier's cassoulet was part of a moral taste for what the cassoulet so beautifully—and beanfully—*meant*.

Or take a touching moment from Craig Claiborne's Time-Life volume *Classic French Cooking,* from the mid-sixties, where he talks about visiting young friends in Mamaroneck, New York, who had taken on the true faith of haute cuisine: "If they have hamburgers, they serve hamburgers *au poivre flambés au cognac.* If they have veal it is served with *fines herbes.*" They make consommé Celestine and sole Marguery and for dessert serve a soufflé Rothschild, and somebody lights a Gauloise and, Claiborne writes, "for one haunting moment I felt as if I were in the South of France." This strikes us as overwrought, but choosing that imaginative Francophile life at that time, too easily nostalgized now, of processed cheese and Corfam shoes was a hard choice, a real choice, a good choice. Moral choices look silly only after others have made them for our benefit.

We have mouth taste and moral taste—and, as Charlie the Tuna long ago discovered, though intricately related they are not quite the same. "Charlie, StarKist don't want tunas with good taste, StarKist wants tunas that taste good," the small wise fish used to explain to the big cartoon tuna, who tried to show the StarKist company, in a series of mid-sixties ads, that he had good taste by wearing berets, hanging abstract art on his wall, and so on, in order—according to the weird convention by which cartoon animals want to be killed and eaten—to convince StarKist that he tasted good. "Guys with good taste always go places no one ever heard of."

About mouth taste we know a lot, chiefly how susceptible it is to framing effects. The order in which a thing is introduced, information about its origin—wines labeled "California" always taste better than wines said to come from the Dakotas—the context in which it's taken, what comes before, what comes after . . . all of this changes our perceptions. Some of these effects—the way that water tastes sweet after eating an artichoke—are purely physiological and well understood. Others, like the ways that labels affect our tastes in wine, are more cagily social. But they are all framing effects in which what we sense on our tongues is secondary to what we believe in our heads.

We know now, for instance, that, in addition to the taste buds in our mouth, we have still more taste buds of another kind in our gut, which cannily regulate and oversee our desires, too, making sure that we eat not just what our tongues like but what our livers need. And we know, too, how much we depend on a kind of eternal game of truth or dare with our brains and their chemistry: we eat capsicum peppers, for instance, only because we know that our brain will superproduce opiates to make up for the burn on our tongue. If it didn't, then chili or curry would be literally unbearable. Whole civilizations every night are head-faking their nervous systems. We learn to use our sensory ability to sense rot in order to relish controlled rotting, as in cheese and truffles and Madirans. We are not slot machines of taste, passively registering information as it arrives on our palate, but poker players, bluffing out our own neurons.

But Charlie the Tuna often was not so wrong. Good taste always starts with tasting good. Moral taste is often an expanded metaphor rising from mouth taste. If metaphors of sight are our pet metaphors of abstract intelligence—our kids are bright, or dim (well, not *ours*), our vision of the future is clear or cloudy, our problems are well-illuminated or dimly understood—then metaphors of taste are our favorites for intuitive sensual experience. The tongue terms speak to the immediate sensual shock: the girl's or boy's manner is so sweet or too bitter, too saccharine or too sour.

The curious thing is that as mouth taste changes, so does moral taste, and on the same cyclical, revolutionary principles. Even in—particularly in—a stable and prosperous middle class, tastes in food, and in dining, change with remarkable speed. When I was a boy, a book called *Masterpieces of French Cuisine,* complete with recipes taken from every three-star palace in France, was among my favorite reading: its cover shows a three-star chef in chef's whites, gesturing haughtily toward the masterpieces contained inside—what now looks like twelve gratin dishes of indistinguishable brown sludge—while inside the recipes from the great chefs of France seem almost unmakeable, not to say indigestible. It's a rule. The good food of twenty-five years ago always looks unhealthy; the good food of fifty years ago always looks unappetizing; and the good food of a hundred years ago always looks inedible. Knowledge progresses, but cooking does not, or only in partial ways. Diet is always the site of ritual convincing itself that it is reason.

The cycles of mouth taste and moral taste are still more evident at greater distance. We know that a century ago the taste for the nonseasonal and exotic defined a sophisticated eater; the man who could get strawberries in December and *poulet de Bresse* on Madison Avenue was the man with taste. Now the same enlightened diner is defined by his rejection of the remote and out-of-season; he's the man who refuses strawberries in December, and wants his chicken grown and strangled in his own basement. Diet changes all the time, and the top diets change as often as the top chef.

Consider the place of seasonality in dining out. In Balzac's *Lost Illusions,* Lucien, after blowing his money on a first-night dinner at the Palais Royal, has to start eating in a Left Bank bistro. Flicoteaux, the *cantine* that poor Lucien is forced to patronize, has *only* local and seasonal produce. Balzac describes in great detail how the owner, M. Flicoteaux himself, keeps down prices by shopping only for what's just off the farms, only cabbage in cabbage season and turnips in turnip time and so on—and describes just as well the shame and suffering that the diners feel in having to eat in so peasantlike a manner right in the middle of Paris. It is part of their sad fate as poets that they have to eat there. Part of the price of poverty was seasonal eating. Now, of course, we pay three hundred dollars prix fixe at Alain Passard's, only a few streets away, to have a single plate of sliced tomatoes—though strictly in tomato season.

These changes not only involve what gives us pleasure—or what we say gives us pleasure—but our whole idea of what pleasure is. Take an instance of the vagaries of taste even nearer, and odder. Read two great British journalists of the 1960s and 1970s, Bernard Levin and Kenneth Tynan. No one did more to break down British puritan injunctions against eating as a humane act, and a kind of art. They were both utterly devoted to great food, which they identified, as most educated people did at that time, with Continental three-star cooking. Their diaries and journals testify to their enraptured love for great French food—and to the constant feelings of sickness and indigestion that all that cream- and butter-based cooking costs them. Yet for Levin and Tynan feeling ill after you ate was not a hint that something might be wrong with the way you'd eaten. It was proof that you had really eaten well. (I well recall my own culinary mentor, Eugenio Donato, a professor of comparative literature, taking pills to stave off a *crise de foie before* he sat down to eat six courses.) This cruel eating even had its tragic side. I once told one of A. J. Liebling's friends how keenly I admired Liebling's food writing, and he shook his head with sorrow. "I can't read Joe on food," he said, "because I watched him eat himself to death." Eating himself to death may have been neurotic, but it was Liebling's conscious neurosis, chosen to make a point. Anyone could diet; it took a real man to die of gout.

This may astound us only a generation later—but the first thing we know about pleasure is that it is intricately tied to perversity. Our own absurd perversities in eating are hidden from us by the fog of our own epoch—it is, after all, always our own epoch that is foggiest to us; the past presents itself with crystal clarity—and as I trudge once more to the farmers' market for hard-neck garlic, I can only imagine the bafflement of my grandchildren. Or think again of salt! We have replaced the ordinary small salt that served our mothers so well with gray and orange and crystal salt, of the kind that one used to find only on soft pretzels. Can we not hear the first faint titters of posterity at that choice?

And we know that such changes in taste are tied to social changes, to questions of class and rank and caste. Who is like- lier to eat today the diet of the American farmer or the Russian peasant of the Old Country—brown bread and freshly grown local vegetables, free-range chicken and raw-milk cheese—the farmer's great-grandchildren, or the professor of comparative literature at the nearby liberal-arts college? All taste is relative in the sense that it is historical, specific, and context-bound. One of the most piquant details in the *Twilight* saga, as any father of a prepubescent girl can tell you, is that the good vampires of the Cullen Clan refer to their voracious consumption of fresh animal blood as "vegetarianism"—and though I suppose some indignant vegetarian has objected, no one within the confines of the series ever disputes the designation. In comparison with the *other* vampire's diet of hot human flesh, killing wild deer with your bare hands and sucking their life out is morally equivalent to eating lentils and greens. Even what you call a vegetable finally depends on the ferocity of your taste for blood.

So it is not simply that tastes, mouth taste and moral taste, change. It is that they change in absolute ways—not incrementally, as we drift toward taking two lumps of sugar in our coffee instead of three, but entirely and radically, and in ways that almost always involve treating as beatific what has been before rejected as base. And they change cyclically—if not predictably, then certainly not haphazardly. That's why we have movements and patterns and periods in the history of cooking. It's why we have a history of culture. Taste is *all* that we dispute.

Well, okay. But they were wrong, and we are . . . *right!* The cost of transporting strawberries in winter from the warm climate to the cool is bad for the fruit and worse for the planet; the poets eating cabbage from Les Halles were luckier than the ones eating imported lobster, a little later on, at Lapérouse. The old taste was bad, artificial, and mistaken, and the new taste is good, natural, and logical. The seasonal is preferable to the remote and exotic for reasons we can enumerate; Tynan and Levin were foolish Englishmen torturing themselves for no reason at all. We now eat the right way—we even have books telling us what the right way is to eat!—with the right balance of healthy organic vegetables and the right suspicion of too much butter and cream covering up the vegetable's natural taste, and the right concerns about keeping our planet and our palate in balance. . . .

No doubt. Very probably so. But it requires arrogance in the face of history to imagine that history has stopped with us. The terrible condescension of posterity is a thing we should avoid, since we are surely those to be condescended to next. Don't misunderstand! I am as partisan about these tastes as anyone else: I evict presweetened food from my children's larder as sternly as Carrie Nation evicted sinners from a saloon; I would, if my children asked to go to McDonald's, say, in the immortal words of Alice Waters, that I would prefer not to get involved in that kind of activity. But I also recognize that these are the tastes of my caste and class and kind, and no likelier to last forever than those of any other, older caste and class and kind.

Presented with these two truths—the never-ending whirligig of taste and our own certainty that our tastes are best and surest—we usually try to escape the contradiction by escaping the problem of taste completely, insisting that we can root our judgment in something that transcends mere fashion. We try to root our tastes in an idea of progress, or in an appeal to nature. We think, Tastes may be trends, but trends trend toward truth. Or else we think, Well, our mothers knew what they wanted, but *we* know what Mother Nature wants. How well have these efforts worked over time to solve the problem of taste?

Before modern times, taste in food particularly was enforced by the two greatest of enforcers: faith and famine, and their not-so-nice foster parent, fear. Dietary restrictions are a big part of most religious practice; kosher and halal rules are the most famous of these, and though various attempts have been made to justify them on rational grounds—pigs eat too much, or are too expensive, or too likely to make you sick when you eat them—few anthropologists take this seriously now. There are too many rules and subrules, covering too many improbable beasts and circumstances. Even the rabbis and mullahs admit now that the purpose of food laws is to create a form of symbolic solidarity that keeps a tribe or faith together. There is nothing so powerful to keep you eating with your family on this side of the river as disgust at what the people on the other side think tastes good.

Faith shapes food, and so does famine. As we've seen, the first birth of "gastronomy" is inseparable from the end of the constant fear of famine that had been part of the European, and particularly the French, condition almost from the beginning of time. Many forces played a role in this transformation, not least new methods of transport that brought food into Paris more efficiently—Les Halles was not then a site of nostalgia but a hub for distribution—and of course new foodstuffs. People who like eating should praise Antoine Parmentier, the father of the French potato, every day. (In a sense, given the ubiquity of the French fry in the world, we do.) It isn't an accident that the one exceptional famine in the West after 1800 was the potato famine in Ireland. With the end of famine in Europe as an immediate, nonpolitical threat—famines afterward would be the work of wars or sieges—came the possibility of a free play of taste. We can say "You are what you eat" only when we have some minimal choice about what we're eating.

With the coming of modernity—which of course came at different times for different reasons, but which we can fairly associate with the growth of science, with its search for truth, and the growth of merchant-economies, with their faith in trade—taste in general and mouth taste in particular had to find another source than faith on which to rest its principles. The 1755 "Essay on Taste" by Montesquieu is the last, classic statement of the traditional, authoritarian view of taste. Taste is produced by education, and the people who have education learn to be tasteful. The best way to be tasteful yourself is to imitate the good taste of your social superiors. (Yet no good thinker thinks just one way. Montesquieu, though he assumes a ladder of taste, also invents the idea of the "je ne sais quoi"—the idea that there is as much delight in disorder as in order.)

It was the great Scottish philosopher of the Enlightenment David Hume, in his 1757 essay "Of the Standard of Taste," who first articulated as a consistent view the notion that taste doesn't depend on the spell of authority, but on the slow acquisition of ideas. Though everyone can see that tastes change, Hume was one of the first to insist that this is the central truth about them:

> The great variety of Taste, as well as of opinion, which prevails in the world, is too obvious not to have fallen under every one's observation. Men of the most confined knowledge are able to remark a difference of taste in the narrow circle of their acquaintance, even where the persons have been educated under the same government, and have early imbibed the same prejudices. But those, who can enlarge their view to contemplate distant nations and remote ages, are still more surprised at the great inconsistence and contrariety. We are apt to call barbarous whatever departs widely from our own taste and apprehension: But soon find the epithet of reproach retorted on us. And the highest arrogance and self-conceit is at last startled, on observing an equal assurance on all sides, and scruples, amidst such a contest of sentiment, to pronounce positively in its own favour.

So how could you make distinctions? Hume thought that you could do it by learning to make ever more minute judgments. "It is acknowledged to be the perfection of every sense or faculty, to perceive with exactness its most minute objects, and allow nothing to escape its notice and observation," he said. "The smaller the objects are, which become sensible to the eye, the finer is that organ, and the more elaborate its make and composition." Practice makes perfect—and what is interesting is that Hume assumes that the best theater of taste is the mouth and the table (though he was born a Scot eating Scottish food, he lived in France as a young man, which may explain it):

A good palate is not tried by strong flavours; but by a mixture of small ingredients, where we are still sensible of each part, notwithstanding its minuteness and its confusion with the rest. . . . A very delicate palate, on many occasions, may be a great inconvenience both to a man himself and to his friends: But a delicate taste of wit or beauty must always be a desirable quality; because it is the source of all the finest and most innocent enjoyments, of which human nature is susceptible. . . . But though there be naturally a wide difference in point of delicacy between one person and another, nothing tends further to encrease and improve this talent, than practice in a particular art, and the frequent survey or contemplation of a particular species of beauty. . . . The mist dissipates, which seemed formerly to hang over the object: the organ acquires greater perfection in its operations; and can pronounce, without danger of mistake, concerning the merits of every performance.

Hume's idea is simple: sensitivity is what counts, and our palates get sensitive by experience. The longer you stand on tiptoe, the easier it is to dance. All taste is acquired taste. Practice makes almost perfect, and practice plus instruction makes as perfect as we can get. A developed palate is more reliable than an instinctive one.

But the most enduring new idea about taste in the eighteenth-century Enlightenment was the romantic move away from *acquired* taste and toward an idea of *authentic* taste—a move that we associate with Hume's great friend, rival, and, eventually, enemy, the philosopher, novelist, and essayist Jean-Jacques Rousseau. Though Rousseau's ideas were not, as is always the case, all his own—others had them before him, and some that we associate with his name were never actually articulated by him—the great change in taste that made the peasant's brown bread as attractive as the prince's brioche *is* tied to things Rousseau asserts in his novels and philosophical books.

Rousseau thinks that taste is not taken from authority, or acquired by educated palates; he thinks that true taste, authentic taste, is derived, somehow, from nature. Rousseau insists that brioche taste is the taste of a corrupt and decadent upper class; if we return to natural man, the noble savage, the virtuous peasant, we find a taste in constant harmony with nature. In a famous letter to Jean d'Alembert he rejects with disgust Hume's love of small discriminations as the basis of good taste. "And what at bottom is this so vaunted 'taste'?" Rousseau asks. "The art of knowing little things. In truth, when one has something so great as liberty worth knowing, all the rest is quite puerile." And in *Emile,* Jean-Jacques teaches his student to feel nothing, but to "fix his affections and his tastes, to hasten to be sure and that he does not search in luxury to find means that he can find best very near to him. Good taste [is] defined very simply as that which pleases or displeases the greatest number." Rousseau loves to describe the joys of a harvest, the pleasures of the vineyard, the superiority of the *terroir* to the city. True taste is popular, near at hand, not the delicate acquired taste of the educated.

Yet this idea of a natural and simple eternal taste, waiting to be found if we could just discard our pretensions, produced, in its own era, very different practices. The natural was as complicated a concept as the acquired. Rousseau's first great public disciple was the Queen herself, Marie Antoinette; his second Robespierre, and his third the man who invented the restaurant, Chantoiseau. Each possessed an idea of simple naturalness, and they gave us in turn the symbol of elite cluelessness, the "rustic village" on the grounds of the Petit Trianon; the symbol of popular terror, the guillotine; and the symbol of common pleasure, the restaurant.

Marie Antoinette built her Petit Hameau in homage to the new cult of simplicity. The Hameau was the first boutique farm where agriculture could be practiced in an ideal and deliberately "antiquated" form and a circle of the rich could restore their inner balance by milking cows and growing carrots. This was mocked at the time, of course, in exactly the same way that the same kind of activity is mocked now: when we insist on an organic garden at the White House or, as many cooks do now, run an organic hothouse attached to an expensive restaurant, we can expect to see it sneered at as a mere plaything of bored privilege.

Yet there is little doubt that Marie Antoinette was perfectly sincere in her beliefs, and that the movement toward *terroir* and fresh produce had a lot to do with what she did. (To deepen the irony of her infatuation, perhaps the most famous culinary imperative—her alleged cry of "Let them eat cake!"—actually *comes* from Rousseau's *Confessions,* where he uses it ironically in reference to an "ancient princess." The connection of Marie and Jean-Jacques ended by connecting her to a cry of indifference that, whatever other crimes she was guilty of, was none of hers.)

The man who took off Marie's head shared many of her tastes. Maximilien Robespierre, the maker of the Reign of Terror, also took his ideas about religion, rectitude, and dining from Rousseau. But where Marie Antoinette had taken the lesson that simple pleasures are natural to life, Robespierre took the related lesson that austere pleasures are necessary for virtue. In an especially creepy note, he had the keepers of the plain rooming house that he lived in prepare for him, night after night, as he came home from the killings, a meatless diet of strawberry jam and white bread. It was left to his great rival Georges Danton to be the *fresser* of the French Revolution—and for his sins he lost his head, too.

But there was also a more enduring relation between Rousseau's ideas and our own food life. As we've seen, Chantoiseau took up the new cult of self-conscious health to make the restorative bouillon that lent its name to that new institution, the restaurant. And the kind of "sentimentality" that Rousseau loved played its role, too: the idea of the restaurant as a public place where women could come for their health without having their morality impugned allowed for a whole new ritual of courtship and sublimated sex. (The appeal to self-improvement is always an acceptable cover for sex; that's why they call them health clubs.)

So from this same simple turn toward brown bread, toward the *terroir* and the authentic, we get radically unlike results: the move among the upper classes toward boutique farming, among the radicals the move away from delectation toward delicacy, and among the middle classes the invention of the most durable of all "bourgeois" institutions, the restaurant. Whatever simple pleasures may be, they aren't simple.

Taste in the Enlightenment belonged to philosophy. In the nineteenth century, the study of taste turned to evolutionary theory and to economics. The idea of the authentic has always been haunted by the possibility that what we call authentic is arbitrary, and in the nineteenth century this instinct was given systematic form by the economist who could be called the Darwin of taste. His name was Thorstein Veblen, and he was a professor who came to fame in 1899 with the book *The Theory of the Leisure Class*. The most original, if the most discouraging, thinker about taste of modern times, Veblen, a passionate Darwinian, must have been well aware of Darwin's writings on that subspecies of natural selection Darwin called "sexual selection," in which Darwin was trying to create a kind of natural science of taste.

What Darwin had noticed was the seemingly perverse elements of sexual display in animals, which seemed to contradict "natural" principles of the efficient use of resources. You might think that animals that used resources most sparingly would live longest and have the most offspring. But in fact, far from existing in a state of parsimonious, peasant-like simplicity which only human artifice and pride disturbed, the state of nature looked more like the rococo interiors at the Nymphenburg Palace than the peasant hut. Peacocks and elks and many other species in the wild indulge in expensive displays of needless plumage and endless antlers: they strut up and down in the lek, to display how much they have to waste. They make themselves as conspicuous as possible in order to show off their goods and get a mate. Showing off, not simplicity, is the rule of nature.

Veblen came from a Norwegian farm family and grew up in Minnesota; a little Norwegian goes a long way toward making you reluctant to put on any kind of display. Inspired in part by Franz Boas's insight that anthropology could explain economics, Veblen began *The Theory of the Leisure Class* with a myth. He imagined that money trouble had begun way back, with the transfer from a state of "peaceable savagery" to one of "predatory barbarism." The peaceable savage was a creature of material appetites who was satisfied when he was satiated. This natural state was superseded by the coming of the predatory barbarian, a category that for Veblen includes the Kwakiutl warrior, the medieval feudalist, and, in America, the businessman—anyone who lived off the labor of others.

The distinguishing characteristic of predatory-barbarian society is a ruling class that doesn't do physical labor—a leisure class. (Even a banker who goes to the office every day is, in Veblen's scheme, a member of the leisure class.) In tribal and feudal societies, he argues, the leisure class had certain occupations—making war, exploiting vast tracts of land, running slave plantations—that gave it prowess and status: its members could fight, and actually owned other people. With the growth of modern industrial society, only the outward show remained, and it became a powerful symbol. In Veblen's scheme, the Ralph Lauren effect is universal: even when membership in the leisure class no longer depends on being able to ride horses and own land, it is still symbolized by polo and ranches. "Manners are symbolical and conventionalized survivals representing former acts of dominance," he writes.

"In large part they are an expression of the relation of status—a symbolic pantomime of mastery on the one hand and of subservience on the other."

The rules of this "symbolic pantomime" became Veblen's subject. It was founded on the practice of "invidious comparison." For preindustrial predatory barbarians, it was pretty clear who stood where: you just counted slaves and acres. For industrial society, though, there is no obvious way to rate predatory barbarians except to see where they shop and what they buy. Since you can't count the slaves or acres of the stranger on Madison Avenue, the only way to know where he stands is to see how much he pays for his cappuccino. In today's terms, if he goes to Three Guys he pays three dollars, and if he goes to the E.A.T. café he pays six. Some would rather pay the six and buy the status. Veblen called this urge to show off your status by spending your money "conspicuous consumption."

And yet Veblen saw that, even among the very rich, conspicuous consumption was usually complicated, involving a tension between the need to display money and the need to be seen to display old money. "Archaic simplicity" had to be evoked in order to demonstrate the age and solidity of your "industrial exemption"—your freedom from the necessity of working with your hands. Conspicuous consumption had to combine "a studious exhibition of expensiveness with a make-believe of simplicity."

Veblen's point is not that we want to separate ourselves from others by showing off while spending a lot of money on big consumer goods: the guy with the giant house in the Hamptons is, to the true uppers, an embarrassment. The point of conspicuous consumption is not that it is more consumption but that it is conspicuous—that is, clearly distinguished from its surroundings, which are the status-manners of the vulgar middles. We want to separate ourselves from the bourgeoisie, and the leisure class does this by taking on the manners of the other exempted people, the peasant or criminal classes. The privileged classes, and their professional attendees, will always struggle to make their true status and income clear by differentiating themselves from the middles. (Already, in 1899, Veblen pointed out that the fashion for candlelight dinners was pure invidiousness; nobody thought candles were romantic until they were archaic.)

Veblen's analysis of taste can be vulgarized, most often in a broad, crude, or merely snide way. But it isn't hard to see how arresting a true Veblenian account of food taste in our time might be. In an era of plenty, when we can't distinguish ourselves by eating more—when obesity has become a sign of the lower-middle classes, not the high uppers—we eat local and seasonal produce in order to annex the exemption of the few surviving peasants. Whole Foods has grown, on Veblenian principles, as more of the professionals and upper-middles try for the same status symbols—and come under suspicion from the true uppers as mere fakery, a counterfeit of "our" beliefs.

Similarly, a Veblenian account of taste can explain apparent oddities: for instance, the question that I raised at the very beginning of this book, and that is the seemingly contradictory trends that have grown up among taste-setters in our own age: the taste for molecular gastronomy, and for slow, peasant food. What they have in common is that they are hard to take part in if you are on a middle income. When Calvin Trillin made fun of the "Maison de la Casa House" restaurant, the typical Continental cuisine spot in Cincinnati or Akron—with its stuff-stuff with heavy cooking—he was noticing, with his matchless eye for the details of American life, that what had been a high cuisine restricted to a handful of people with access to New York or Paris was now a common ideal of the middle classes—which meant that it would now have to be rejected quickly and completely by the uppers and the pros. And so we came to the end of even real French cooking, to the French restaurant, with its velvet banquettes, to the disappearance of all those "Le" and "La" restaurants in New York; no more Le Cygne, La Caravelle, or Le Lavandou.

They've been replaced by single words and numbers—Basil, Butter, Cilantro—which suggest the elemental ingredient derived pseudo-peasant style.

The molecular—or "techno-emotional"—cuisine depends on resources for travel, and on machinery for making, that are also outside the range of all the middles; the localist cuisine depends on resources that take more organization, and more time, than money, but the two are the same in many ways. It would be no surprise to the Veblenian that the new "best restaurant," taking the place of all those old French temples, is René Redzepi's Noma, in Copenhagen, which combines extreme localism with high molecularism, a double whammy of Veblenian achievement: René stores vintage carrots for years—the ultimate peasant tribute—but also manufactures potato chips that taste like chocolate and raw soil that tastes like caviar and so on. You win the triple: you get to eat local, you get to eat high, and you have to go to Denmark to do it.

For Veblen, it's *all* status and symbol; it isn't possible to have an authentic response to food, much less an altruistic one. We are social creatures driven to confer status on ourselves. Every taste choice we make is a status choice in a not-very-hard-to-see-through disguise.

Veblen's theory was that there were large areas of real life that defy free-market theories, and that what we call taste is like the antigravity mineral in *Avatar,* the thing that makes it all float up. There are antigravity zones made by the acceleration of taste, where we pay more to get less and the rain falls up and the grass grows high in winter.

Yet the most influential American economist of taste in the century since Veblen was writing has been the University of Chicago professor Gary Becker, who in 1992 won the Nobel Prize in economics, for *his* studies of taste, time, and money—in fact, the paper he cowrote, called simply "De Gustibus Non Est Disputandum," is one of the most cited papers in the literature. In it, Becker insists, a little shockingly, that there is no such thing as taste, and that all tastes are all the same. By this he means not that they never change but that, from the point of view of an economic model, they can all be mapped in the same way. Where earlier economists would say that changing tastes violated or overthrew classical laws of supply and demand, Becker insists that that's not so: it doesn't matter what it is you want, the ends of wanting are all alike. People make rational decisions to invest in what they like and what gives them pleasure; the mistake is thinking of the product and not the entire social process.

Why, Becker asks, if you have two restaurants across the street from each other, serving comparable food, do the normal rules of economics not apply? Why doesn't the one with the long line each night expand its premises, or raise its prices? Why doesn't the restaurant across the street lower its prices? Veblen's answer is that we have been coerced by capitalism into imagining that people will envy us if we are standing in the right line. Becker's answer is, in plain English, that the line is what we're paying for. It is the sum of the experience, which is the experience of standing in a line with people. The presence of other people makes the product more desirable. This explains why crowded restaurants don't expand, and why, in New York, they often set up obstacles—private numbers, snooty young women maître d's—designed to drive away customers. Knowing that the chances of staying in fashion are very slim, the best strategy is to milk as much money as you can from the intimidated consumer now. Keeping customers out is a very good short-term strategy for making a profit, so long as you can keep the other customers coming in.

Or take that E.A.T. cappuccino; the Veblenian explanation is that it's an irrational perversity imposed by status overriding economic sense. Becker's explanation is that the six-dollar cappuccino *is* good economic sense. The price is a rational price given that what you're paying for is the social interaction—and though this sounds like the same thing said in a different way, it is different inasmuch as Veblen thinks the cycles of taste are silly and to be escaped from, if you can, and Becker thinks that they are part of the rational logic of markets. Seemingly irrational phenomena of mere taste are actually completely rational phenomena of utility. The cappuccino is correctly priced, in its own weird way. Veblen thinks that people adopt silly tastes because they're driven to do it by capitalism; Becker thinks they do it because the market frees us to be honest in our likes and dislikes, and then reveals them as they really are. What we call educating our tastes is merely maximizing our utilities, and all utilities look about the same seen from a sufficient distance. All rat races look the same to everyone but the rats who are running in them.

Now, in real life we don't live within one model of taste, but many. We may each be, by turns, Montesquieu and Rousseau and Veblen and Becker at a single dinner. Many of my friends who run restaurants race through these roles every day: in their role as cooks they are Rousseauian optimists, in their view of their customers Veblenian cynics, and in their view of their business partners Beckerian realists. They want their food to be authentic and pure and natural; they know their customers will come only if they think it's hot and hip; and they recognize that the best way to persuade clients that it's hot and hip is to have someone else say it is. They want to serve the best steak they can but they know they're selling the sizzle; they want the sizzle to last as long as it can by making people hear it.

Though the thinkers are various, and the views complex, the common point is simple: wherever we stand, we cannot escape the cycles of symbolic social life—whether they are driven by invidious comparison, self-interest, imitation, or utility. They may derive from our desire to keep up with the Joneses, or from our urge to find out what it is the Joneses are keeping up with themselves—in every case, the romantic idea of true taste as a thing revealed after false taste and fashion has been stripped away fails. What we find when we look at taste—from the viewpoint of sociologists, psychologists, economists, and novelists alike—is a system of imbalances, asymmetries, persistent illusions, turning cycles, tail-biting serpents, deferred self-interests, not just wheels instead of ladders but gyrating spirals instead of simple wheels. None of us can escape the web of competitive, cyclical, counterintuitive, imitative relations that shape the social role of taste. There is no privileged space from which we can look down and say, Your tastes are trends, my tastes are truths. All taste effects depend on contexts. The smell in our nose changes the taste in our mouth, and the length of the line outside the restaurant changes our view of the taste of the food we're waiting for, and even how much we'll spend to eat it. We are what we eat? Probably closer to the truth to say that we eat what we are: the total self we bring to the table shapes the way we choose, and even how we chew. Our morals and our manners together drive our molars.

There is no true or "natural" taste outside the circles of social ritual. You, me, the guy at McDonald's, the kosher butcher down the street, and the evangelical vegetarian actress on television, the locavore and the mad seasonalist and the organic shopper and the crazed carnivore—we are all part of an inescapable network of social relations that shape our tastes in ways small and large. Our circumstances whisper in our ear what we ought to eat and what we ought to like and why we ought to like it. To insist that *ours* is true simplicity, true taste, that we at last know the right way to eat, is to lobby for an exemption from history that history will not provide. It is even to imagine that we can escape the effects of living among our own kind—our humanity. That was Rousseau's mistake, and Robespierre's sin.

Yet I know from long and sometimes painful experience that this truth often goes down *very* badly, or is taken to mean that all our tastes are just delusions. Take, for instance, the obvious smaller truth about the social texture of taste—the experimental truth that wine tasting is a social ritual as much as it is an objective rating. We know that the taste of wine is heavily dependent on all kinds of social cues—the order of glasses, color, place, expectations, labels . . . even experts do no better than random chance in determining between a glass of white and a glass of red in a blindfold test. We see "Rousseau effects" in the trend toward organic and biodynamic wine (biodynamic viticulture combines organic treatment of the vineyard with a spiritual aspect), which *must* taste better; we see Veblenian effects in wine tasting (the bottle of Cristal or Pétrus has become marked as nouveau riche, so better buy the biodynamic ones); we see Beckerian effects (the price is justified by our chance to take part in the community); and so on.

Doesn't this mean that you're saying that it's all phony? That it's a fraud or a fake? Just the opposite; what it shows is that the experience of taste is like all of our other experiences of meaning, produced by complicated frames and interactions and effects and all the richer for it. Wine writing or tasting is no more fraudulent than music criticism or art appreciation, which are also crucially dependent on context and expectations, on social context at least as constricting as those that govern mouth taste. All the things that make us human—the nature of our social lives, our taste for competitions and our capacity for learning new games—make the distinction between acquired taste and authentic taste, trendy taste and true taste, meaningless in any discussion about real life.

Yet, just because they can be partly explained as conspicuous display doesn't mean that our tastes are without value, meaning, importance, or integrity. The naïve naturist believes that insistently asserting the sincerity of her values places them outside the realm of mere style; the naïve Veblenian believes that having shown that a thing has an element of style is enough to empty it of any sincerity at all.

In truth, much, perhaps most, of the good in our lives comes from recognizing the fragile and temporary basis of what we choose to do, and then doing it anyway. We don't have to believe in natural or absolute grammar to believe in beautiful sentences. We don't have to believe in natural monogamy to work at a happy marriage. All the good stuff is at once universal and over-whelming, and local, tempered by taste, finely articulated to the place and moment. When we have a child in a foreign country, it is all foreign and all child. When we have an omelet in Spain, it is all Spain and all omelet. When we eat beautifully in 2011, we are both free diners and prisoners of the table of our time.

So the choice between an authority to tell us what we ought to eat and the anarchy of warring fashions is a false one. Between authority and anarchy falls *argument*, and though arguments aren't always better for being ended, they're always better for being addressed. What *"De gustibus . . ."* really means is not that taste is not *disputable* but that it's not *decidable*—if you don't like Brussels sprouts, I can argue you into trying them but I can't argue you into liking them. But that's an argument worth having. We have it every time I put them on the table.

What the arguments do show is something deeper, and vital—that behind nearly all taste squabbles are value disputes. All morals manifest themselves as manners, and all manners have a moral locked inside. We know the values that we want to uphold on the "green" side of the fence: community, tradition, care, sus-tainability, and pleasure above all else. But on the "industrialized" side there are values, too: efficiency, prosperity, ease of choice, and abundance. This is a case where the seeming "left" is entirely conservative, while the industrial and populist right, as happens so often in the capitalist regime, is essentially progressive—say good-bye to the family farm, the slow-cooked chicken, and in exchange you get, or hope to get, what we have not had ever before on this planet: cheap meat for everyone. Organic, local, slow—if this is what we want, it is, the counterargument goes, the best way to go hungry. There is the silent spring of industrialized agriculture, but there is also the long silent summer of natural starvation.

On the other hand, or in the other fork, there is the truth that the diet of grease and sugar and salt, produced by reducing living things to machines, creates the overfed, glazed, and ill American majority. The argument is that cheap meat for all will end with no cheap meat for anyone; the argument in return is that the threat of no cheap meat means that we must find ways to make more. The animal Auschwitz meets the silent clearing of the Congo. That there are no simple solutions to be had does not mean that there are no good arguments to be made. All good arguments have no end, only provisional settlements.

One thing is for sure: these questions won't be solved by a nostalgic appeal to nature. The appeal to nature is *always* a false appeal. Every appeal to nature or the natural way or the way we were meant to do it has always failed in the history of human thought and action. If anything is natural, it is the flight from nature. If anything is genetic, it is the willingness to be fascinated by the elaborate, the deceptive, and the deliberately overcharged. Birds in the lek were Barcelona chefs long before there was a Barcelona. If anything is efficient, it is waste. The peacock's tail, which does nothing except show the peahen how much he has to throw away, is as good a model for a natural life, or diet, as the happy Paleolithic eater sharing the healthy diet.

There is no right way to eat, spell, get dressed, wear clothes, make love, listen to music, drink wine, raise children, because there is no natural way to do any of these things. Every attempt to say what nature wants us to do turns out to be what someone thinks we ought to. There may be nature-based explanations for why some ways are taken more frequently than others, but they fail at the moment of specific choice, and the specific choice is all that counts: we can explain why people like music, but we cannot explain why some prefer Barry Manilow to Mozart. That lies beyond reason.

Nature does, and makes us do, many good things and many horrible things. Nature gives us the bounty of the fields; it also offers the slavery of agriculture, and the cruelty of animal slaughter. Nature lets worms eat other animals alive from the inside out. As John Stuart Mill said, what matters is not to discover what nature does, but what it is good to do. (In any case, we generally argue that the tastes we already have are the ones that will save the world to come: people who believe that the answer is to reduce consumption don't much like the culture of consumption in the first place—they're *already* living in Vermont.)

This isn't a counsel of despair. It is a counsel of devoted detachment. Let me now offer the secret of life—or, rather, what James Taylor calls, in his fine song of that name, the secret o' life. The secret of life is having enough intellectual detachment from our tastes to see their absurdity, while taking enough emotional fulfillment from them to grasp their necessity. We *are* absurd followers of the fashions of a time and place and class; we are also wise worshippers of ideas. We need not flee manners to embrace morals. The morals are the manners in more complicated form. If we lack the proper distance from our tastes, we can't see things as they are; if we lack the emotional attachment to them, we see things *merely* as they are. With mouth taste as with moral taste, we cannot escape a frame of ritualized context; but with mouth taste as with moral taste, the frame is what contains the feeling, and leads the eye. (Wallace Stevens put it nicely: "The final belief is to believe in a fiction, which you know to be a fiction, there being nothing else. The exquisite truth is to know that it is a fiction and that you believe in it willingly.")

I spend, for instance, a large portion of every day of my life worrying about the shape of sentences. Semicolon or period? Replace a polysyllabic word with a monosyllable for drop-shot effect, or replace a monosyllable with a polysyllable for ironic overcharge? And I patiently follow the rules of English grammar. "That" or "which"? Where's the antecedent? What's the rule here? I believe in the one right sentence, in the one way to write, just as passionately as anyone can believe in the one right meal. Yet my mom, as it happens, is a linguist, and when she wasn't teaching me how to cook she taught me the one hard truth: there is no natural grammar, no "right way" to write. She taught me that rules and practices and usage change all the time, and dramatically, and that "prescriptivism" in language is as bogus a concept in linguistics as green cheese is in astronomy. There is no grammar of the gods, just as there is no timeless taste.

So why do we stick to the rules? We dutifully follow the rules of grammar not because the rules are right, or fixed, but to show to others our love of language and our regard for a tradition. It's a signal, not a slavish act. The green eater, in her secret heart, is doing the same thing: not eating what she should, but eating in a way that shows who she is. By eating the "right way," we communicate to the other people at the table our passion for food and our willingness to look a little foolish in showing it. Obvious fictions often have important moral points—that's why Jesus, that apostle of the open table, always spoke in parables. You needn't prove to me that this grass-fed veal is healthier for me; you need say merely, the grass-fed veal symbolizes the kind of world I want to live in, and the meat from the industrial abattoir does not. It's a symbol not of a natural order but of a community of belief.

So perhaps we're now in a better state to say what we mean when we talk about taste. By "taste" we mean the social customs and practices that let us negotiate between our fashions and our values. A taste is more durable than a fashion, more mutable than a value. Taste is an argument compressed into an instruction. It is complicated, ironic knowledge turned into a choice on a menu.

The idea that on one hand there are mere fashions and on the other hand enduring values is false. The best way to get people to change their values is by first changing their fashions, and it takes a new taste to do that. We show people that organic apples taste better, and we hope that the values of sustainability and true food will penetrate; we want people not to bait bears or hold cockfights, and we make it unfashionable before we can make it immoral. The fashionable chef knows to serve wild salmon; the one with values knows why wild salmon is better than farmed; the one with taste knows that if you are serving wild salmon you ought to serve it with rhubarb and organic quinoa to make a proper meal. In life, as on the plate, there is a constant interchange between fashion and value, between "surface" and "substance"—and taste is what carries the charge between them. *That's* why it's never at rest.

There were, I wrote, *two* famous Latin tags that everyone knew. The other, of course, is what was once the national motto: *e pluribus unum*. Out of many, one. It is a supremely democratic slogan, since it does not pretend that the one that is made loses its plurality, but speaks to the closest thing we have to a secular miracle: that we do pull along, most of the time, and that we can manage.

What isn't well known is that it is a *culinary* metaphor. It comes from a recipe for salad dressing—or so you'll be told if you pursue it—taken from a Latin poem called "Moretum," long attributed, probably wrongly, to Virgil. Actually, it's a recipe for pesto: a peasant cook is pestling together cheese, garlic, and herbs and oil. When it all comes together, well, *e pluribus unum*.

> (. . . *Symilus the rustic husbandman* . . .)
> *Th' aforesaid herbs he now doth introduce*
> *And with his left hand 'neath his hairy groin*
> *Supports his garment; with his right he first*

The reeking garlic with the pestle breaks,
Then everything he equally doth rub
I' th' mingled juice. His hand in circles move:
Till by degrees they one by one do lose
Their proper powers, and out of many comes
A single colour, not entirely green
Because the milky fragments this forbid,
Nor showing white as from the milk because
That colour's altered by so many herbs.

Now, as anyone who makes pesto knows (I make mine with lime; I'll give you the recipe), what makes it interesting is that unlike a hollandaise or a crème anglaise, it's just like in the poem—it takes on a composite character different from its starting elements, but the elements remain alive within the mix. The cheese and basil and garlic all come together, and yet they all remain distinct. Choosing this for their motto, the founders chose well, and with good taste: pesto *is* a model for a composite country.

And for a civilized one. For what, after all, is the purpose of this peasant poem? To show how complex, how far from simple, the simple life is. The poem shows that each time we cook we enact the means by which life is lived: through blending, unstable compromise, uncertain joining together of unlikely opposites. It is exactly against the idealized vision of the Georgics and pastorals of Virgil, where the shepherds live in ideal leisure. The peasants in "Moretum" are not blissfully enjoying the fruits of nature. They are at work, and their work, even making a salad dressing, costs them tears, takes time, and is the result of a thousand small decisions—tastings, in the literal and most exalted sense—that produce an eerie impression of unity.

Not from many things one fixed thing, but from many things one thing that—if you just work it hard with a pestle—holds together well enough and long enough to taste good. The truth of all of us who live in our kitchens, whether as pros or dads and moms, is that we know the place of taste as a set of steps, not a series of diktats—an ongoing permanent negotiation between values and fashions, between fundamentally different views of what we want from life and what the plenty of nature can give us, where the child who hates broccoli meets the parent who fears malnutrition and where our belief in saving the planet meets the reality of the half-hour deadline. And where every time we make a plate of pesto we are wowed all over again by the sheer complicated weight of tradition, knack, and knowledge it demands—the way that principles of practice as old as the Roman empire meet particulars of practice as fresh as today's basil and the price of pine nuts. We have our orders, like classicists; go to the market for organic basil, like Rousseauians—want to show our diners that it's real pesto, not from a jar, so we add a ragged leaf or two, like Veblenians; and we recognize that we are investing not just in the scrumptiousness of the dish but in a set of values about jarlessness for our kids, and hope it pays off later on when in our toothless age they will invite us over for a jarless dinner.

Chop wood. Carry water. Bake your cake. Then you have it. Then you eat it. The only thing to *do* with a cake is eat it. The submission to sequence is the source of the sublime. Taste *is* only "the art of knowing little things." That's what makes it big. In republics as in the kitchen, it's the little things, respected for themselves rather than puréed into sameness, that make the finest sauces. Taste begins at the door, and ends in our dreams. It is not on our tongues, or in our hearts, or in our minds or our social roles, but everywhere at once. Taste is choice. Taste is labor. Taste is work. And taste is everywhere and results from everything. Taste is the totality of our lives. No surprise, surely. That taste is not a set of principles to be applied by rote but a daily negotiation among practices, prices, promises, and possibilities is what even the most peasantlike home cook knows. It's the working chef's wisdom. They should teach it to philosophers.

5

E-MAIL TO ELIZABETH PENNELL:
Lamb, Saffron, Cinnamon

Dear Eliza:

My goodness, are we still alive—or, in your case, comfortably dead—after all that argument! Lime pesto, I promised at the end, and so now I shall present it. It is part of the summer run of things, something to serve with grilled food. I love to grill, and the grill is the one part of cooking that I think opened up most since your time. Perhaps I'm wrong, but I don't think that there was any real grilling going on in your day. Beautiful pictures of picnics abound, of course, but I think they were all sandwich-and-cold-chicken affairs. I suspect that the central summer sight of our day—the middle-aged man surrounded by smoke—was completely unknown in yours.

Anyway, here it is. I like to serve it with grilled salmon. It's simple. In a blender—yes, yes, I know that you should do this all by hand, with a mortar and pestle, with virtuous small steps, but, well, really—you take a nicely scissored mix of the three summer herbs, basil, mint, and cilantro, and add some chopped garlic, about one clove, and lots of fresh lime juice. No other sour thing—fresh lime juice, at least two and perhaps three limes' worth. Then you take half a cup of pine nuts—yes, you can use walnuts, although it really isn't as good, but I don't think you have to toast the pine nuts for it to work out well—and whiz them together, and slowly stream in about three-quarters of a cup of good olive oil. Then you grate in as much Parmesan as you think right, grating it over the blender and mixing it in with a wooden spoon. Salt a bit if you like. It's brighter and somehow cleaner tasting than other pesto. Is there anything made with lime that doesn't taste good? Perhaps it's the history of scurvy, buried in our blood, that calls for citrus?

The more I learn about you the more extraordinary you seem, and the more weirdly parallel our lives become, despite the century and sex that separates us. You come, it turns out, from Philadelphia, or were born there, as was I, and kept such an affection for it throughout your wanderings to Paris and London that it's said you wrote a book about it! There's a Philadelphia flavor to your work. You spent your best working years in London, but then returning home to America, you came to New York, and died in Brooklyn Heights, the most London-like part of New York, perhaps—certainly now, with its color-named streets and leafy rows of brownstones. So your triangle, the tripod on which you stand to eat—Philadelphian by birth, Francophile by choice, and New Yorker by default—are all mine, too, or nearly so. And then I like that you call cooking "cookery"— "Writing articles on cookery led me to buying books on cookery, also to receiving them for review." As "Tigger" robs "tiger" of its teeth, and "Tyger" in Blake adds to it its mystical ferocity, the word "cookery" turns cooking from a pastime or chore to a craft: "He was wise in the ways of cookery," something they teach at Hogwarts.

I like your Francophilia, too, and that you lived in exile for so long. Greedy people who care about what you call "cookery in a

philosophical frame" care most if they are partly exiles, permanent expatriates. The home diner knows what he likes; one of
the reasons for the efflorescence of French writing on food, back
when, and its partial absence now, is the effort of definition—
Who are we? What shall we eat? You disapprove of Brillat-
Savarin, as a bit of a tourist trap: I think this is a good judgment,
in its way. Certainly Grimod's was the wittier pen. When I'm
eating, or shopping, I carry on a conversation with you, trying
to see if, by explaining what's different from our time to yours,
I can explain to myself what really counts. I imagine calling
you, spiritlike, from a kind of Limbo renamed, say, Gumbo, and
explaining more to you of how eating has changed since last
you ate.

Spices—now *they've* changed. The strong ones are back in
favor. In lots of ways, the revolutions of the nineteenth
century—the restaurant revolution, the recipe book
revolution—all turn around a revolution in spices and spicing, a tsunami in whose wake you still rock, but which has
now, so to speak, rocked back. Throughout the medieval and
early-Renaissance period, and of course going further back into
the Roman, sweet and strong spices were the staff of life, the
way food was, the way food tasted. Some spices were so strong
that we have lost track of them today, so that they live on only
in strange bestiaries. There are spices that have just vanished.
We read about the lost spices of antiquity with the same wonder that occultists feel when they read about the (supposedly)
sunken islands. Silphium, the legendary root spice that the
Greeks used as easily as we use nutmeg, disappeared sometime
in the first century A.D., and hasn't been seen since, losing for us
an entire range of flavors, a whole scale in the kitchen's music.
(Though if it's true, as legend also has it, that the nearest thing
to it is that other strange and smelly spice, asafetida, or hing,
then it may be very well lost.) In any case, we'll never taste the
Roman delicacy of sea squirt and silphium. And what of balsam

of Mecca, and what of tejpat? Both savory spices, once loved, now lost or cast aside. Thinking of them makes our regular diet of salt and pepper and the same six green herbs seem as limited as those pallid white marble neoclassical statues, compared with the polychrome and bronze surfaces that were the true marvels of antique art.

The reform against sweet and savory spices—the banishment of cloves, the expulsion of cinnamon to a slightly disreputable, confined life in the dessert menu and the holiday punch bowl—was one of the rocks on which French cuisine, to which you so emotionally and naturally pledged yourself, was built. The great codifying chef Carême substituted the green plants for the brown spices, tarragon in reduced stock with cream for cloves in simmered red wine with cinnamon, and a new taste was made, one that lasted longer than most. The perceived virtues of the new green cooking—green in this herb- and plant-based way—probably had something to do with a kind of weird reorganization of taste: you had meat here, vegetables there, and you put them together on a single plate. There's certainly nothing grander, is there, than the moment of the garnish, when a simple pot roast of chuck becomes a *boeuf à la mode*—when all the sparkling green peas and bright orange carrots gather around it, the sauce gleaming with the gelatinous shimmer of calf's foot? Clarity, freshness, intensity of natural flavor instead of its concealment by spice—all of those virtues, more than the supposed ones of cream and butter, were part of the French revolution in cooking when it first happened. Food had been muddy as a city river; now, suddenly, it ran clear as a Swiss lake.

But there was more to it than that, wasn't there? There was a kind of maturity of taste in play. Kids like sweet tastes. To banish sweet and strong spices was to end the childhood of cooking. And primitive people, earth's children in the eighteenth-century view, were thought to like strong flavors.

Transcending our urge to eat sweet and spicy things was a way to transcend our infantile, barbarian past. Sweet and sour and spicy, molasses and lime and chili—all those were just too *easy*. Grown-up taste, studied taste, was subtler than that. You write about it quite directly, referring to your collection of cookbooks, and how the cooks of old practiced by "adding such a wholesale mixture of cloying sweets and rank spices that, as I read, I can but wonder if in the old days meat and poultry were not apt to be tainted and the cook's art needed to disguise the fact. These were the horrors from which the French delivered the world."

But now, you see, the horrors have returned. The notion that spices were once heaped on tainted meat now seems false; at least, so the new culinary historians say. There's no evidence that meat was more tainted then than now; it's just another case where we regulate our prejudices in the model of our tastes— where we pretend our prejudices are the truth of healthy eating. People ate spicy food then because they liked the way it tasted. Now, you see, Elizabeth, people who think about food think the green herb and thick cream and white pepper and melted cheese taste which seemed so sophisticated to your time is itself infantile. It's too easy, too, well, bourgeois. So the old brown spices your time banished to the nursery return in my day to the main table—but under another guise, as the banished so often do when they return, and that is as dashing foreigners. Tastes that were routine in premodern days, nutmeg and cardamom and molasses, are back, but as emissaries of the Great Khan. Returned under the demand for exotica, returned in the guise of travel.

The pair of old spices I find irresistible is saffron and cinnamon. I don't think that there can be anything—rice, chicken stew, flank-steak braise, even a tuna in tomato sauce—that isn't better for having a touch of saffron and cinnamon. How did they come home? By way of North Africa, of course, where they were never lost. So I take lamb—I like gigot for roasting, of course, but lamb shoulder braises best. And here's the thing: with this dish, with the dark, dense spices, it doesn't really matter if you brown the lamb first or not. I know, that doesn't make sense—it violates the cook's first law, that browning at length is the key to "caramelizing" and to making things tender. We have a mental image, I think, that *sounds* right: the brown crust "seals in" juiciness. Of course, anyone who actually braises and stews stuff knows that juiciness isn't sealed in. It leaks out, right out into the bouillon, which is why the bouillon tastes so good. Reducing the bouillon is what makes the thing great. It's simply the taste of the browning we like best, and, if your nose and mouth have enough else to occupy them, it doesn't matter. So you . . . just throw the things together. Two to three pounds of lamb chunks, and an onion, peeled but not chopped, and the holy trinity of cilantro, basil, and mint tied together—if it gets loose you have to strain it afterward, which is just a small step, but still—and a fresh fragrant stick of cinnamon, broken in two, with each half stuck in on either side of the lamb chunks.

Yes, yes, I know: there are many different kinds of cinnamon. There is the true cinnamon of Sri Lanka, the strong Saigon cinnamon, and a kind of strange Chinese relation, cassia. I like to go down to Kalustyan's on Lexington Avenue and shop for spices, make notes on the varieties and verities. Now that all the record stores are closed, and the bookstores are closing— oh God, you caught only the very beginnings of the record industry, and can't imagine the glory of the record store at its height!—the spice stores are the last browsing places left. If we were truly virtuous, we would smell and taste each kind, and note the differences—I'm sure they exist—and do a cinnamon tasting, as, at the fancy places now, they do tastings of red volcanic salt against black basalt salt, or whatever.

Anyway, you let the lamb very gently braise for about two hours, until it's tender. I bought one of those elegant Chinese-hat *tagines,* and it works well, but no better than a normal Dutch oven. (The high-steepled shape is meant to draw up and reuse moisture in a North African climate where water is scarce, but the key to a good *tagine*, to a good stew, is *always* to use less liquid than the recipe says, and make the oven or burner heat even lower than it suggests. Simmer and braise, never stew and boil.) Then—this is ridiculously simple—you boil down the liquid, add a teaspoonful of honey, some prunes ("dried plums,") or the apricots in water, and at last the little saffron stems. They're not really stems at all, they're threads. It's intoxicating—sweet and spicy, meaty and fruity. Kids love it and adults, when you add harissa paste to it, they die. It's never missed for me. And yet it's the kind of taste that was banned for so long, as sex outside of marriage was banned for so long.

What's lost, of course, is rigor: the sense that we are doing right by eating well. We show our maturity by rejecting the easy pleasures of obvious mouth tastes as cloying and too rich, and transmute the judgment into a moral taste by insisting that the limited flavor of a few herbs is morally superior to the wide-open spaces of many spices. Moral taste works by rejecting a delicious *tagine* as *slack*. Of course this lamb tastes good! I hear you cry, newly awakened out there in Gumbo. How could it not? But the taste is not a taste coaxed and respected and teased out of a natural thing; it is an infantile taste imposed on something, indifferent to that something's subtleties. *Anything* would taste good dipped in honey and saffron and cinnamon and fruit. That isn't cooking, that's just . . . *eating*, eating as "primitives" do, as children do, even, perhaps, as animals do. You write about this with indignation and intelligence, describing bad hosts.

In excess they would emulate the banquets of the ancients, though they are too refined by far to revive the old vomitories— the indispensable antidote. Before dinner is half over, palates are jaded. "Fine shades" can no more be appreciated, every new course awakens fear of the morrow's indigestion. Art despises show, it disdains rivalry, and it knows not excess. A Velázquez or a Whistler never overloads his canvas for the sake of the gorgeous detail. To the artist in words, superfluous ornament is the unpardonable sin. And so with the lords of Gasterea, the tenth and fairest of the muses. Better by far Omar Khayyam's jug of wine and loaf of bread, if both be good. Neat in mind the master's model luncheon and its success. No menu could have been simpler; none more delicious. The table was laid for three, a goodly number, for all the slurs cast upon it. At each plate were "two dozen oysters with a bright golden lemon"; at each end of the table stood a bottle of Sauterne, carefully wiped all except the cork . . . after the oysters roasted kidneys were served; next truffled foie gras, then the famous fondue, fruit followed and coffee; and last two liqueurs, "One a spirit, to clear, and the other an oil, to soothe." Be not content to read, but go and do likewise.

The "master" you refer to, by the way, is, as I finally figured out, Brillat-Savarin—odd for you to honor him so, since you have the right literary prejudice in favor of Grimod, though perhaps your politics got the better of your taste. What *are* your politics, by the way? Are they *bien-pensant* liberal-socialist, like Brillat-Savarin's and your friend Oscar Wilde's? Or do they turn, as your beloved Whistler's did, a touch toward the irascible right? I wonder . . .

Well, you knew that all tastes are compressed arguments, arguments reduced to sensual instructions, moral cases made by pointing at the menu. And the taste argument you're making is plain enough. Saffron and cinnamon, you think, are to taste as gold thread and lapis lazuli are to the eye—of course they delight and entice, but they are a cheap form of seduction, compared with the solidity of massive form, compared with the ability to paint one gray sky as it is.

Yet look at the luncheon you point to as the model! And consider the complexity of it—sweet white wine with oysters (that would seem to us now as cloying as honey with lamb seems to you), where we could drink only a flinty Chablis or a brut champagne. So once again the march of progress becomes the circle of argument, and we are drawn back into the past to find that it was more advanced than we are. History comes back to bite itself on the tail, and all we can hope is that the tail is well seasoned. Saffron and cinnamon always delight. That, your time says back, is just what's wrong with them. And to that we have no answer.

In any case, those are my four secret, or at least semisacramental, ingredients: bacon and anchovies, saffron and cinnamon. And do try the lamb; it's best with couscous and a red wine from the region, something that the three kings would have drunk: a Château Musar from Lebanon, or, though it's from a different continent, an Australian Shiraz, which at least has a name that sounds of the region. Shiraz could have been the name of a Fourth Wise Man, now forgotten, who made the first spice-giving journey. In eating much depends on names.

Ever,
A.G.

6

Meat or Vegetables?

ON AN OVERCAST, gray-to-white London summer morning, the British chef Fergus Henderson is standing and staring reverently at the edge of Smithfield, the great meat market in the East End. If it is still reasonably early by restaurant standards, it is late in the day by those of a wholesale market; though Smithfield, an arcaded nineteenth-century affair of bright-painted cast-iron arches and venders' stalls, is beginning to close for the day, it still hums with a sense of sociable business ritual. Wholesalers in straw hats pack up their bacon and chops and trotters, some in Cryovac, some in shiny brown butcher paper. Henderson's relationship to Smithfield these days is largely spiritual—he gets most of the meat for his nearby restaurant, St. John, from private country suppliers and small boutique slaughterhouses—but it is still an enchanted place for him. "It's a bit of a closed society, with its own customs and traditions," he says. "And it represents a certain tradition that began before pink-in-plastic." ("Pink-in-plastic" is Henderson's dismissive name for supermarket meat.) "For centuries, using the whole beast was the common sense of the market. Embrace your carcass and you'll be richer and happier."

Fergus Henderson is a man in love with meat. He even looks like an English butcher. His face is florid, with the raspberry blush that one associates with the kind of all-right-then-dearie butcher who might appear in a Boulting Brothers comedy of the fifties. Since he opened St. John, in 1994, he has become famous for his devotion to the odd bits of ordinary animals. Ox tongue and tripe, lambs' brains and pigs' heads, stuffed lambs' hearts and rolled pigs' spleen: St. John has returned them to the repertory of the world's "high" cooking, while Henderson's book *Nose to Tail Eating*—which for a long time had to be bought in the United States on a gray market of second-hand copies, where prices could sometimes reach a hundred dollars—has become the *Ulysses* of the whole food–Slow Food movement, a plea for the fullness of life that begins with a man eating innards. (It has at last been published in America, under the slightly cosmeticized name of *The Whole Beast.*)

Henderson starts walking the block and a half back to his restaurant. "The squirrels, I suppose," he says, after a moment's pause. He has been asked if any particular adventures in heterodoxy caused comment in London. "Squirrel is delicious—like an oily wild rabbit. We had some that had been trapped by keepers in the country, and I decided to do a whole plate of them. Re-create the forest floor: wilted greens, to suggest the bosky woods they come from. Rather poetic, the whole thing. But somehow serving squirrels created quite a stir."

St. John, a converted nineteenth-century smokehouse, has two rooms: a twenty-foot-high sky-lit, cathedral-ceilinged front room, where the bar and bakery are, and the dining room, just beyond. The dining room is large and whitewashed; a row of knobs and hooks for coats goes around the room, giving it the air of an eighteenth-century eating house or tavern, though the open space is unlike any actual eighteenth-century tavern—it's more Saatchi collection than Cheshire cheese, a hint, perhaps, that archaism and modernism are in more complicated relation here than is evident at first glimpse, or smell. The kitchen seems to be visible from the dining room, but, as Henderson says, "It's a very tricky kind of openness. You can't actually see inside. It's the Mount Fuji principle borrowed from Japanese prints. You should never see the whole of Mount Fuji, you know." Henderson shows off the restaurant's tiny, cool larder. Inside a steel drawer, a suckling piglet lies waiting to be eaten, its feet curled up comfortably, its eyes closed, its face smiling. It has been specially ordered, and will be roasted and served later that week, nose to tail.

Over Hobbit-like elevenses (seed cake and Madeira), Henderson begins to talk about the ascent that has turned him, at forty-two, into a public figure widely viewed in his homeland as a cross between Jamie Oliver and Sweeney Todd—an image that he sustains with a complex and comic irony. "Isn't the approach to lunch the most wonderful time of day?" he asks. "Lunch is a choice, a decision of a sort. At dinner one must eat, but at lunch one chooses to eat well. There's a certain excitement in lunch." An assistant brings him the day's menu, and he looks it over. Though he no longer works in the kitchen, he still oversees each day's choices. Today's menu, written a little defiantly in nothing but English (only "crème fraîche," an adopted phrase, breaks the Anglo-Saxon attitude), is a calm, squirrelless document: there is to be middle white—a kind of northern pig—and also deep-fried tripe, veal-tail broth, deviled kidneys, and ox heart with beetroot and pickled walnut. The desserts are English, too, or Englishy— Eccles cake and Lancashire cheese, and even something called Eton Mess, which some people have suggested is not food at all but a succinct explanation of the sex lives of many British politicians.

In spite of his matey, Ealing Studios manner, Henderson is actually a former architect, with almost no formal training as a chef. "My mum was a good cook and my dad was a big eater," he recalls, "and both of them were architects"—well-known second-generation modernists, in fact. "I trained as an architect, but I found lunch in architectural offices discouraging. People ate at their desks. Then, with a friend, I began doing big peasant dishes over in a restaurant in Covent Garden when it was closed. We did cassoulet or pot-au-feu and would have forty or fifty people come and sit at a common table. That led to my finding work as a chef, even though I didn't have the training. I became the cook in a couple of places—I was lucky not to have to work for other people—and then I met my business partners. We found this place, and I began cooking here. We opened, got warm reviews, and, very quickly, turned the corner. I don't know what that corner was, but we turned it." (Henderson opened St. John at the height of the "mad-cow" disease scare, which made him modify his menu slightly; to this day, lambs' and calves' brains are out.)

Henderson had always liked innards, but it was only as he began to cook that he came to recognize the absurdity of our usual meat-eating, which clings to a few square feet of animal muscle near the skeleton, as timorous natives might cling to a few miles of coast on an island while avoiding the volcanic mountains inland. "There were all these wonderful, splendid bits of the animal being wasted, thrown out, while we were eating nothing but the filet," he said, pronouncing "filet" in the English manner, with a hard last consonant. "It seemed positively insulting to the animal that one had raised to treat it with such contempt. So many wonders there. Spleen! Spleen is a very fine, perfectly framed organ. In fact, your spleen swells when you're in love! How can you resist an organ that does that?"

He believes not only that animals should be made happy by being raised well, slaughtered humanely, and eaten entirely but that you can taste the emotional state of the animal on your plate. He senses this with hares. "Rabbits, when they're wild, have a very different temperament, which is expressed in their muscles. Welsh rabbits used to have a certain . . . tension. You could taste their tension. Now we've been using more relaxed Yorkshire rabbits, which are splendid in their way, but not as tense and interesting as the Welsh rabbits."

Henderson's devotion to the bits of the animal that other people tend to throw away or make faces at is partly a revivalist aesthetic, a tribute to peasant traditions, but it is closer to certain weird outer ends of conceptual installation than to anything nostalgic. The more time one spends with him, the more inclined one is to think that certain of his American devotees can miss an edge of irony and po-faced British wit in his approach. This is not to say that he doesn't think that noses and tails and heads and spleens are good to eat—he does think that, absolutely—but he also thinks that the idea that noses and tails and heads and spleens might be good to eat would be interesting even if they weren't as good to eat as they are. He grasps that even sincere gestures in the kitchen become social symbols on the plate—that the idea of eating rolled spleen and pig's tail has resonances and challenges apart from the taste of rolled spleen and pig's tail in the mouth. He is, as an ironist, close to the artist Damien Hirst, an inventor who plays on the line between display and disgust, and yet Henderson steps soberly over that line to the constant edge of delight.

Henderson's attitude toward the Englishness of his food is complex. Despite that menu written almost entirely in English, and English English, at that—no ricotta ravioli, no noisettes—the wine list is exclusively French. ("Of course, there's the Aquitaine connection," he says.) Yet when pressed for his influences he cites the Italian Marcella Hazan, and his favorite experience of eating is the walk in Paris through the Palais Royal toward the Grand Véfour on a sunny afternoon. The book that lurks behind his approach is Elisabeth Luard's *Sacred Food,* an eccentric polemic for a kind of universal home cooking, a transformational grammar of whole beasts and comforting puddings, rooted in the conviction that a restoration of this kind of cooking, in each of its regional guises, is essential to the recovery of a whole civilization.

The most famous dish that Henderson has created is a study in the invention of English tradition through multicultural wit: a salad of bone marrow, parsley, and capers, which, though it seems today to be as rural and English as Eccles cake, occurred to him a decade ago after watching a French film, *La Grande Bouffe.* "It has that scene where the man delights in marrow bones," he recalls. "And a friend had come in and all I had left were the marrow bones and the parsley and some capers. I thought that they would make a splendid marriage. I love the idea of food in which you participate. The singe is very important, getting the right singe on the bones. And the parsley. Vegetables these days are chopped into tiny grass. We discipline the parsley, so that it's chopped, yet still parsley. And capers are so important. They're the 'Nyeh!' factor in the dish." He makes a kind of complaining, whinnying noise. "You always need a little 'Nyeh!' on the plate. Pickled walnuts do the same thing for ox heart."

He sighs and looks over at the kitchen. "I wish I could stay in the kitchen through the service, but I'm not really trustworthy with this ropy left side of mine," he says. For the past few years, Henderson has been struggling with Parkinson's disease, which courses through his body like a lightning storm in summer, sending his left arm and hand into paroxysms of uncontrolled movement. He is neither melodramatic about it nor showily brave. "It was a bad day," he says of the moment he learned from his doctors about the disease. "My hand had been moving steadily to my chest, John Wayne in a Western movie, and I thought, How odd! And then it turned out to be this.

"I sat down and had a good lunch and felt somewhat better." His wife, Margot, and his three children, he says, have come to accept his "ropiness." (Later that year he had experimental surgery to place electrodes in his brain to try to control it.) "Disgust is always rooted in a perception of asymmetry," he says suddenly. "Geometry cures it. Take the haggis, for instance. It's made of sheep's stomach and sheep's lights, but people will eat it because it's comfortably round. Sausages have always been allowed in, because of their shape. People are somehow reassured."

Disgust, the psychologist Paul Rozin has suggested, may be a kind of optimal strategy for solving what he calls the "omnivore's dilemma": animals that can eat everything have to be especially cautious about what parts of other animals they eat. The default assumption seems to be that all animals are disgusting, and we have to learn an item-by-item list of what's acceptable. In this way, we enclose our children in our own double wrapping, composed of both common sense and collective neurosis. Yet it is also obviously true that the mind overgeneralizes its fear of the unshaped, and knows it. So along with the "Don't eat it!" impulse comes a "Dare you to eat it!" impulse, and it is between these two impulses that Henderson dances.

By now, lunch has progressed through many meats, with various quick detours into the vegetable world—St. John serves leaves, and even excels at them—and there is the promise of an unequaled dark-chocolate ice cream ahead. Henderson finishes off his ox heart with pickled walnuts. "The heart is the most expressive muscle in any animal," he says as he cleans his plate. "It's amazing, a muscle that works so endlessly and tirelessly to keep us alive. And yet it emerges tender and distinctive. Each animal heart is resonant with its animal. Ox heart has an honest beefy quality, lamb's heart rubs up against you. Each heart tastes like the animal that depended on it."

In Henderson's own heart there is, one senses, a harmony between man and his food that comes from eating all of the animal there is to eat, a mysticism rooted in fatality and the fact of our being, head to toe, animals, too. We are all meat, trembling and fresh, dying and spasming, and we enter into our humanity, as we leave it, by way of our animalness. We are beasts eating beasts, and the real bestiality, he suggests, lies in avoiding the truth of it. "Taste that!" he says, pressing a bit of fatty middle white on the visitor from New York. "It comes from a happy pig. You can taste the difference. People eat meat. You can be an unhappy carnivore, and eat pink-in-plastic, or a wise carnivore and eat the animal with care and respect. To eat the whole beast is to accept existence. Embrace your carcass! It's simply common sense."

On a hot, white-and-gold French summer afternoon, Alain Passard is standing in his kitchen garden on the grounds of the Château du Gros Chesnay, in Fillé-sur-Sarthe, about two hundred kilometers southwest of Paris, near the racing town of Le Mans. A few years ago, Passard, the owner and chef of the restaurant L'Arpège, on the Rue de Varenne, in Paris, which since 1996 has had three stars in the Michelin Red Guide, bought the château in order to create a *potager,* an organic vegetable garden. He bought it through a uniquely French practice, in which a younger person buys the property of an older one while the old person is still alive. This gives the older person a cash infusion, and the new buyer gets at least a little use of the property while he or she waits to get it all. The practice can create a situation as intensely delicate as a Roman imperial adoption, since the buyer becomes nearly a son or daughter of the house as he begins to occupy it, or bits of it, while, by ancient French cynical conviction, the sudden onset of money combined with the power of spite extends the life of the older person out to the demoralizing edge of immortality.

Passard, fortunately, had bought the place from Mme Baccarach, an impeccable French grande dame whose family has owned the château for centuries but who, as it happens, lived for thirty years in Grosse Pointe, Michigan, and with whom he has a perfect long-term relationship: she loves to mind the house while he is content to work the grounds. While Madame prepares a table in the dining room, he begins the tour of the *potager,* with one of his gardeners, Mohamadou, a severe Frenchman of African origin.

"It is an organic garden but not merely an organic garden," Mohamadou says. "It's a vegetable garden controlled by the beasts. Do you know a garden only by its sights and smells? No. You know it, too, by its sounds. Listen!" The New Yorkers visiting cock their heads in the gasping heat and hear the sounds of birds flying to nests specially provided for them in the orchard; the distant croaking of frogs in the pond that Passard has had dug in order to have natural predators for crop-eating insects; and, off in the further distance, a lovely, slightly ominous buzz of bees. The garden has a set of wood-frame hives; the bees make honey for the restaurant. "Those are the sounds of a true garden," Mohamadou says. "We're bringing the birds back, and vipers to eat the mice, and frogs to eat the bugs. . . . It's a balance."

Alain Passard is a man in love with vegetables. For most of his career, though an infinitely inventive cook, he was famous for his roasts: particularly roasts of veal and lamb, cooked for six or seven hours *sur la plaque,* on the stove. Then, in 2000, he startled his diners, and his staff, by announcing that he would no longer cook red meat in his restaurant, and that he might phase out animal protein entirely. Today, though he will still throw a few *moules* or langoustines into his dishes, and there is usually fowl available for the incorrigible, the menu he prefers is made entirely of vegetables.

His garden in Sarthe is a showpiece of "permaculture," a system of intensive small-plot rotation that is intended to preserve the energies and resources of the soil. All the planting, for instance, is prepared traditionally, by horse-drawn plow, in order to prevent the soil from being torn up too deeply, as happens with tractors.

Mohamadou looks at Passard. "I saw you on television, *chef,*" he says. "I approved of what you said about the single gesture." On a television program the night before, exploring the new, rococo cooking of the Spanish chefs, Passard had said that a single gesture on a plate was the right direction for the future of cooking, that one properly sliced tomato was a higher accomplishment than a tomato confit, that to get the single gesture right was harder than to make a set of gestures on the plate.

"I believe it," Passard says. "I believe it utterly. One sincere action from the garden is worth six skilled actions in the kitchen.

When I'm in my kitchen, I shut my eyes and think that I'm here."
He points all around. "And, by seeing myself here, I see what
I want to do with the gardens." Passard is a handsome man,
light on his feet, younger-looking than his fifty-odd years, with a
French schoolboy's face: hair *en brosse*, expression intensely earnest and open. "The other day I made a plate of tomatoes—just
these tomatoes, sliced the right thickness, salted, and with a dab
of balsamic. It was perfect." The gardener nods seriously. "Of
course, one gesture on the plate demands a thousand acts here in
the garden," he says, and Passard nods in response.

Passard offers a comprehensive embrace, taking in the garden and the frogs and the birds and the budding vegetables. "I
chose this place for many reasons," he says as he walks through
vine-covered trellises. Off in the distance, golden cattle low. "It
was important to be here in the Sarthe, in part because the soil
is promising, neither too sickly rich nor too poor, and in part
because it gave us excellent access to the TGV"—the high-speed
train. "That means we can pick vegetables at seven in the morning
and have them in the kitchen to start making lunch at ten-thirty,
and on the diner's plate at noon." He shakes a finger beside his
nose, impressed by the efficiency of his own system. "They don't
have to be refrigerated for their journey and they lose nothing,
or nearly nothing. This fall, we're going to start selling what we
don't use for the restaurant at a little counter at the Grande Epi-
cerie at the Bon Marché, so that people who can't eat at the restaurant can still have an experience of true garden vegetables."

Passard continues his tour. "It's an experimental garden, too.
We're trying to revive some of the great heirloom varieties of
tomatoes and potatoes. We're trying to see what might happen.
The beet, for instance, has never been completely appreciated."
He leans down and gently brushes the dirt from a fat, dark beet.
"We're raising larger, richer beets, and they have a potential that
is vast! Enormous!" The new beets have inspired Passard to make
an imposing plat in his kitchen: the beet is cooked in a crust of

gros sel, as duck and lamb have been for centuries, and then the crust is broken with a flourish and the beet is delicately sliced and served, with a light *jus,* as the main course.

For lunch, in the château, Passard prepares a few single-gesture plates from the garden outside: tomatoes, potatoes, and a fine Comté cheese and a bit of country bread from his city restaurant, with a red wine from the Gascogne country, on a table that Madame has set beautifully with old china and etched glass and white linen.

"It was many things," he explains earnestly to Madame B. and his visitors, talking of his conversion experience, five years earlier. "There was the fear of B.S.E. [mad-cow disease]. And for years I had been seeing new dimensions in vegetables when I cooked: green beans with peaches and almonds. Seeing them, but not seeing them all. But, especially, it was because I no longer wanted to be in a daily relationship with the corpse of an animal. I had a moment when I took a roast out into the dining room, and the reality struck me that every day I was struggling to have a creative relationship with a corpse, a dead animal! And I could feel inside me the weight and the sadness of the *cuisine animale.* And since then—gone! All the terrible nervousness and bad temper that are so much part of the burden of being a chef: that was gone with the old cooking. I entered into a new relation to my art, but also to my life. Everyone in the kitchen commented on it. And the lightness of what I was doing began to enter my body and my entire existence, and it entered into the existence of the kitchen. Digestively, yes, of course, but also spiritually, a new lightness of step and spirit that entered my life. It was like a light that I saw, and a door that I walked through. One day, I found myself regarding a carrot in a different light, and I saw the *cuisine végétale* ahead of me through an open door."

"Of course, we have always had many beautiful vegetables here in France, as they do in America," Madame B. says, in the classic style in which mannerly French people search for polite

consensus while still speaking the truth. "But in America vegetables were always horribly overcooked. There would be this, and
then that, with special utensils to fish them out."

"There have been great vegetable dishes in France," Passard
says. "But no great vegetable chefs."

"Very true!" Madame says. "Not before you, monsieur."

Alain and Fergus represent the two extreme poles of the great
meat-eating debate that divides our day: at one end, no meat at
all, no daily relation with a dead carcass; on the other end, the
whole of the whole beast the whole of the time. Taste, we've
said, is an argument compressed to an instruction—so what
exactly must the no-meat-evers be arguing?

The most impassioned and eloquent, if at times chaotic—the
better to press home the urgency—anticarnivore polemic is Jonathan Safran Foer's *Eating Animals*. Foer is not afraid to use big
words when talking about dead birds. We are, he says, "making
war" on seafood. The intensity of the language may make us
doubt as much as assent. After all, we wonder, have cats really
declared war on mice? Have foxes made war on chickens? Preda-
tion is surely different in kind from persecution. This doesn't justify its cruelties, but it does point toward its complexities. Nature,
we may think, isn't "cruel," since cruelty depends on understanding. But then, nature certainly isn't kind. Foer's arguments ultimately depend on the likeness of animal feeling to human feeling,
and how great we think that likeness really is. "KFC is arguably
the company that has increased the sum of suffering in the world
more than any other in history," he writes. The complaint is easily made that this kind of thinking projects human feelings onto
animals, while ignoring the actual sufferings of humans. The suffering of shrimp is a metaphysical question; that of the Sudanese
is not.

What are the *best* arguments to be made for not eating dead animals? The arguments seem to come in three tiers. The first argument is that killing animals for food causes pain, and that we have no right to inflict pain on another living creature just because it can't speak out or fight back. We shouldn't cause pain to weak or mentally slow members of our own species, and to cause pain to nonhuman creatures because they cannot speak or even reason is no better. Yet this argument leaves us with at least the exit of painless slaughter: if we kill kindly, and somehow without warning or notice, so that the animal knows no panic or fear, then can we kill to eat?

This in turn leads to a second, fiercer argument: that the act of animal slaughter is *essentially* cruel: no living thing wants anything but life, on pretty much any terms it can get it, and to execute inarticulate and helpless animals for our pleasure because they can't speak, organize, or struggle is finally as cruel as executing babies would be because *they* can't speak or struggle. That we enjoy eating them is neither here nor there; we might enjoy eating babies or chimps if we tried them, too. The attempt to justify murder by insisting that the soon-to-be-dead don't know that they will die, or that they do die without pain, is no better, the argument goes, and finally no different in moral kind, than the attempts by the SS to anesthetize or justify their own atrocities by insisting that they were being kind to the Jews by telling them that they were going to the showers: such kindness exists only in the minds of the killer. (I'm not proposing, or endorsing, this analogy, only saying that it is one, very often prompting the use of the term "animal Auschwitz" to refer to particular farms or, indeed, the whole meat industry. Google it!)

The third argument is that we shouldn't eat dead animals even if they are painlessly slaughtered and go to their death without fear because raising animals for food on big industrial farms is itself cruel and, by its nature, resistant to change. This argument is more utilitarian than moral. The meat industry, with its vast inefficiencies, its reliance on antibiotics and other drugs, and its hideous distortion of sustainable agricultural practices, is inherently destructive, wasteful, and polluting. Even if animal killing could be justified on moral grounds, meat-eating can't be: it is a luxury that no one who cares about the future of the planet can indulge. Even eating locally raised, grass-fed, "sustainable" animal meat makes at best a marginal difference. To this argument add another, still utilitarian but more selfish, that meat-eating is violently unhealthy for humans in its current everyday form, involving a kind of self-injection with all the dreck we feed to animals. It would be better to eat grass-fed beef, but we would still be eating more fat and protein than nature ever meant us to.

The arguments from suffering seem serious; those from inefficiency and disease much less so, since these are all things that could be remedied, and, if they were, would leave you with the same sad pig. Foer, to his credit, embraces and investigates humane farming methods with considerable respect; he rejects them, though, as an excuse for meat-eating, and finds that his revulsion is not ended by the kinder practice of a Niman Ranch—to him, eating meat is always degrading to people and inherently cruel to animals. He makes a distinction, crucial to his view, between those who care about "animal welfare" and those who care about "animal rights." The animal-welfare movement—insisting on more space in chicken batteries, more room for animals to roam, more humane slaughtering—is merely alleviative. It eases pain without ending killing. Animal rights are more substantial than that: if we accept that animal rights exist, then we can't morally "make war" on tuna or conduct a "daily massacre" of cows, any more than we would make a genocidal war on or conduct a daily massacre of people. That we treated them "humanely" before the killing started wouldn't alter the crime. Murder is murder.

And the arguments *for* eating meat? Perhaps typically, the arguments for doing something that we already all (or nearly all) do, which ought to be weighty and well made, given that they govern our behavior, barely exist. We don't make arguments

for things we do anyway; we only make arguments to stop ourselves from doing them. Proslavery arguments appeared in the
American South not in advance of but only in reaction to abo-
litionism. Women's inferiority was so self-evident even to our
great-great-grandfathers (if not their wives) that they had only a
handful of old saws and religious injunctions to point to to justify it; it took John Stuart Mill and Helen Taylor to end it with a
fiendishly well-formed case. We don't need an argument to eat
cheeseburgers until we stop eating them.

The taste for meat-eating being so intuitive, or seeming so, we
make a new argument for it just by doing it again. And so the
new anger at animal-eating has been countered by a new gusto
in meat-*choosing,* evidenced in the work of Anthony Bourdain
and Mario Batali and Henderson, which has produced a practice
of aggressively celebrating strange or special meats—face bacon
and braised spleen, cuts of Spanish black-footed pigs and French
blue-footed chickens—in order, in effect, both to defend the carnivore and insist that he is more than just a dumb consumer of
those dead carcasses, that there is honor among butchers, too.
There are mere meat-eaters, and savvy carnivores, and canny
ones compliment their meat by eating it properly. (Remember
when Hemingway used to write that way about hunting and fish-
ing? The animal *liked* to be killed by someone as impressive as
Hemingway was.)

Yet we can find, or make, several good, articulate arguments
for meat-eating. Animals raised for slaughter are an intrinsic part
of the cycle of all traditional agriculture—for feed, manure, to
trim the grass. It isn't realistic to think of sustainable agriculture
without the interaction of animal and vegetable, and to keep the
animals only as mowing machines without using them as protein is wasteful and unreal. An ideal sustainable cycle in farming,
though very different from the one we see in practice now, would
still be ineluctably carnivorous.

Second, animals raised to be slaughtered are in a real sense *meant* to be eaten: we can demand kindness and consideration for goats, sheep, and calves, but they exist at all only for the table, and to stop eating them is not to give them or their descendants a better life; it is to give them no hope of life at all. The analogy with slaves dies right there (the argument goes): the emancipated slave goes on to make his own life, however hard; the emancipated animal, with a few feral exceptions, is in every sense a dead end. There would be very few pigs at all if we did not eat pork chops.

Third, eating animals is, however hedged the concept may be, and however many qualifications we wreathe around its middle, *natural* to humans, as it is indeed natural in the rest of creation. Big fish eat little fish; lions eat gazelles; humans eat pigs. I have written such harsh things in this book about the appeal to nature that to insert it here even as a plausible hypothesis seems rank hypocrisy in search of a hamburger. Yet arguments from nature that say we ought to do something—eat one way rather than another—are different from those that warn how hard it is to stop ourselves from doing something that our bodies are designed to do. We can eat the way we choose—but we can't choose not to eat. We can't *not* have sex—at least not as a society—nor not shit. Is meat-eating perhaps one of those necessities, sad or sublime, take your pick, in which it is frivolous to insist on abolition when the best that can be hoped for is improvement?

Yes, of course, "Nature" does many cruel things that we no longer do. But there is a difference between improving on nature by eliminating its cruelties, and defying nature by ignoring its needs. Evangelical vegetarianism, on this view, is closer to the Shaker prohibition on sex than it is to the abolitionist war on slavery: it does not ask us to be better than we have been. It asks us to be other than we are. That our grandparents ate steaks is not in itself, perhaps, an argument for our eating cheeseburgers—our grandparents also took, or were, slaves. But that *all* human beings in *all* contexts since even before there were human beings have eaten some kind of meat in some kind of circumstance provides, if not grounds to foreclose the debate, at least some kind of sanction from the sweep of time. (There are, after all, very good arguments against having sex, too, and lots of people who don't. We still regard the attempt to make that practice universal not just as likely to fail but as completely unrealistic. That there are now no Shakers left to shake is itself an argument against Shakerism.)

One of the better arguments I have come across for ethical meat-eating comes, of all places—or perhaps, given his gifts, not so surprisingly—in Lewis Carroll's *Sylvie and Bruno,* that odd and beautiful amalgam of fantasy, sentiment, and somber Victorian moralism. Carroll's argument derives from the argument over vivisection. Carroll's German professor, clearly speaking for the author, submits that while we have absolute mastery over nature, and therefore the right to eat or experiment on animals, the right brings with it an equally absolute responsibility to refrain from giving them pain: the exquisite ethical dilemma, as with most of them, is to exercise the right while honoring the responsibility, which is always, and in every ethical case, much harder than it looks. (Carroll, good Christian clergyman, took it for granted that that "mastery" was a gift from God; even if we imagine it only to be a long-term accident of history, the case still holds.)

The very strongest argument I have found for animal-eating is based on what always comes back to haunt us in every dilemma in life, and cooking, and that is the nature of mortality. All animals die. The choice for a pig is not between painful death and perpetual life, but between one death and some other. If we ate only animals that died naturally, then could there be any rational objection to our eating them—to eating their flesh in celebration of their life rather than burying it to rot or merely burning it? Could we rationally object if, after *we* died, presumably at the end of as long and rich life as we could have, people ate *us*? (Surely not. Indeed, some of us are "eaten," consumed, in the form of eye and liver transplants and so on, and many regard this as a great good.

So if we could engineer a pig to die naturally at, say, prime eating age—would it be wrong to eat him then? What difference would there be between the first case, the pig scavenged, and that of the pig killed kindly—or perhaps in this thought experiment, by the action of his own genes—after a happy life? (Obviously, we would want him to die painlessly, which nature does not assure at all.) All animals die, and mostly quite young. What's the morally relevant distinction between "road kill" and animals slaughtered humanely? The length of time they have been given to live? Well, by "old age" we surely don't mean a number—it varies too much—but a general condition. When we say that someone has died of old age we mean as painlessly and peacefully as possible after a productive life. Natural death, after all, is a complicated concept: we could easily imagine that pig designed to die at a moment of maximum succulence by the action of its own genes. The two cases seem indistinguishable—and so we realize that our real complaint is not against inevitable death, but against avoidable pain. (Curiously, if you think about it, what this proposes as a kind of moral ideal is not slaughter but *scavenging*. We see the carrion-eaters gathered around the dead zebra with a revulsion so deep, pit-deep, that we use the very names—vultures and jackals—in ways that we rarely use those of other predators. We find it far worse to be a vulture or jackal than a lion or tiger; there are few stuffed vultures in children's cribs. But on this view their carnivorism is *more* moral than the other kind, and the closer we replicate it, the better we are.)

The point isn't that we should breed animals in this way (though perhaps we could) or that we should wait for lambs to die in motorcycle accidents before we eat them. It is that once we accept the principle of animal scavenging, it becomes plain that the real issue isn't eating animals but the way in which animals live and die—it becomes plain that "animal welfare" isn't some secondary, ameliorative concern, but actually the big one. In this case, animal welfare and animal rights collapse into one another:

if we can create a condition in which animals live peacefully and die painlessly and then are eaten it is hard to see how anyone can object, any more than we object to the consumed carcass of the road-killed deer or to our own decomposition. It is then incumbent on us to see that animals die as naturally as possible—I will not put scare quotes on "naturally" here, since we have to accept that, in the case of animals-to-be-eaten, that which is natural is that which already has been intricately wrought, and by us—and as painlessly as possible. But if we do, then the difference between the animal dead of old age and the animal dead of induced old age is so minimal as to be meaningless, and we can eat them with joy and respect. (This position, or one like it, is Fergus's intuitive case.) Joy in the mourning, one might say. This argument *for* animal-eating rests on a recognition of our common mortality, just as the argument against cruelty rests on our common capacity to suffer. The recognition that all animals die leads us to the recognition that it is not wrong to eat them when they do, and so the question turns to how and why and in what way they die. We have thus won ourselves the right to eat meat if we respect the responsibility to be kind.

What would the rational vegetarian say to this? I think she would answer that no one actually dies of old age by being stunned and slaughtered; the old-age analogy is the truly abstract one. And then, at a deeper level, that the very act of making subjects with feelings into objects to eat is degrading for the eater and the eaten alike. Foer, for instance, is particularly repelled—I share his repulsion, merely reading it—when he, bravely and correctly, visits a slaughterhouse and sees a pig's face casually split in two: it seems worse than the death itself, since it shows such contempt for the intelligence of the animal, so evident in its eyes and mouth and brain. It is turning a living thing into a commodity that is the real offense of the abattoir. Raising a living thing as an object to be mutilated is the moral wrong, and engaging in an elaborate pretense of "natural scavenging" can't alter it.

Like most of us, I suppose, I find myself swinging back and forth among these various cases while still eating steak. There are moments when I am fairly sure that "veal chop" will sound to our descendants as brutal and as barbarian a phrase as "public hanging" does to us. That we can live so easily in the presence of calf-slaughter will be as baffling to them as it is to us that Adam Smith and David Hume and Dr. Johnson could live so easily a few hundred yards away from the gallows at Tyburn, where teenage boys were hanged for petty theft.

There are other moments when the space between my appetite for meat and the arguments against it seems to be in itself an argument for eating it: an appetite this strong, this old, and this natural cannot be immoral, or, if it is, then existence itself must be in some sense immoral. Whoever made us, or whatever historical process produced us, meat-eating was part of it. (Then I think again of the vampires in *Twilight* and hear them argue that, after all, they were made to drink human blood.)

In any case, and for the time being, at least we can see this: that the new enthusiasm for "whole-beast" eating, with its various tributaries in Spanish pigs, blood sausage, face bacon, and so on, is, effectively, an attempt to argue for carnivorism by making it the opposite of "pink-in-plastic." It is a new form of Hemingway's argument for hunting: killing is honorable so long as hunting is *hard*. Eating meat is good so long as it is urgent. Fergus Henderson's cuisine, in a kind of weird, conceptual way, involves a form of animal-eating so demanding that it is on the edge of becoming a paradoxical variant of vegetarianism. Fergus believes that if we are to ask of animals (who are raised to be slaughtered, and will die in any case) that they give up their lives for our food, then we must not treat their gift lightly, or with the indifference we give to mere commodities. To eat another animal is a high calling, and we need to honor its sacrifice by eating it all—eyes and tails, brains and spleen, calves' feet and squirrel liver. Only in that way can we recognize the enormity of the act, and turn it into something—half folk sacred; half Damien Hirst occult—that honors our own shared animalness. Embrace your carcass. If you aren't prepared to eat hearts and hooves, then you aren't fit to be a carnivore. One might even argue that the man who eats the whole beast, and the man who eats no beasts, are engaged in the same kind of ethical inquiry. But one would probably not argue this way if one were a pig.

Another question rises to the mind and mouth of a greedy man or woman: can a plate of vegetables really be enough to support a whole high style of fancy food? Like all classically trained French chefs, Passard has the sensitive, quick-turning eyes of one who learned at an early age, and from tough masters, that the world is not always easily at your service. (Passard apprenticed as a chef when he was fourteen, and subsequently worked for Gaston Boyer in Reims and, most important, for Alain Senderens at the old L'Archestrate, whose premises L'Arpège now occupies.) He therefore takes his preeminence as a chef seriously, but almost egolessly: that he has something special to contribute to French cooking is a fact independent of his desires, not so much an accomplishment as a grace. "It is the good fortune of vegetables to have at last found a great chef at the height of his powers to explore them," he says. He isn't being immodest, just truthful.

A typical *cuisine végétale* menu at his restaurant these days might include a tomato gazpacho with mustard ice cream (Passard makes the mustard himself); a gratin of white Cévennes onions with black pepper and baby lettuce; a langoustine bisque with a speck-scented cream; a consommé of cucumber with ravioli stuffed with lemongrass; a light soup of mussels with yellow flowers, ginger, and coriander ("The cuisine of flowers has hardly been touched, even by me," he said later); and a plate of summer root vegetables—carrots and new potatoes and small golden beets—dusted with couscous. For dessert, he offers a chocolate-and-avocado soufflé, the dark chocolate swirled into the rich and slightly eggy avocado, and a simple black-currant sorbet, made from black currants that were just in season in Sarthe.

In his new style, Passard has achieved a level of cooking that surpasses even his earlier excellence, a fact that can be acknowledged even by those who think it prudent to eat an entire *côte de boeuf* the night before having lunch at his place. If some people will never quite get his cooking, his stature in France is indisputable, and with good reason. Cooking is both an expression of the essence of the ingredient and an attempt to turn it into something else; it's both melodic and harmonic. The old French cooking was all harmony, with the chicken breast or the sole treated as the bass note, and everything coming from what went on top. The new cooking, which has spread from America and Australia out into the world, is almost purely melodic: the unadorned perfect thing, singing the song of itself. Passard is among the few to cook both ways at once; one is intensely aware of the thing on the plate, and intensely aware of the mind of the chef that gets it there. The very best of what Passard is doing—say, the cucumber broth with herb ravioli—is as straightforward as a vegetable garden and as complex as the system that makes it run. (And not cheap, either, of course. Lunch costs a couple hundred dollars per person—not surprising, given that the beet on your plate took the TGV to Paris that morning.)

He sharply distinguishes his *cuisine végétale* from vegetarian cooking. He is not a fan of raw vegetables, or of a health-conscious cuisine. "The real malady and unhappiness of vegetables has always been the vegetarian restaurant," he says. He sees cooking vegetables as an aesthetic challenge before anything else. "The white of chicken, or even a filet of fish, cooking these things can be taught. But sautéing white onions, or a pan of turnips—that calls on every bit of the wisdom and knowledge and skill that a chef has accumulated in his training. Everyone in the kitchen has to pay attention in a new way. My team is alert and awake now in a way that it could never be before."

Passard's sense of purpose is undiluted by irony; if the objects of his cooking are beets and roots and tomatoes, the subject of his cooking is France. It is the French cooking tradition, the great tradition that began after the French Revolution, that he embodies. When, at L'Arpège, the single beet comes out of its crust of salt, or the cauliflower emerges from under a silver bell, where once there had been a rack of lamb, there is no conscious parody, but there is certainly an element of play, of a quiet joke—not at the expense of the old grand style but about the wit required to continue it by other means.

Cooking, we are told, ought to be a sensible craft, a peace-making practice, a human act of reconciliation and repetition, like gardening or popular song, rather than a place for experiment and extravagant imagination. Yet there is another kind of cooking, whose point is to press borders, turn corners, suggest extremes—extremes not merely of possible palates we might possess but of possible positions we might yet take. It is in these extremes, Carême's edifice-building or Escoffier's encyclopedism, that cooking touches the edge of something more. Both Henderson and Passard speak in conversation the language of realism: of the sensible, the healthy, the logical, the natural. But one feels in both, finally, an adherence less to a moral logic than to an aesthetic illogic: Passard was once Henderson, Henderson could easily become Passard; their real morality is neither that of evangelical vegans nor beautiful beast-eaters but simply that of the extreme case taken seriously. So perhaps one may be forgiven if one feels, in their single-mindedness, not common sense at all but something of that appetite for perversity which is at the root, and forces the flowers, of art.

7

E-MAIL TO ELIZABETH PENNELL:
Chicken, Pudding, Dogs

Dear Elizabeth:

I have read and reread your chapter on the perfect dinner many
times. And I like it. How hard we have to work to make perfection, and yet when it happens, the truth is that it falls on us like
grace. For instance, I made the best meal of my life tonight,
and it happened more or less by chance and is unlikely ever
to get made again, or not so well. Grace just falls on the head
of us amateur cooks sometimes—like anvils on the head of
silent-movie comedians: for no reason, life's like that—after
absenting itself for months. I think it's true of all committed
ham-handed, clumsy cooks that the best meals we make are
never the meals we serve to guests. We struggle with something
fancy and tricky—chicken with roasted lemons, or a poached leg
of lamb with whisky-mint sauce, or the like—and it all comes
out okay, but we're worn out and the guests are oppressed by
the fanciness of it all. Then, over twenty-five minutes, with the
radio playing Christmas songs, we hit gold. Tonight, I made one
of my set-piece meals: fresh tuna *au poivre,* with basmati rice and
green beans—an ordinary weekday dinner, but a happy night,

Christmas week, best week of the year, time to open a bottle of champagne and enjoy. And . . . everything worked. Every night I struggle with rice—how to do it in that nice pilaf way, where you cook the rice in spices and hot olive oil for a few minutes before you add the water, which boils furiously as you add it, and then simmer it. I've tried all kinds of spices: cinnamon, of course, and cardamom and a Cajun mix and whole cumin and Chinese five-spice mix . . . it's all okay, and I *always* add turmeric, partly from superstition—it's supposed to be the ultimate anti-inflammatory, all-purpose, Alzheimer's-stopping miracle spice—and partly from cosmetic scruples: it does add a lovely yellow tone to the rice.

Tonight, I don't know why, I reached in and decided to toast together turmeric and not spicy but *sweet* curry and black, African cardamom, the musky, dense, mysterious primitive relation to bright, intelligent Indian cardamom. African cardamom is to Indian cardamom, which I love, as a tribal nail fetish is to a lecture by Krishnamurti: one is lethal, the other lilting. It was perfect, the best rice I'd ever done, and I added frozen baby peas at the last minute, which added color and green meaning. The tuna I did four minutes on one side, three on the other, which I find, don't you, is almost always the perfect balance for any protein thing without a bone you have to cook?—and did it with a dense coating of hashed black and pink peppercorns in oil. The sauce was a quick reduction with cooking brandy and then supermarket veal stock—though you could have used plain bouillon from a cube, it would have been just as good, and half a cup of crème fraîche. The beans I just steamed for eight minutes, which brings out their beany taste, with fresh ginger grated over them. It was all good food—the cardamom spoke to the fresh ginger, the crème fraîche negotiated with the black pepper, the yellow and soft-green rice stood nicely against the brown and pink tuna. It was nearly perfect, the children liked it, in the absentminded way children like things—only grown-ups say "Oooh!"; children say "Oh!" and then it's all gone.

For dessert we had butterscotch pudding, which Olivia and I had made earlier in the day in honor of her new Havanese puppy, whose name is Butterscotch. Nothing could be simpler, and nothing could be more quietly demanding: just as the key with a good penne *all'amatriciana* is the fusion of pancetta and onion, so the key to a really good butterscotch pudding is burning the one and a half cups of sugar to caramel without scorching it, so that it has a deep, residual flavor, without an unpleasant burned taste. But once that is done, the only other trick is adding the milk and melted butter soon but not too soon: you want it to bubble with the super-hot sugar, but not explode out of the pan, as has happened to Olivia and me before. Then it's just egg yolks mixed with cornstarch and whipped with a whisk until it boils and thickens. The cornstarch is key—a humble, forgotten thing that creates pudding as efficiently, though with far less diva-like self-dramatization, as egg whites create soufflés. Then you chill the pudding, and serve it with freshly whipped cream. Nobody doesn't like it; it is the ideal recipe to represent a small, sweet, happy dog; you can't help but like it, you can't resist it, it makes no demands on your mind, only on your heart.

Having a dog in the kitchen, by the way, is the best way to understand what it really is to be a person in the kitchen, don't you think? The key to *dogginess* is that dogs are pure creatures of sensation. By that I mean that they absorb life as vast, intriguing, and vaguely replicable clouds of stuff, endlessly interesting—smells and places and actions and times and above all foods—without breaking it down into neat causal sequences of act and effect. Every dog delights in food, but no dog could cook dinner, which depends on remembering which comes first, the caramel or the cornstarch. When Butterscotch sees me come home with bags from the grocery store, she leaps with joy as her memory tells her that something good will happen, that there is some vague connection between this thing and the tastes she loves and needs. But what the sequence is, where it starts and where it ends, obviously baffles her, just as she knows that some cloud-nexus of taking elevators and putting on leashes and making phone calls produces a chance to play with Lily, the Havanese upstairs. But exactly how this works eludes her: some days when she hears the name Lily she rushes to the door, sometimes to her leash, sometimes goes to the elevator and sometimes to the door on our floor that corresponds to the door on the eighth floor where Lily lives. It is a joy, obviously, to live life in this way: her head is, in every sense, in the clouds. The life of pure appetite and affections, where Butterscotch resides, is obviously a happy one, free not just of intimations of mortality but of any intimations at all: it is all just stuff rolling at you, some predictably nice, some usually nasty, all rolled up in a big ball that you can eat or push or chew to pieces, as the occasion demands.

Our life, in contrast, is not really that life of the appetites but the life of desire, a different thing, as Brillat-Savarin understood. Concepts come between our hungers and our pleasures. Our desires make us scrutinize the sequences of life to find out their small conceptual secrets: what comes first, the butter or the scotch, the caramel or the cause? The cause, it is the cause, my soul . . . our life is spent breaking and making codes, cooking being one of them. For animals, there are no codes, because there are no causes—codes are possible only because we know about intentions and disguises, smiles and masks—there is only sensation and the scary, the delicious and the disgusting, which comes at you as it will. The "second mirror" of self-consciousness, the mirror we have that faces the mirror in our mind and lets us see ourselves as we think, is not in the mind of the dog. They see, they sense, they live. We cook in order to reenter the world of pure sensation, but we only do it by stringing concepts and causes together in the form of steps and spices: first this, then that, and then more. The state in which Butterscotch lives naturally, where tastes just fall out of the sky, in a happy, humming paradise of sensation—we have to sneak up on that state from behind, with the help of a glass of cold champagne and a handful of cardamom. Butterscotch is joyful but never surprised by joy, as we are, we creatures of codes and plans, who are shocked when everything comes together, because we know how hard it is to get the sequence right, and how lucky we are when we do.

We follow codes and plans, and, sometimes, invent them. You recall, back when I first wrote to you, that I mentioned that I had invented one new thing in cooking? Well, I have, truly, though it is a bit of a Blotting Paper Pudding. I think every home cook has one Blotting Paper Pudding, don't you? By Blotting Paper Pudding I refer, of course, to the White Knight's recipe in Alice, which, you will recall, was the cleverest thing he had ever invented, and which he thought up during the meat course in time for the dessert course. The pudding was never actually *made,* as he explains—and yet it was a very clever pudding to invent. "It began with blotting paper," the Knight tells Alice, and then gunpowder and sealing wax were part of the recipe, too, all mixed in. All of us amateur cooks invent things in our heads as we go about following the rules we find, and we are sure that they are clever, but it is probably just as well that they never get made.

My first Blotting Paper Pudding was an actual pudding, or a sort of pudding, anyway. One week, when we were children, my older sister and I, having been somehow delegated the week's worth of desserts, made Jell-O one night (the box, hot water, mix and refrigerate), then Jell-O pudding the next (the box, warm milk, stir and refrigerate), then Jell-O again the night after (I see green—could it be lime?), and then pudding again, and then on the last decided to combine our genius and make a mixed Jell-O and Jell-O pudding, with results you can imagine.

Since then, my best Blotting Paper Pudding has been an idea

I've had for a new kind of béarnaise sauce, one that would be made just like a normal béarnaise sauce—tarragon, shallots, white wine, and vinegar reduced to nothing, then emulsified with egg yolks and butter—only with the wonderful Thai mix of herbs in place of tarragon: cilantro, mint, and basil. I think of this sauce all the time, because I love that trio, and because it has such a beautiful inner logic to it. It should be excellent with salmon, for instance, or with chicken, and perhaps with lamb, too. (Mint béarnaise already exists, though I've never tried it.) It has logic, fusion, and a certain originality to it, and I will confess that there were moments in the past when I *talked* about it with other people as though I'd actually made it when what I really meant was that I had *invented* it, and intended to make it soon. Sometimes purely intellectual acts can feel so present that we confuse them with sensual ones, though this leads us down long ramps of the Internet where we should not go.

And then, just the other night, I made it at last, and it was fine, very good, call it Bangkok béarnaise—catchy name, too. I have never been to Bangkok, I probably will never go to Bangkok, and though I may get to the Béarn someday, I haven't actually been there, either. But now I had invented and made a sauce that combined the herbs of one with the style of the other, and put it on grilled salmon. If I ever open a restaurant, in another life, it will be a specialty of the house, and meanwhile I will casually yawn and mention it if I have the chance. Bangkok béarnaise, my one true thing. The White Knight would be proud.

Yet, as I suspect the Knight intuited, it was, on the whole, more fun to have invented, and imagined, than it was to eat. Not that it wasn't good—but thinking about food, though never as satisfying as eating it, is often just as interesting. Just as we have to read *past* certain classic texts, we *eat* past certain new recipes,

registering the excellence of the idea as much as the deliciousness of the dish. Parsnip steaks and eggplant desserts, turkey
tartar and duck confit sorbet—these things are excellent, but
they are excellent as my Bangkok béarnaise is excellent. They
are Blotting Paper Puddings.

This is a term, I think, that can be extended far beyond the
confines of the kitchen: there are Blotting Paper Puddings in
many walks of life. Most of these new Brooklyn-incubated
speculative novels, six hundred pages long, strike me as Blotting
Paper Puddings: I don't believe most of them will ever be read,
but who can deny that they were very clever puddings to invent?
All political platforms are Blotting Paper Puddings: they will
never be cooked, but they, too, were very nice to contemplate.

For the first time, though, I find myself eating Blotting Paper
Puddings in place of real puddings. When you go out to eat
dessert, you find yourself not with a cake or pie or real pudding,
but with some strange collision of unlike parts—mousses and
gels and foams and vertical biscuits. But then, nothing is the
subject of as much mockery as innovative cooking. I suppose
in a sense all avant-garde activity is a set subject for satire—the
all-black painting, the silent concerto—but they tend to take on
aggressively a little bit of the aura of avant-garde purpose; you
have to be a bit of a dope to make fun of John Cage. Yet the
intuition that originality in food will run in narrower paths than
originality in any other art is not false—and is, in truth, one of
the things that make cooking other, though not lesser, as an art.
We dream of making Bangkok béarnaise, and end up making
Blotting Paper Pudding. Then we find out that Bangkok béarnaise *is* Blotting Paper Pudding, and we turn back to the
Jell-O box.

While we are on the subject of simple classics, I suppose I
should say something about roast chicken. Was there a cult of

roast chicken in your day? I don't see it in your pages. Perhaps it was still a luxury dish, not easily set apart from all the other ones. But in ours a whole cult of roast chicken has grown up, a literature in which roasting a chicken right becomes identical with acting virtuously. Well—as Humpty Dumpty says, when it comes to reciting poetry, I can do it as well as other folks. "It needn't come to that," Alice says, hurrying to stop him from starting, but she can't. When it comes to roasting chicken, I can do it as well as other folks—and I shall not be stopped, either, any more than Humpty could.

I do roast chicken three basic ways, and I do them often because both children treat roast chicken as the default birthday and holiday meal—or, perhaps, being pestered to say what they want, think of roast chicken in lieu of anything better. Though I'm a crazed briner, salt water and juniper and sugar dripping from my roast pork and Christmas turkey like the weird encrusted stuff in *Pirates of the Caribbean,* I find that for a normal chicken, brining merely "koshers" it without actually enriching it. So I don't bother.

My basic roast chicken is like everyone else's, though simpler: the lemon-up-the-bum chicken beloved of British cooks. (Martha *hates* it when I say lemon-up-the-bum chicken, though, as she hates when people say a pregnant woman has a "bump.") The one trick is to use a *very* hot oven: 400° is good, but 425°, if you watch the skin and cover it with parchment or foil to keep it from burning toward the end, is still better. The one biggest difference between pro kitchens and home kitchens, truly, is the heat they can muster in their ovens and ranges. If there is a single kitchen secret that I have learned from hanging out with real cooks, it is that the real cooks either go very hot or surprisingly cold: they roast at 400°, 450°, or even higher, and they braise at 275°, 250°, or even lower. They can do this because they have time—time to braise, space to take the bird out and let it rest after it roasts. "Three seventy-five is death," Dan Barber told

me once, meaning that in that homey zone where almost every
roasting or baking recipe takes place, birds dry out and become
dull. So I roast in a very hot oven. Simple chicken is best with
a *small*, blue-foot-type bird; I learned to do it with the *poulet de
Bresse* of France, but since you can't get them here—someone in
Quebec was breeding them, and shipping them to Fairway, but
then they were stopped, perhaps by a sudden explosive descent
of French paratroopers protecting the name—I use the little
D'Artagnan birds, which are excellent. The nice thing about
this chicken is what you can do all around it: put it in a cast-iron
pan to roast with a little film of olive oil on the base, and you
can put in cubed potatoes, whole shallots, cloves of garlic (late
in the process so they don't burn), and everything comes out
lovely. You can't really do a sauce from the drippings, if you fill
the pan with extras, but my kids love a simple mustard–crème
fraîche–white wine sauce with chicken anyway. (You just don't
mention the white wine.) Make carrots with cumin and orange
juice on the side, which is easy but tastes hard, and a broccoli–
crème fraîche purée; the colors, bright orange, pale green,
brown-chicken-skin caramel, are lovely together. Feed to teddy
bear. Of course, cooking for children is not simply a matter of
pressing the right button and getting the right response; children
like what they like and they can't be persuaded to like what they
don't like. We drag our educated palates behind us like Marley's
ghost drags his chains. What children like is various. But it's
what they like.

The second method I use—and this would work well on a
rotisserie; in fact is made for one—is the method they use in
Paris. This involves no lemon—stuffing for a chicken is like
hoop earrings with a black dress, I always think, too much,
though Martha sighs at both thoughts with desire—again very
high heat, but lots of duck or goose fat and salt slathered on the
chicken before you roast it. You can use butter, but the duck or
goose fat (which you can buy packaged these days from various

places) gives it a luxurious wow! quality that is much prized. The trick, though, is to keep the secret ingredient secret from the diners, lest you run into this kind of conversation:

CHILD DINER-TO-BE: What are you making for dinner, Dad?
DAD-COOK: Roast chicken! Your favorite!
CDTB: Oh, good. (Long pause) What's that white stuff you're putting on the chicken, Dad?
DC: Oh, it's duck fat, baby. It makes it delicious.
CDTB: (Deeply suspicious) What do you mean, duck fat? How do they get fat from the duck? It's, like, wool from a sheep?
DC: (Honesty is the best policy—or maybe sadism is the best entertainment) Not exactly. When they slaughter the duck and filet its breast and so on, they squeeze all the fat out of it and refrigerate it so it can congeal.
CDTB: (Long pained pause) You're really going to eat that?
DC: We all are.
CDTB: Not me. Can I have my slice without the duck fat? Luke! Daddy's putting dead duck fat on the chicken!

And so on.

I might add that CDTB is sometimes MDTB—Mom Diner-to-Be. So keep the kitchen door shut, roast for an hour, and they will love it. If you do this in a pan, and pour off just enough of the fat in the pan to keep it from being too greasy, the browned bits and the duck-fat renderings just dissolved in a bit of pure water, nothing more, make a wonderful simple sauce. This is great with potatoes also sautéed in duck fat and then roasted in the oven. (A light meal? Well, no, not exactly. But a good one, and who goes to roast chicken on a diet anyway?) It's particularly delicious with a Rhône Valley red, for some reason—I suppose pepper and fat make a nice team-up. I always think of this as bistro chicken; the first kind somehow for me is farm chicken.

My third method is to make a paste out of mustard, olive oil, tarragon, and—secret ingredient—just a touch of soy sauce. I slip my fingers beneath the skin of the bird, beginning at the base and moving toward the breast, slowly working it loose from the raw meat, gradually slipping back down toward the thighs to open the skin there as well. Then I dip my fingers in the paste and slowly rub it in the space between the raw flesh and the loosened skin. This needs to roast in a slightly "slower" oven—400°, not 425°—so the paste doesn't burn. It makes for a wonderful chicken, especially if you keep some of the paste aside to use as a condiment. Serve with a purée of potatoes, very simple with cream and butter, so that the mustard-soy-tarragon flavors dominate. Great with a good Pinot Noir, the velvet of the wine melting into the silk of the mustard paste.

And then, let us not forget *poulet crapaudine*—the chicken split down its back and done facedown in one iron skillet while being pressed down from above by another iron skillet with a brick or something else heavy in it. "Chicken under a brick," as the Italians call it. It's nice to bread-crumb the breast first. Also very good with a shallot–white wine–mustard sauce, and curiously nice with a rosé wine. The children love this, as they love chicken pot pie, and I have a theory that it is the names, as much as anything, that move them—a "pot pie," "cooked under a brick," a vocabulary of hide-and-seek, and things buried beneath things, that appeals to them. Tastes that hide under bricks, in pots and pies, in crusts and gratiné; things that are scalloped and mashed and made cheesy. Delicious words all start with *s*, just as funny words all end in *k*. Scalloped potatoes, steak with sauce, salmon, syllabub, sassafras, saffron, salsa, and salads; though the *ch* and *k* sounds have their little charm (chocolate, chicken), it is the *s*'s that carry the day. Seared sole; sautéed sole; filets with oysters.

The sounds of words, the roar of language, comes between

us and the sensations that dogs enjoy. Butterscotch does not care, or know, what her chicken is called. But the concepts have their own pleasures. The hint of the plural, present in all *s* words, suggests plenty, and the hiss of the *s* suggests insinuation and promise. "Sweetbreads," as a word for glands, proves this— as does its French equivalent, *ris de veau*. And the soluble *s* sound raises brains in France from oddity to delicacy—*cervelles*. "Ice cream" is another instance where it is buried as a soft *c* but sings the same way. The whispering sounds of secrecy and succulence combined. Henry James said that the most beautiful words of the nineteenth century were "summer afternoon"; the loveliest words of the kitchen are surely "ice-cream sundae." They breathe between their teeth but do so sibilantly, like smiling sinners, not like serpents.

All best,
Adam

8

Near or Far?

TWELVE-THIRTY on a beautiful summer day, and the chicken committee of the City Chicken Project is meeting at the Garden of Happiness, in the Crotona neighborhood of the Bronx. The chicken committee is devoted to the proliferation of egg-laying chickens in the outer boroughs, giving hens to people and having them raise the birds in community gardens and eat and even sell the eggs ("passing on the gift," as this is called in the project), and thereby gain experience of chickens, eggs, and community—or fowl, food, and fellowship, as one of the more alliterative-minded organizers has said. It is the pet program of Just Food, a small organization that is administered by a startlingly young-looking woman named Jacquie Berger, who is silently monitoring the proceedings.

The Garden of Happiness is a sunny community garden with vegetable plots, a chicken coop, a corrugated-tin shed, and a few chairs beneath a grape arbor, where the chicken committee is meeting. The chicken committee is a lot more committee than chicken, its deliberations filled with references to "existing chicken situations" and "pursuit of newer egg opportunities," and the slightly skeptical neighborhood people have to be gently won over by the carefully beaming professionals. They provide the nudging, let's-get-back-on-track counsel that community chicken organizers have to give potentially disorganized community chicken-carers.

"It's, like, a long questionnaire, you know?" one of the neighborhood people says, about a form to be handed out to potential chicken-carers.

"Well, don't you think that someone who isn't prepared to fill out a few questions isn't—don't you have to question their commitment to caring for a chicken over the winter?"

"Yeah, I guess so. But it's a long thing. All these questions."

The Garden of Happiness has the semimagical ability, common to any place in the city with trees and plants and animals, to secede from its environment and become what most of the world is, a bit out in the country somewhere. A hen in the coop starts clucking. A scruffy pit bull in a neighboring yard begins to growl and then bark. Undiscouraged, the hen goes on clucking, and a second hen joins her. Together they drown out the dog. The sun shines down through the arbor on the chicken committee, and the animal sounds drown out its complicated pleadings.

I had come to the Garden of Happiness not only to see a New York City chicken committee in operation but also to get myself a chicken to roast. This was why, a few moments later, I was trying to arrange, privately, for a hit on a fowl. Getting a chicken that has been raised and slaughtered in New York City is harder than it might seem, with laws and bylaws entangling the transaction: I wanted to eat a chicken that had been raised in the city, and insiders who cannot be named said that, though the City Chickens are raised strictly for their eggs, in private a poultry whacking could be arranged, for a price. I had been set up with a chicken keeper I'll call Freddie.

"Looks like you've got, you know, chickens," I said, sidling up to him in what I imagined to be the best Washington Square marijuana-buying manner, as we stared at his coop.

"Yeah." Long pause.

Euphemism, I saw, would get you only so far in the poultry-whacking game. "I was wondering if maybe, on Friday or Saturday, you could get me a chicken," I said. "You know. The kind that people can eat." I tried to give the words a *Sopranos*-like significance.

"Yeah, I understand," Freddie said, not making eye contact. Another long silence.

"So." I took a deep breath. "So, uh, you think there'll be a chicken?"

After another pause, he said, with exactly the kind of ominous serenity you want in a hit man, "Why not? Come on Saturday. You be there. There'll be a chicken."

I felt unreasonably pleased with myself; the chicken was going to be hit, and I would pay for the action.

I was arranging to kill a Bronx chicken as part of a project that I had begun a month or so before—to spend a week eating only food grown or raised within the five boroughs of New York City. "Localism" is a movement that has rules, Web pages, and books devoted to it. Its central idea is that one should try to eat only things grown within a narrow "foodshed" around one's own home, and in the past decade localism has been the subject of a couple of folksy, how-we-did-it books, records of how their authors nailed down their diet to the local goods: *Plenty*, by Alisa Smith and J. B. Mackinnon, which recounts the authors' yearlong experience of eating only from a foodshed around their Vancouver home, and *Animal, Vegetable, Miracle*, by Barbara Kingsolver, which tells of a similar dogmatic diet, undertaken for a year around Kingsolver's house in southwest Virginia.

The point of localism is to encourage sustainable agriculture by eating things that nearby friends and farmers grow or raise and that don't have to be shipped halfway around the world, guzzling fossil fuel, to get to your table. The rules generally involve eating within a radius of a hundred or sometimes three hundred miles, and are undertaken in places, like Berkeley and the Pacific Northwest, that have a lot of nice produce and plump animals within their circles.

You go local in Berkeley, you're gonna eat. I had been curious to see what might happen if you tried to squeeze food out of what looked mostly like bricks and steel girders and shoes in trees. I wanted to do it partly to see if it could be done (like an episode of what would be called on ESPN "X-treme Localism"), partly as a way of exploring the economics and aesthetics of localism more generally, and partly to see if perhaps the implicit antiurban prejudices lurking in the localist movement could be leached away by some city-bred purposefulness. If you can eat that way here, you can do it anywhere.

I enlisted Gabrielle Langholtz, then of the Greenmarket, a young woman of awe-inspiring purposefulness, and she at once came up with a list of possibilities: vegetables from farms in Staten Island and Brooklyn, honey from rooftops, and eggs seemed plausible, too. It was the other proteins, she noted, that would be the problem, and this had led me to the chicken committee.

We began with honey. David Graves is a keeper of rooftop beehives in New York City, tending fifteen hives and colonies around town. His rooftop honey is one of the ornaments of the Greenmarkets, and so he is a walking human-interest story, who trails his news clips behind him as bees do their sun dance. We were looking at a rooftop vegetable garden, on the eastern fringe of SoHo, that belonged to the film producer Chris Goode and his wife, Lisa. The garden, which stretches across the entire rooftop, just under the watchful gaze of the clock on the old Police Building (which stopped a couple of months earlier, one of its faces at 3:40, the other at 4:35), grows tomatoes and basil and zucchini and squash and green beans and watermelon—enough for a SoHo sect of survivalists. It also hosts one of Dave's beehives.

"It could be a little strange if the bees swarmed," Dave admitted. I had asked if his bees ever alarmed anyone. "I mean, that could be a little unnerving to people on a city street. It's not dangerous at all, but it would look like hell—a bunch of bees swarming around a stoplight."

Bees, Dave explained, fly two to three miles each day in search of nectar and then return to the hive. In New York, they favor the nectar of ginkgo, sumac, linden, a tree called Chinese Scholar, and Japanese knotweed. New York honeybees live for around forty-five days, and their queen for two or three years. "New York honeybees have the same life span as other honeybees, but they work longer hours," he said. "You can get between sixty and a hundred and forty pounds of honey per season from one rooftop hive. My record is a hundred and forty, from a hive on the Upper West Side."

The beehive sits at the center of the roof. Dave opened it, cautiously, and we looked in together. It was like looking down into a New York office building from above: several thousand bad-tempered coworkers racing around and muttering. Dave tasted the honey. "That's linden," he said. It was New York honey: strong, spicy, and extremely sweet. He looked slightly abashed. "I didn't use to like the taste of it. And it's definitely not the Berkshires."

There was a time, not so long ago, when New York City was far more self-sufficient in food. As Marc Linder and Lawrence S. Zacharias document in their fascinating book *Of Cabbages and Kings County,* Brooklyn not only was the breadbasket of the city, well into the late nineteenth century, but also made a quick, successful agricultural right turn, replacing grain with intensive vegetable and fruit cultivation. It was only with the coming of the truck farms in New Jersey and other points west, in the early twentieth century, that New York became largely dependent on imports; in recent years, thirty percent of our fruits and vegetables have come all the way from California.

New York's abundance lingers on as rumor and memory, but the city's ground is intrinsically fertile, and I decided next to get a sense of the natural wealth of New York by eating things that are growing here by accident. "Why don't you try foraging Central Park with 'Wildman' Steve Brill?" Gabrielle suggested. Steve, she explained, could point to everything savage that there was to eat in the city. I was taken with the idea of using the Park as a kitchen garden, like those country friends who scamper into the yard for fresh-cut basil.

A Sunday or two later, I found myself, with my children, following Steve on one of his encyclopedic tours of New York's edible nature. The children had been ornery when I announced my local eating plan.

"I'll eat New York food," Olivia, who was then seven, said. "But pigeons I will not eat. Squirrels I will not eat."

"Squirrels make a very delicious dish, called Brunswick stew," I offered. "And pigeons are squab. You see them on the best menus."

"Anything city-colored, that looks like it could actually live in New York, is being thrown out," said Luke, who was twelve. "Gray things. Brown things. We don't eat anything that blends in with the sidewalk. It needs to stand out from its surroundings." The strictures seemed daunting but the possibilities fresh.

"Now, this is wood sorrel," Brill was saying, bending over a little patch of weeds at the edge of the path that led toward the Park entrance at West 107th Street. "These are completely delicious! They taste just like lemonade!"

Everyone knelt down to taste them. A few meditative moments, ready to spit it out. Then: "Hey, this is good! It does taste like lemonade."

Wildman Steve Brill looked pleased, but unsurprised. He has had the fortitude to eat out of the Park for decades. Mushrooms and black cherries, field garlic and sassafras—he can construct entire meals around things he finds growing ferally near West Seventy-second Street. He is known for his Smokey Bear hat, his baggy pants, his borscht belt jokes.

"This is lamb's-quarter," Steve was saying, clearing a path to what, to the unknowing eye, looked just like the desultory weeds where the softball ends up after the fat kid with glasses you've stowed in right field watches it go by. Lamb's-quarter turned out to be a matte-green plant with arrow-shaped leaves.

"But now you have to be careful," he went on. "You see this?" He picked through the underbrush and found, alongside the lamb's-quarter, another, equally agreeable-looking weed. He held it up. "This is white snakeroot," he explained. "White snakeroot is completely poisonous. In the early days of the country, cows would eat it and it would get into their milk, creating what's called milk sickness. A fatal disease. Who knows how this changed American history?" No hands went up. "Abraham Lincoln, that's how. Abraham Lincoln's mother died of milk sickness caused by this very root. So you have to be careful to distinguish between lamb's-quarter, which is good, and white snakeroot, which, if you eat it . . ." He paused and then played Chopin's Funeral March on an improvised kazoo made of his lips and his right hand.

The children looked dubiously at the plastic bags they carried, stuffed with wood sorrel and lamb's-quarter. New York kids, they had learned the logic of safe and shaky blocks, but the logic of poisonous plants alongside wholesome ones was outside their experience.

Wildman Steve Brill went on to show us an almost unbelievable variety of edibles in Central Park: purslane leaves, the Asiatic dayflower ("tastes like string beans"), poor man's pepper ("tastes like radish"), sassafras ("tastes like root beer—you can actually make root beer out of it!"), field garlic, even a kind of "artist's mushroom," which you can't eat but makes a wonderful sketchbook if scratched on.

"We should ask him what pigeon tastes like," Olivia said darkly. "He looks like a pigeon-eater."

"He'd probably say it tastes like chicken," Luke told her. "That's what they always say."

Finally, it was time for a lunch break, and Steve and his dutiful followers settled down on the rocks and the lawn near the 107th Street entrance to eat what they had gathered plus a few slices of healthy-looking whole-grain bread. Luke stood up. He pointed with the urgency of a shipwrecked sailor spotting a sail. Just visible at the edge of the Park was a sign reading "West Side Deli." The Deli in the Distance! While our wholesome fellow-scavengers were looking elsewhere, we sneaked out of the Park and returned to hide in a small copse, so that the kids could gorge on a turkey hero with mayonnaise and potato chips and Snapple drinks. Then they returned to the group, a smear of orange around the mouth the only sign of their impiety.

Localism is a movement made of pieties. The cult of seasonality was a taste that evolved into a politics; localism is essentially a politics attempting to create a taste. It is built on the conviction that the industrial economics of food growing and delivery are bad for us and bad for the planet, but it also has an implicit moralistic attitude that prefers small country patches over big urban deserts.

It is possible to have localism without nostalgia, though, and Gabrielle urged me to look into the tilapia-farming program at Brooklyn College. I took the subway out and met with Martin Schreibman, a biologist who has helped pioneer an ambitious project to create an enclosed system of fish farming, which could serve as a model for urban aquaculture in the future. If the ethic of the pure localist is in part reactionary, Schreibman's is scientific-minded, with Lex Luthor–like overtones: he dreams of giant translucent fish tanks surrounding our cities, where we would breed our own dinner in a ring of virtuous water.

"The demand for sustainable protein is *the* demand of this century," Schreibman told me. "Somehow we're going to have to produce enough protein to feed our population, and we'll have to do it in urban locales, because the costs of transportation are going to become prohibitive." He has spent most of his life at Brooklyn College, beginning as a student, in the fifties. He had been interested in problems of endocrinology and had started using fish as genetic models ("Rats are just terrible to work with," he said, a New Yorker's reaction), and then he had become as interested in the problems presented by raising fish as in doing the experiments the fish were being raised for.

"Tilapia is one of the easiest fish to raise," he explained. "It's an ancient, ancient fish—it's the fish eaten at the Last Supper. It's a warm-water fish, and it's not carnivorous, so you don't get the problems of input that you do with, say, salmon." As critics of the aquaculture industry never tire of pointing out, far more fish-mass has to go into feeding a farmed salmon than you get from the salmon itself. "The green revolution presented problems," he said. "Hey, we're still dealing with the *mishegas* presented by the Industrial Revolution! That doesn't mean we should reverse the Industrial Revolution, since it was a solution to the problems of poverty that preceded it. Does the blue revolution"—addressing global water issues—"present problems? You bet it does! Does that mean we should give up on it? Of course not." Schreibman has a vision, oft-repeated in his writings, of reviving the dying cities of New York State by making them centers of aquaculture, so that Rochester tilapia would be a government-certified item, like Bresse chickens, but he has had a frustrating time getting the state government to adopt it.

"Meanwhile, we're getting flooded with Chinese aquaculture, and we have no idea what the fish are fed or what conditions they're raised in," he said. "This"—he made a gesture taking in the farmed fish—"is going to happen, and it's going to happen quickly. The question is if it's going to happen here, and happen in a way that we can oversee and control."

Schreibman showed me around the Brooklyn College fish farm, which feels, well, very basement: high windows and humid air and the whiz-kid sense of somebody's science-fair project percolating downstairs, below the kitchen. There is a Rube Goldbergian series of barrels and pipes, which bring the water into the fish tanks and cycle it back out again into shallow basins, where it gets used to grow plants, which can, in turn, be used to feed the fish—or us. There are even some related projects, where "ornamental" fish, seahorses and clownfish, are being raised. The tilapia swim in dense, dim schools within their barrels—oddly ominous shapes in the green water, the future in fish. Schreibman gave me a few filets for the urban table.

As we got ready for our week, we had Greenmarket herbs growing on our windowsill; knew we could forage in the Park, and so had a source for homemade root beer; were pulling plenty of local honey; owned some tilapia. But we wanted produce from a real farm, too. So, on the Fourth of July, Gabrielle and I and the children went out to the two working farms that we had found within the city limits: Decker Farm, in Staten Island, and the Red Hook Community Farm, in Red Hook, Brooklyn.

Decker, fifteen minutes across the Verrazano-Narrows Bridge from midtown, is a small place, smelling of damp earth, that is farmed by a handful of Mexican émigrés who work in a pizza parlor nearby. The Mexicans discovered, upon arriving in Staten Island, that they missed farming—missed Mexican things like jalapeños and tomatillos and fresh cilantro. They work their plots on days off, nights, and weekends, and they loaded us down with poblanos and hot and sweet peppers. (The only farm-grown food used at the pizza place is basil.)

The Red Hook Community Farm, just around the corner from a new Fairway Market, is more socially ambitious. It is a three-acre urban farm reclaimed from an old asphalt playground, with soil piled high. It looks like a Bruce McCall drawing of a pastoralized New York, the asphalt playground with a farm just dropped on top, and a twenty-foot-tall chain-link fence running around it. Begun as a kind of reclamation project for young people, it has become a farm that supplies many of the local epicurean joints with arugula and collard greens. "Twenty teenagers work here each week for a ten-week session," Ian Marvy, the farm's director, said. "We sell to the community, and we also sell, at a good profit, to the restaurants that have come to Red Hook in the past few years. Farming in Brooklyn reconnects kids to the earth. We bring schoolkids here from all over the city for a day's program. Most of them have no idea that vegetables come out of the ground."

Ian went on, "We try to run the farm organically. Our compost is composed almost entirely of manure from the Bronx Zoo. We use the manure of herbivores, like zebras and elephants."

I looked at him for a moment, wondering if this was an urban-farm poker-faced joke, but he assured me that it wasn't. I asked if we could taste the elephant manure residually in the food.

"Yes, you can," he said. "I mean, we have a dark chlorophyll flavor in all of our vegetables, and I really think that you can taste the concentration of nitrogen. It's a New York taste." I looked at the turnips with new respect. Along with turnips, we collected super-spicy arugula, squash, and green beans, and drove back home.

With the Red Hook and Decker Farm vegetables on hand, I decided to make Saturday dinner the centerpiece of our local-eating moment, featuring one blowout meal of good things from around the boroughs. But I was more determined than ever to collect that chicken, and, with my friend Peter Hoffman, the owner of Savoy and Back Forty, and a devotee of localism and seasonalism both, drove up to the Bronx to get it. We pulled up at the meeting spot I had chosen with Freddie, near the coop, and there he was.

"So, you got the chicken?" I said, looking up at the sky in my sunglasses.

"Yeah, I got the chicken. This one." He pointed down at one of his handsome whites. The chickens pecked and clucked.

"Oh," I said. "Well, I was hoping you would, you know, make it ready for us to eat."

For the first time, Freddie turned toward me. "You want me to kill it?" he said. "I don't—I can't kill my chickens! I raise 'em. I love 'em. I thought you wanted it—you said you wanted a chicken." We looked at each other head-on. "It's, like, all bloody and all, I don't like to do that," he said, with apology and annoyance mixed. Then a little anger crept in. "I thought you wanted a chicken. To raise! Not to kill!"

I withdrew with what dignity I could, and left, expelled from the Garden of Happiness. Peter and I drove over to Arthur Avenue, where venders make their own ricotta, and sausage hangs from the ceiling, and started to head home.

Just then, bombing down Third Avenue in the Bronx, we caught sight of the biggest, gaudiest, most *alluring* slaughterhouse either of us had ever seen. Musa's, it was called, with a broad, wooden front painted rather in the manner of Haitian folk art. Lambs and goats gazed through wooden slats onto the sidewalk, where local children fed and petted them. A giant hand-painted "Lookee! Lookee!" sign pointed to the young animals, and a frieze of paintings above suggested all the kinds of animal you could have killed for your dinner.

We went inside. It wasn't just a slaughterhouse but more like a pagan temple: the small animals awaiting sacrifice, calves and kids and lambs. We picked out a chicken from a coop crowded with whites and browns and reds. It was white-feathered, and protested briefly with a squawk as it was selected, weighed, and disappeared into the back room. The smells of a slaughterhouse—not horrible, really, just deep, a farm smell in the city—filled the air. A few minutes later, a bag came out, with the chicken, still warm, cut up inside. It wasn't, of course, precisely the city chicken that

I had hoped for. It was an upstate chicken, most likely, that had come to town just for the hell of it, but its life cycle—born elsewhere, arrived in hope, lived in cramped quarters, ended its New York existence violently and unexpectedly at the hands of someone with a fatal amount of money—seemed to make its life local enough to qualify. I took it home to roast.

Localism, like its companion, seasonalism, has become so much a part of the equipment of the conscientious eater that it is difficult to sort out its rights and wrongs with any kind of detachment. People get worked up about it. When I mentioned my local-eating escapade to some of my friends who are most attached to the slow-food movement, they were, I could sense, a little upset, even offended, at what they saw as the frivolity of the attempt. Localism's no joke. I could see that they thought this, and though I certainly didn't mean it as a *jeer*, I did mean it as a small joke, not at the expense of the values of the localists, which I share, but at the expense of some of its pieties.

It seemed to me that the real spirit of localism—the thing most worth taking from it—*is* the joke: the playful idea of the pleasure of adventure, the idea, at the heart of most aesthetic pleasures, that by narrowing down, closing up, the area of our inquiry, we can broaden out and open up the possibilities of our pleasures. We live in a food world where everything is possible—every day we see arriving at the supermarket green beans from Kenya and oranges from South Africa and chickens from God knows where. And where everything is possible, little registers. To return to a world of limited choices—these Brooklyn eggplants, this Staten Island pepper—was to once again force the flower of invention, to make the cook, even one of limited powers, think again, act more resourcefully, invent rather than merely imitate.

For the plain truth is that the ecological merits of localism are more disputable than its supporters allow. There is a sane set of counterarguments that insist that local eating only *looks* green.

Critics point out that the "carbon equations" of local food eating, which insist that transportation costs are necessarily hugely wasteful, are dubious. In a now famous—or notorious—op-ed in *The New York Times,* the historian James E. McWilliams, who calls himself a lover of farmers' markets and even a locavore, insisted that careful researchers, in peer-reviewed studies, "found that lamb raised on New Zealand's clover-choked pastures and shipped 11,000 miles by boat to Britain produced 1,520 pounds of carbon dioxide emissions per ton while British lamb produced 6,280 pounds of carbon dioxide per ton, in part because poorer British pastures force farmers to use feed. In other words, it is four times more energy-efficient for Londoners to buy lamb imported from the other side of the world than to buy it from a producer in their backyard. Similar figures were found for dairy products and fruit."

Though some of this criticism sounds oddly strident, and suspiciously serves all too well the interests of the big industrialized agriculture, it does recall what have turned out to be persistent truths about prosperity. The central truth of our food-time is not that we have moved from efficiency to waste, but that we have moved from general famine to what is, in historical terms, abundance. What may really matter most for the world's food efficiency is exactly the "division of labor" that Adam Smith in the eighteenth century rightly saw as the birthright of modernity, and the birthmark of increasing wealth. If some in New Zealand raise lambs, while others in New York eat them, the whole may be a far more efficient use of resources than if we tried to raise sheep on our fire escapes in holistic self-righteousness. It might *look* more efficient, but it would just be frivolous. Adam Smith's central refutation of the "physiocrats" of France, who insisted that the wealth of a nation all derived from its farms, was to show that wealth derived from productivity alone, and that the division of labor into small component tasks, though it might seem ugly and inefficient—wouldn't it be better to have one shed making pins than to divide the labor of pin-making across Europe?—was actually far more productive. It is still somehow counterintuitive to think that it is more efficient to divide food production into many sheds among many people, some very far removed, than to concentrate the work all in one place, but it is certainly so.

There is also, in some of the slow-food and localist rhetoric, in a fashion that also dates back to Adam Smith's time, a kind of hovering puritanical-cum-Catholic suspicion of imported goods, and particularly imported food, as *inherently* decadent and wasteful. Smith used the example of wine to show that there was nothing effectively "decadent" about buying from abroad, any more than if Champagne were still part of Britain. (It is not an accident that Smith chose wine, since few of his British readers could imagine a life without it, and they all knew that it couldn't be made on their island.) The consumer benefits most by buying goods from wherever they are most cheaply made. That principle holds even when the costs are counted in carbon miles. If Kenyan green beans take less total energy than Plattsburgh tomatoes, then we should revel in them no matter how far they have to travel.

And then, apart from the inevitable statistical tussles about exactly how much fuel is used for how much food, the one word that never occurs in the evocation of the lost world of small cities and nearby farms is "famine." When it comes to local eating, we *have* been here before. Our peasant ancestors, who lived locally and ate seasonally from the fruit of their own vines and the meat of their own lambs, were hungry all the time. There is, in the localist, slow-food, seasonalist, and even organicist literature, a disturbing whiff of anticosmopolitanism, of the old reactionary-agrarian dream of giving up urban mongrelization for pure peasant life. It's perhaps too little noted that while President Obama has become an apostle of localism right down to a vegetable garden in the backyard, the real epiphany of his fine first memoir occurs when he goes to Kenya in search of his roots on a plate, and discovers that there is no "authentic" African food—that it's all a hybrid mix of seasonings and methods, of styles and influences and borrowed practices, some of them only half a century old, and all mixed up; the primeval pot is a naïf's fantasy.

It is even perilously easy to construct a Veblenian explanation for the vogue for localism. Where a century ago all upwardly mobile people knew enough, and had enough resources, to get their hands on the most unseasonable foods from the most distant places, in order to distinguish themselves from the peasant past and the laboring masses, their descendants now distinguish themselves by hustling after a peasant diet.

The best argument for eating the local tomatoes instead of the African green beans is that they really do taste better. We hear a lot about the "fact/value" distinction: the famous philosophical idea that distinguishes "what is" from "what ought to be" and insists that no fact, no matter how strong, can determine our values. But we should perhaps pay as much attention to what we might call the "act/value" distinction—the distinction that makes us see that it is not necessary for a thing to make something else good happen in order to be good in itself. What if, after all, all our beliefs about sustainability and the planet and food turned out to be false, or redundant, or of very minor value? Would we then give up going to farmers' markets and stewing organic lamb and all go out to Wendy's? I think it would still be worth cooking slowly, shopping locally, using the whole beast, not because these are acts that will demonstrably do something good but because we believe these things are good in themselves. We like them now. They don't ward off our later ills; they provide our present pleasures.

Or what if the truth was that we could take a single small green pill that would give us all the nutrition we need and help sustain the planet at the same time? Would we gladly give up dinner in order to take it? This idea isn't a joke or even a far-fetched thought experiment: the best evidence of the moment is that an extremely low-calorie diet *is* by far the best "life extender" we know. How many of us take it up? Not many; the loss in the meaning of the table is too great. Like the pig, we'll all die anyway.

The act/value distinction is a helpful one. It keeps us in the present tense. "It's good for you because it tastes good," though far from perfect, is generally stronger wisdom than its opposite, "It ought to taste good because it's good for you." Stronger because it appeals to an increase in joy, because it addresses the fact of appetite, stronger because it speaks to first principles of pleasure. The fragility of life means that our goal is not to extend it but to enjoy it, for the simple reason that we can't really extend it and we know right now if we're enjoying it. The fiercest arguments about ways of eating tend to be the hardest to settle, while the most "frivolous" ones are the most definitive. You should drink wine, eat chocolate, have dessert, fill your plate, even have that steak, because they fit your hunger. And you should eat locally because it connects you to your landscape, city-bred or countrified. We can at least be definitive about that—that a life lived with a face on our food is a richer life than one lived without it. We can have our cake and eat it, too, if you are willing to see that the only point of having cake is to eat it.

We can never know for sure what is cause and what's just correlation—what's merely the happenstance of simultaneous acts and what is the true order of virtuous succession. Perhaps red wine makes our hearts healthier; perhaps it is only that wealthier people with already healthy hearts are the kinds who choose to drink red wine. We don't, or rarely, know for certain what makes things happen. We do know what things are like when we eat or touch or watch them now. The best argument against violent video games isn't that it makes kids violent later; it's that it shows kids violence now. It isn't what it does; it's what it *is*. We don't know, for certain, what food will do. We do know what dinner is. That's enough.

·   ·   ·

So I made our local dinner. Gabrielle, her boyfriend, Craig Haney, the Hoffmans, and our family gathered around the table. We had Bronx chicken with Staten Island peppers, sweet and hot, and rooftop basil; tilapia *tagine;* a big pot of green beans; turnip purée, redolent of elephant dung; super-spicy Brooklyn arugula salad. Aside from the spices and the olive oil—which we allowed ourselves under what the writer Bill McKibben first called a "Marco Polo exemption," common to localism—everything in the dinner hailed from, or had at least seen its first or last days, within the city limits of New York. It was subway localism, short-term localism—a quick sprint, rather than the more dutiful long haul. But it could be done.

If there was something to be learned, it's that the question of locality is one that can be either narrow and parched or broad and humanizing. As usual, the frivolous reason is the better reason, and the "better" reason looks a bit frivolous. To shorten the food chain is to pull it close, close enough to put that face on one's food and a familiar place on one's plate. To eat something local is to meet someone nearby. We had put the city, from Brooklyn ingenuity and Bronx Zoo manure to a slaughterhouse on 168th Street, on a plate, and eaten it up. The plates had stories, where they normally have only food.

The one thing that puzzled me was why Olivia, normally a major *fresser*, hadn't eaten any of the chicken dish; it was a touch tough but, still, tasty. She had, instead of eating, done some highly skilled, three-card-monte-style food pushing around the plate. (Seven-year-olds know that you won't get busted for food-pushing-on-the-plate, only for food-rejecting.) "I did try it," she told me at last, the next day. "The problem was, it tasted just like pigeon."

9

E-MAIL TO ELIZABETH PENNELL:
Salt, Pork, Mustard

Dear Elizabeth:

Today I want to write to you about salt and family, perhaps not
in that order. Of all the meals I make, the one I think the children like most is an odd one, not predictable: long-brined pork,
served with Brussels sprouts braised in balsamic vinegar, which
sweetens them, and mustard-shallot sauce: salt and pungent,
mustard and brine. It isn't what one thinks of as child-friendly
food, necessarily, but there is something about the assembly of
pungencies that appeals to them.

Was mustard as much a symbol of France to you as it is to
me? Someone told me once that you could make anything taste
French simply by slathering it in mustard, and, quick to believe,
I began to do it. Salmon covered and broiled in old-fashioned
whole-grain mustard; tuna in dry mustard mixed with water and
honey; there was a broiling period in my life. I think of our first
days—I mean, Martha's and my first days—in our tiny, six-foot
basement apartment, and I smell the smell of Paul Corcellet
mustard sauce.

And when did brining start? In one way, of course, it started long ago; kosher folks and kosher butchers all salt-brine their food. My own cooking mother would have despised the idea, draining juicy blood and replacing it with desiccating salt. I first came across it where I think my generation did, in *Cook's Illustrated* back in the early nineties, in a famous piece on roasting turkey. The brine solution to keeping turkey moist seemed absurd—we all believed in basting then. I would baste the turkey for hours and hours, with carefully composed solutions of tangerine juice and olive oil and cloves . . . all to absolutely no effect. The baster merely paints the skin of the bird, and whatever goes on underneath goes on.

So brining overtook basting—dunking our food instead of drawing on it. (If Roland Barthes were alive, he could get paragraphs—no, pages; no, *pieces*—out of that difference.) The turkey was the first to go, into kosher salt. The salt fetish is, as I've said, in part a reflection of our urge to turn ourselves into pro cooks—who salt their food with a heavier hand than we do—and partly an urge, I think, to restore, at least unconsciously, some of the old grandmotherly kitchen, where things brined and marinated and pickled and altered, while the family waited.

Family food, I suppose, is what I mean—brining is for family food. So, with family thoughts in mind, I approached the sauce. First you dice shallots. (And I hear my mother teaching me: first cut, slice; next cut, chop; next cut, dice.) Then—and this I think is so important; it's the one thing I know to do that isn't in all the books—you have to slowly sauté the shallots before you put them in the pan that you've cooked the meat in. If you put the shallots into the super-hot pan where you've sautéed the loin, the way it always says to do in the books, then all they do is scorch and remain slightly raw. If you cook them first for, say, eight or nine minutes, slowly, so that they're already sweet and even slightly caramelized, and *then* put them in the pan where the meat cooked, you can cook them in that hot pan even more,

till they're really browned and nice, and then instantly deglaze
the pan with the red or white wine. It makes a perfect shallot
base. Then you cook the wine right down till it's almost dry, and
then you add about a cup of chicken stock. (I like the expensive
but silky veal and chicken stocks that Eli Zabar sells in New
York, but the truth is that any decent supermarket stock will do.
I know there are people who make their own, and that's admirable, but, as so often with cooking, the gain in delight is not truly
worth the expense of labor.)

Anyway, you then cook it down till it's the right sauce thickness. That's tricky, you know: you want it not the least bit soupy,
but on the other hand you don't want just a glaze of shallots.
You ought to stop it just half a minute before it's right, as it will
go on reducing a bit. Then you can add mustard. It's nice to
chop in some tarragon, or just brush in some thyme—you know
the way, treating the thyme like a toothbrush, turning a couple
of stems upside down and then pushing down with your thumb
and forefinger in a circle, so that all the little leaves rain down
into the dish. If you let a bare stick fall in, too, I don't think it
changes the flavor, and it looks kind of pretty and country that
way.

So that's the sauce. It interests me, you know, that it is
another three-step process: wine, stock, and mustard. Or, to go
with chicken or steak, just wine reduced, crème fraîche added
and cooked down, mustard stirred in off heat. The rule of
three seems to be the rule of cooking. There are some two-step
dishes, and a few—a very few—worthwhile four and fives. But
mostly, the good things to eat take three steps. Three steps to
pan sauté: the sauté, the reduction, and the finish. Three steps to
make a cake: the liquids, the butter, and the dries. Three steps to
stew (brine, braise, reduce) and three to make a pasta sauce: the
spice base, anchovies, and garlic; the tomatoes; the scissored-in
herbs. Three steps to grill: the marinade, the grill, and the salsa.
Even rice and beans. . . . The spice base there, too, then the rice,

then the beans. Let us mark it down as another secret o' life: the rule of three will always rule.

Is there a pattern of making here, more universal than it might at first seem? Jasper Johns once said, with the high, significant disingenuousness of faux-naïf genius, that the way to make art is to take something and do something to it and then do something else to it. And this is true—nine times out of ten, when art fails to satisfy, it is either because the artist has merely taken something and done something to it (as in illustration and bad conceptual art) or else because the artist has taken something and done something to it and then done something else and then done even more. The rule of three is the rule of life, even when cooking for four.

I suspect that this is so because the rule of three really expresses the three stages that are always at the base of any good thing we make, from soup to David Salle: there is first the raw thing, then there is the transformative act, and then there is the personal embroidery. The rule of three applies, because it captures an enduring truth of life, that, at best, people always have three terms to play with: what I take from nature, what I've learned from my tribe, what I do myself: nature, culture, me. Something borrowed, something done, something only I can do. Nature's Way; Our Tribe's Way; My Way. Or else History, My Time, My Talent. The chicken that grew on a farm upstate, the sauté pan I was given at our wedding, the sauce made just as I choose to make it. The fish from the cold ocean, the oven inherited from the previous tenants of this apartment, the lemon and olive oil I bought tonight to pour over the fish. The rule of three is the rule of making.

Yours,
Adam

PART III

Talking at the Table

AFTER THE napkin has been unfolded and the menu scrutinized and the choices made, what is there to do but talk? The test of a good meal is the loft of the talk around the table, the way that it rises with the heat of conversation and debate. "I dogmatize and am refuted," Dr. Johnson said of this, "and in this cycle find my delight." And what better thing to talk about than … food, and all its meanings. Each time we do, we talk about more. "In every home I've ever known / the living room's a tomb," the little bit of rhyming runs. "In every home I've ever known, the dining room's the room."

10

In Vino Veritas?

SOMEWHERE in the middle pages of *1984*, Winston Smith is being inducted into the shadowy and, as it turns out, nonexistent "Brotherhood" of resistance to Big Brother, and, to celebrate, the Inner Party member O'Brien pours him a glass of wine. Winston has never had wine before, but he has read about it, and he is desperately excited to try it, since he expects it to taste like blackberry jam and to be instantly intoxicating. Instead, of course, the wine tastes the way wine tastes the first time you taste it—a bit acidic and bitter—and a single sip, or glass, isn't intoxicating at all. The intensity of this experience as a model of disappointment was significant enough for Orwell that he inserted it in his dystopia right there among all the greater horrors—as though the future weren't bad enough, that whole wine thing will go on, too.

Sixty years later, we live in a wine world where, for the first time, there are wines that do taste like blackberry jam and are instantly intoxicating, or nearly so—I mean all the wines of the "Southern" regions, the New Zealand Pinot Noirs and California Zinfandels and Australian Shirazes—and a literature has grown up to try to sort them out in relation to the tastes of the Old World. "Wine," Saul Steinberg once said, "is the only thing that makes us happy as adults for no reason." Wine books, on the other hand, find a hundred ways of making us unhappy for lots of reasons. The space between what the wine writers say and what the wine novice tastes is a standard subject of satire. (The best was written, exactly contemporary with Orwell, by Stephen Potter in the "Winemanship" section of his peerless *Lifemanship* books.)

Some of the weakness of wine-writing is complex. Being an expert on wine and writing about it is what the English call "naff," embarrassing and uncool, while being a nonexpert on wine and writing about it anyway sounds merely boozy. No subject produces a literature so anxious, expressed not so much in its grandiosity as in its defensive jokiness and regular-guydom. A book on wine will always begin with the assurance that it is not like all those other books on wine, even though all those other books on wine begin by saying that they're not like those other books on wine, either.

Running through most of the best wine writing of the past decade, though, is one story, a common time frame and a central fable. The time frame is the past thirty years, and the central fable is the defeat of the French tyranny over wine values, first by American wines, then by American experts, and then by the world at large. And what one sees, again and again, in book after book that tells the tale of the French decline and the American—and more latterly the Australian—rise, are all the pieces of a first-class Henry James comedy about the brutality of New World innocence, the helplessness of Old World sophistication, and the need for intoxicants that are always called by some other name and claimed for some other purpose.

The story always opens in the early 1970s, when the cult of claret—well-aged Bordeaux wine—was locked in place, especially in England, which dominated the wine trade as the Germans had earlier dominated the champagne trade. Bordeaux produced hard, tannic wines that often took a decade to be good to drink. (Then they were really good to drink.) Even when they weren't good, though, everyone went on drinking them, because they were claret. The best wines, if far from cheap, were available, not collector's items: anyone with a taste for wine could expect to drink Château Margaux or Château Cheval Blanc more than once in a lifetime, and the lesser *grands crus* were there for everyday drinking. The preeminence of French wines was simply taken for granted, like the skills of Jewish internists. Within Bordeaux, the classification of 1855—which had fixed the vineyards in a hierarchy of first-, second-, and third-growth classes—still hummed along, dominating everything.

Into this story come two new forces: Japanese money and American numbers. In the mid-seventies, the Japanese developed a taste for expensive French wine, and for buying the big names. This vastly expanded the market and seemed to justify investment in higher yields: more grapes, and more land. But this meant that the lower reaches of second- and third-growth wine were now all that most Americans could drink, though in a less equable and accepting mood. In 1976, in Paris, an American Cabernet beat the French Bordeaux in a blind tasting. This was not quite the event that it has since come to seem. To the French winemakers, it was more like an American loss to the Lithuanians in basketball— wrong game at the wrong time—but it did mark a trembling of the earth beneath their feet.

More significant, a lawyer named Robert Parker, from the suburbs of Baltimore, began to mimeograph, and then publish, his own newsletter, *The Wine Advocate,* listing all the châteaux and grading them on a hundred-point system. His virtues were limited: he was a very ordinary writer with few pretensions to the grace notes of French, or even English, wine writing. What he brought to the table was what Americans always bring: encyclopedic ambitions and a universal numerical system. Not since Bernard Berenson made his lists of true and false Italian pictures had an American expert on the arts so fundamentally changed the economics of European culture. As with Berenson, what mattered was not so much that the list was right—who could tell for sure?—as that the list existed.

In retrospect, it seems that Parker was doing to wine what Bill James was doing to baseball in the same years, and in the same way. Both Parker and James began, in the late seventies, as unknown amateurs with privately printed newsletters, rapidly found a hungry and enthusiastic audience, and by the mid-eighties had become the reigning authorities among people impatient with the old wisdoms. Both were uncannily successful because they were apostles of a radical American empiricism—an insistence that facts and numbers could show you what was really going on, against everything tradition told you. James was weakly predictive, but brilliantly analytic: his explanations of why things had happened were mesmerizing and convincing, but his guesses about what would happen next were often wrong. (His system had the Brewers winning the '82 series.) Parker was weakly analytic but brilliantly predictive; he could never really explain why wines tasted good, but he claimed that the '82 vintage was going to be great, and it was.

The difference was that Parker's game had always belonged to the French. And from the French point of view he was poison. Like all Henry James heroes, Parker was a true American innocent, meaning only to help and purify his European friends. The wines that receive the most consistent and adulatory praise in his system are the conventional favorites of conventional French taste: Château Margaux and, Burgundy, Domaine de la Romanée-Conti. No one could have been more single-mindedly rapturous about Château d'Yquem. In France, though, the greatness of those wines was accepted not as effort well rewarded but as the natural order of life. There had to be not-so-good wines below to have great wines above; the hierarchy was part of the pleasure. Parker assumed that if some wines were not as good as others it was because some winemakers were not doing as good a job.

Although, in a defensive move, the French government gave him the Légion d'Honneur—he cried when he received it—his Francophilia did him no good with the French; the vintners set dogs on him. In a Henry James story, he would marry a French *comtesse* with a fading château, and have to decide whether to be true to his system by rating her wines properly or be true to her and lie. (In the James story, he would lie, and suffer.) Without intending to, he was wrecking the second rank. He was able to do this because, for the first time, there was a solid second rank of claret-style wine in the world, and it wasn't the second growths of Bordeaux.

One common complaint has been that Parker's idea of good was too narrow. People who know wines now disparage Parker for preferring "flavor bombs," big wines that are exploding with fruit and alcohol, and which showed up better in tastings—with the not very convincing implication that there is something second-rate about liking such blackberry-jam wines. But the essential "character" of many of the wines that he ruled out was the quality of not being very good.

Meanwhile, beginning in the 1980s, there was more good wine around than ever before, and most of it was coming, as it still does, from the then-underexploited warm-weather vineyards of other continents. It is hard to find a less than delicious bottle of Australian Syrah or South African Cabernet or California Zinfandel, or, these days, New Zealand Pinot Noir. Even southern Italy, and Sicily in particular, began to fall into line. Mouton Cadet, the old standard Bordeaux plonk, has almost disappeared from dinner tables.

In this way, Parker's achievement wasn't so much to Americanize French wine as to southernize northern palates—to favor the fruitier and more forward wines common to South Africa and California and Australia over the drier and more astringent tastes of young Bordeaux and old Burgundy. He liked wines that tasted good. His favorite French wines, the ones he loves from the heart ("This is the kind of wine I would drink if I were not always tasting," he once wrote plaintively, apropos of a simple Guigal Côtes du Rhône), are southern, too, from the Rhône Valley. An "educated" palate may seek to explain why this is a limiting taste, but is unlikely to win over the Winston Smiths. It is a little like the educated eye trying to explain why Poussin is better than Rubens; people may listen, but they look at those thighs, and doubt.

Once Parker had established his reputation, the French had to decide whether to fight or to change, and they changed. William Echikson's heroes, in his book *Noble Rot*—the story of the ins and outs of the family who own Château d'Yquem but more broadly about post–Parker Bordeaux—are the *garagistes* and "right bankers," the winemakers from the wrong bank of the Gironde, who, one by one, are either taking control of old estates or making their own wine in the backyard. Following his heroes from château to château, Echikson gives a strong hint throughout that making good wine is more like making good peanut butter than it is like writing great poetry. Low yields (meaning not too many grapes per hectare), sweet fruit allowed to ripen as long as possible (there is always pressure on growers to harvest early, because of the threat of a late rain or an early frost), no stems, minimal "handling"—the formula is pretty simple. Wine is good grape juice gone bad, and, as many of the new French winemakers seem to suggest under their breath, there is something to be said for the Australian system where grapes are collected from around the country, sorted through, and fermented in great big well-controlled vats, and *terroir* be damned.

Yet the reader, even one with Parkerized tastes, may, on reflection, find the French objections to Parker's lists and numbers more complicated than many of the critics allow. The debate is not about whether the numbers are right but whether it is right to have numbers. Everyone agrees that Parker is, on his own terms, a completely honest scorer; but by scoring he intends to serve the consumer, and makes the wine drinker into one. What consumers want is reliable beverage products, and, once wine is a reliable beverage product, it isn't quite wine.

Demanding absolute excellence on an unchanging universal numerical scale is not, after all, our usual measure of sensual engagement. A man who makes love to fifty-some women and then publishes a list in which each one gets a numerical grade would not be called a lady's man. He would be called a cad. And that, more or less, is how a good many Frenchmen think of Parker: they don't doubt his credentials; they question his character. A real man likes moles and frailties; a real man marries his wine, as he marries his wife, and sees her through the thin spots. Being impatient with the tannins in a Margaux is like being impatient with the lines on your wife's face. They are what makes it a marriage rather than a paid assignation.

For one of the defining characteristics of many French *terroirs* is not to make very good wine. To alter that is to put them in the beverage business. No one says this, exactly—but when you are handed a glass of thin and astringent country wine in France and asked to admire it for its character, there is a reasonable point in which its character does consist in its having some. The French connoisseur believes that, with his glass of turpentiney Gascon wine, he is in a truer relation to history and reality than the American searching for his jammy high-scorers. I wouldn't actually drink like this, but I understand it.

Of course, if the ladies were offering their favors at forty dollars a go, it would seem fair for somebody to grade them, and that is, more or less, what Parker's defenders say: a product that is being bought and sold should be subject to the market discipline of all other things that are bought and sold, and all the guff about earth and history and ineffable singularity is just a way of avoiding giving the customer what he ought to get for his money.

. . .

Well, what does make wine taste bad or good? Is there really a standard, or a way to agree on one? Within the heart of every wine drinker there is the suspicion that no one really knows. I was once at a dinner in Paris, seated by a big "name" in wine tasting, and, along about the third bottle, she leaned in and announced, half gaily and half conspiratorially, "You know, it's really all about the same." Of course, she didn't actually believe that—but I also had the sense that in another way she *did* believe it, that she was confiding something significant about her own profession. She didn't mean that it all tastes the same—obviously, it doesn't—but that, stripped away from its elaborate rituals, the distinctions that her livelihood depends on would be a lot muddier and mixed up.

The French cognitive psychologist Frédéric Brochet has done pioneering, if disconcerting, work on this subject. It was Brochet who first discovered that if you simply put red food coloring in white wine even experienced drinkers can't tell it from red wine. What we see shapes what we smell. But his work goes further than that. In another study, he offered, at a week's interval to a constant group, the same mediocre wine, first labeling it a *vin de table* and then as a *grand cru*. Predictably, the subjects' tasting notes conformed more closely to the label than to what was "really" there. Nor did anyone seem to detect that it was the same wine with a new label. Once again, the frame frames. We lean on what we see, what we read, to create a context for what we think we taste and smell.

Nor does "expertise" seem to alter this effect very profoundly. Studying tasting notes from forty-four professionals at a wine exposition, Brochet discovered that "when a taster experiences a particular wine, the words they use to describe it are those that they link to this sort of wine." That is, even the expert tastes what he expects to taste, and says what he has said before. If you called the last Côtes du Rhône "rich and peppery," then that is what you will say about the next one; the words make the wine before the wine produces the words. What's more, and it's a slightly scary thought, Brochet showed that when you look at MRIs of the brains of wine connoisseurs who use different pet phrases to describe their wines, different areas of the brain light up—they are actually experiencing different things. To the degree that any "fakery" is going on, it is entirely sincere self-delusion.

According to scientists who study smell and taste, that's just the beginning: the duplicity reaches from the organizing mind deep into the experiencing senses themselves. Rachel Herz, a professor of psychology at Brown, conducts research into the effects of "frames"—context—on the perception of smells. (Wine tasters are "noses" first of all.) Smells, she reports, "are so malleable when it comes to verbal context that when reasonable verbal information is available it will override and even replace the olfactory information." The effect is pronounced when the smells are, in some way, ambiguous—tell people that they're smelling vomit, and they'll smell vomit; tell them that the same smell is Parmesan cheese, and they'll smell Parmesan cheese. With wine, the most basic verbal categories (it comes from France, it comes from America, it's cheap, it's expensive) seem to be able to throw even an educated nose off track. The illusions, Herz suggests, "work the way, in a familiar illusion, arrowheads either going in or feathering out extend or shorten straight lines. Word labels on smells are the same kind of context effect, and these context effects are markedly more powerful with nose sensations than they are with other kinds."

To make things worse, the nose turns out to have the shortest memory of all the sense organs. A simple experiment, Herz suggests, shows just how powerful nose amnesia is: Think of a familiar tune—say, "Yesterday." Now think of a familiar picture—say, the *Mona Lisa*. Now think of the smell of a tuna-fish sandwich. You can do the last, of course, but where the other sensory memories are strong, clear, and sharp, the tuna-fish sandwich smell is general and vague. What the nose knows, in effect, is not much, and that soon forgotten. (Wine lovers protest violently when they are told this, but their protest, from the academic point of view, is a bit like the protest of eyewitnesses who are *sure* they saw what they say they saw, even if they didn't.) Yet to accept this is not to say that the elaborate language of wine evaluation is necessarily or even remotely phony. It is exactly because smells are so labile and hard to grasp that they need more help from words than other sensations. When it comes to wine, we are all like early-Alzheimer's patients who have to be coaxed into memory and appreciation. ("Remember, Dad—that's the woman we saw on the beach at Wellfleet." "Oh, yes! Her.")

The real question is not whether wine snobs and wine writers are big phonies but whether they are any bigger phonies than, say, book reviewers or art critics. For with those things, too, context effects are overwhelming. All description is impressionistic, and all impressions are interpretive. Colors and shapes don't emerge from pictures in neat packages to strike the eye, either, any more than plots and themes come direct to the mind from the pages of books. Everything is framed by something. Once again, the essential dialogue between the frame of our expectations and the experience of our senses is not the thing to be defeated when we talk about our hungers, but the thing to be celebrated: it is what gives shape to our sensorium.

It is perfectly possible—in fact, almost certainly true—that given the wrong frame, or no frame at all, all of our responses to wine would vanish into one big buzzing confusion. If all the grape juice in Bordeaux or Napa were poured into vats, without labels or corkscrews or prior knowledge, it really might all taste the same. Anyway, no elaborate rhetoric of compliments is meant to be "accurate"; it is meant to be complimentary. When Shakespeare compares his lover to a summer's day, he doesn't really mean that she (or he) is like a summer's day in that she is hotter in the middle and cooler at the ends—though, then again, he might. Wine writing is of the same type: a series of elaborately plausible compliments paid to wines. When the French wine writer Eric Glatre declares, say, that in the aroma of a bottle of Krug "intense empyreumatic fragrances of toasted milk bread, fresh butter, café au lait, and afterthoughts of linden join in a harmonious chorus with generous notes of acacia honey, mocha, and vanilla," he is suggesting that, of all the analogies out there, this might be one that expands our minds, opens our horizons, delights our imaginations. He is offering a metaphor, not an account book.

In this way, the intersection of French sensibility and modern science suggests not so much the limits of Parker as the limits of naïve American empiricism: numbers and honesty and transparency only get you so far in the world. Our experiences of everything are too mediated—by contexts and intentions and likeness—to be summed up in a number. It is exactly the disputable quality of the compliments we pay to wine that makes them touch the lower edge of art. Once again, *De gustibus solum est disputandum*. Only matters of taste are worth arguing over.

Between the rhetorical and the real lies ritual. And wine is a ritual thing before it is any other kind of thing. The history of wine provides the not surprising but always reassuring news that there is, from the very beginning of viniculture, no sorting out the need for intoxication from the necessity of ritual, the desire to drink from the debt to structure. The story of wine seems to begin someplace out in the "Transcaucasus"—today's Georgia, Armenia, and Azerbaijan—when the first *Vitis viniferas* grapes got grown. The astonishing thing about wines is that they are like dogs: there is endless apparent variety we can squeeze from what is, in the end, one species. Had Darwin been a wine-drinker, instead of an English port man, he might have chosen to use the varieties of wine, shaped by man from one unchanging grape into a thousand *terroirs,* to make his point about variation produced under selective pressure. (Actually, Darwin *did* do important work in the history of wine, and not just because he was one of the first Englishmen to taste New Zealand reds. He made the essential point that the grapevine will produce tendrils, to climb with, or grapes, to reproduce with, and that this is a vestige of the vine's ancient forest habitat, where it could "choose" either to climb higher to reach sunlight, or stop where it was and make fruit. And, not coincidentally, he helped save French wine. It was Darwinian evolutionary principles that helped French biologists discover, at the time of the great phyloxera crisis of the late nineteenth century, the one thing that might save French wine. They realized that, since the root louse causing the plague was American, the American vines on which it must once have lived must surely have evolved resistance to it—and it was the grafting of New World roots onto Old World vines that saved Burgundy and Bordeaux. Before Darwin, it seems likely that the last thing vintners would have done is go back to the same vines that had carried the plague to supply the cure.)

What we find in all the ancient wine cultures is not a slow growth from a disorganized Bacchanalia to an evolved ritual practice, from simple intoxication to information system. On the contrary, wine ritual and wine-drinking seem to have been inseparable from the very first. Wine, after all, though a natural product, isn't a simple one: even the plainest garage wines demand a complex grasp of a multipart process; leave it in the vat and let it rot doesn't work very well. You have to think it even as you drink it. So it's no surprise that everywhere we turn, even in the most ancient wine writing, we find gods and demigods, vessels and special glasses—the absurd paraphernalia of the wine lover, with his tasting glasses and little fridge, stretches back to the beginning of time.

From the beginning, wine and wine culture has been a halfway house between the sacramental and the social. In Neolithic cultures there are already inscriptions and decorations on wine vessels. As the scholar Patrick McGovern tells us, at the end of Old Kingdom Egypt, around 2200 B.C., there is already a system of "AOC," *appellation contrôlée*, designations of the kind that France arrived at only in the nineteenth century: wines in mortuary tablets seem to be grouped around the names of well-known wineries in the Nile Delta. They are called Northern wine, *abesh* wine, and *sunu* wine. In New Kingdom pottery inscriptions, referred to as *ostraca* and dated to around 1350 B.C., wines are rated as "genuine," "good," "very good," and even "very, very good"—a blunter and more useful system, in its way, than the French "Grand Cru Classé" and our own regional markings. "Wine snobbery" of this sort, a compulsive need to rate and class and compare, far from being a late invention, seems inseparable from the activity itself. It is as if from the start wine-drinkers grasped that without a mental frame of comparison, without words to structure tastes, the pleasures of wine drinking would be lessened. Egyptian wine-drinkers wanted to know if they were drinking *abesh* or *sunu,* and they wanted to know if it was merely genuine or very good—and doubtless they then turned toward each other in profile and said, "They're calling this *abesh* 'very, very good'—but then, Parker *always* overrates *abesh.*"

The question about such judgments, mixing snobbishness and sense, is not whether they exist—they exist in the minds of the people who feel them; that's enough—but what they are *about.* For the true wine snob, they are about the ability to make them, and this is just sad. For the French wine critic—a generalized type, but one who exists—they are about the ability to make a map inside your mind: to taste tastes and see places. For the American wine critic, they are about the ability to offer consumers a quality beverage. What they rarely seem to be about is drinking wine. Paul Draper, the great winemaker from Ridge Vineyards in California, has had the honesty to say that he wishes there were more drinkers in the wine world and less tasting. He means by this not that more people should get drunk, but that more people should accept the totality of the experience of wine as it really is, instead of amputating one bit of the whole activity and fetishizing it.

Remarkably, nowhere in wine writing, including Parker's, would a Martian learn that the first reason people drink wine is to get drunk. To read wine writing, one would think that wine is simply another luxury food, like smoked salmon or caviar or chocolate; the one idea that is banished is that it is a powerful drug, which can wash away, in a few minutes, the ability to discriminate at all. The end of food writing is to turn eating into a metaphor for wanting, of all kinds. The end of wine writing is to turn drinking into a metaphor for judging. Since we know that this is false, we feel the falsity, and the pathos of the falsity.

For it is not wine that makes us happy for no reason; it is alcohol that makes us happy for no reason. Wine is what gives us a reason to let alcohol make us happy without one. It's the ritual context that civilizes the simple need. Yet there is still a strong taboo in place among even the ritzier reaches of wine writing about addressing this untroubling truth. It is true, of course, that the professional wine-taster tastes and spits. And I am told that there are wine-tasters who are allergic to alcohol. But the specialized bits of the activity would not exist without the totality of the larger truth: if wine were just better-tasting grape juice, we wouldn't have the books or the background or the bards.

Our experience is whole. We can take one moment, the mouth moment, from the whole experience, but we would not relish the moment if we did not keep the whole experience in mind. If we were not warmed by wine, we would not take the trouble to categorize its tastes. (And even if we didn't others would do it for us; there's a social dimension to wine, a division of labor, à la

Adam Smith, in which the tasters do some of the work, and the drinkers do the rest; if there were no drinkers, there would be no tastings for the tasters.) Men like to look at nude pictures of pretty women—or perhaps that should be, at pretty pictures of nude women—without necessarily having (or feigning to have) sex with them. But it is only the wider experience of sex that lends the pictures their punch and their point.

The strident denials on the part of the wine connoisseurs that their experience has *anything* to do with that other experience of getting tipsy reminds one of nothing so much as the earnest insistence, on the part of Victorian aesthetes, that the nude in art had nothing whatever to do with sex, and that if it did "it was bad morals and bad art." To which Kenneth Clark replied, mischievously, in his great book *The Nude,* that if the nude in art *didn't* have some relation to sexual desire, then it was bad morals and bad art. This doesn't mean that Clark wanted to make love to the Venus de Milo (though given what we know of his avid sex life, maybe he did). It just means that the idealizations and the "aesthetic" pleasures, the gentle flow of curves and breasts and rear, in the Venus is an extended, heightened, crystallized form of desire—desire transformed into art, but still desire at, er, bottom.

The wine expert can create a new space, between intoxication and discrimination, and then perform in it—just as the fun of being a connoisseur of the classical nude, à la Rubens and Titian, is to play in the space between the erotic and the pornographic. But the hunger for the comfort drug lies at the root of one activity, as the hunger for the human body lies at the root of the other. The reproductive instinct is at the start, though by no means always at the finish, of our love lives. Divorcing sex from reproduction in everything we write about it—if only to counsel birth control—would not strike us as elegant; it would strike us as unreal. And the same is true of wine. If wine did not warm, we would not want it.

The mixed-up sensations of wine do not make a case for the

superfluity of wine writing; it is the case for its necessity. Without wine lore and wine tasting and wine talk and wine labels and, yes, wine writing and rating—the whole elaborate idea of wine—we would still get drunk, but we would be *merely* drunk. The language of wine appreciation is there not because wine is such a special, subtle challenge to our discernment but because without the elaborate language—without the idea of wine, held up and regularly polished—it *would* all be about the same, or taste that way. Wine talk and wine ceremony are not simply snobbish distractions that lead us away from the real experience; they are part of what lets the experience happen. Once again, our contexts and our convictions are in constant play. We believe in the virtue of some kinds of wine, we bounce with joy at the tastes of others—our tastes and our temperaments debate even as they dance.

To turn wine away from happiness is the drinker's sin, as turning food from gusto is the eater's. A good fruity bottle of a Santa Barbara Pinot Noir, with a pretty label and a decent story, makes us happy, and happier than that we don't really deserve to be. In that Henry James story, of course, the innocent empirical American's reward and punishment would come when he marries that *comtesse* and retires to her château, where they spend the rest of their lives drinking nothing but water, for their health.

11

E-MAIL TO ELIZABETH PENNELL:
Potatoes, Steak, Air

Dear Eliza:

I notice that, in your essay on the perfect dinner, you dish-drop *pommes soufflées*. Of all the dishes that are out there, and that I dream of making, *pommes soufflées* is perhaps the first on the list. The dish was popular already in your time, which is why you refer to it—that might have been its heyday, actually: potatoes are sliced about a quarter of an inch thick, then twice deep-fried. The first time preps them at a lower heat, the second time—done right, done fully, done with luck—the potatoes blister and then blossom, popping up and filling with air, so that they are delicate little balloons of potato and salt and the lingering taste of the oil they were cooked in. They are, if not the immortality of potatoes, as cheese is said to be the immortality of milk, then at least the elegance of potatoes. Parmentier, the great French agronomist who brought the potato to Paris, thought of it as a plebeian dish, and we eat it mostly in that manner, mashed or roasted or boiled. But the fried potato, absurdly ubiquitous as it now is, once was the royalty of the line, and the *pomme soufflé*, if you can find it, keeps some savor of that stature.

They don't seem to make them anywhere in New York these days, though I have read that they were still available in the fancy places in New Orleans until recently, along with crêpes suzettes and flambéed duck and all the other ancient dishes of the old theatrical cuisine. I think the only one I have ever eaten in New York was a one-off. I was in a burger-and-lobster sort of place along Second Avenue, thirty years ago, when the eastern avenues of Manhattan were lined with glass cafés and the phrases "singles bars" and "brunch" still resonated. Ordering sautéed potatoes, I saw that one had swelled and risen, just like a *pomme soufflé*. It must have fallen into the oil twice, by chance, and inflated by accident. It was, exactly, a "hopeful monster," of the kind that evolutionary biologists, Stephen Jay Gould prominent among them, were talking about in those days—the one lucky potato slice dropped by accident twice in the ever-hotter oil, suddenly inflated and ballooned.

It was evidence, though, that they can be made. So the other night, following a recipe in one of the old, sixties-era French cookbooks I like to collect, I neatly peeled some firm russets—the books emphasize that you can't use new potatoes, or baking potatoes that have gone too soft—and then sliced them into what I measured as a template of three-eighths of an inch. Then I poured canola oil into two Dutch ovens, took out the candy/frying thermometer, and turned on our (unfortunately electric, and slow-responding) stove. I decided to serve them, for safety, with one of the meals that I knew in advance the children would love: a rib steak done with a red wine and shallot sauce—sauce Bordelaise, as it's called in the old recipe books, a classic three-step sauce: shallots, red wine, veal stock. I made the steak with my "consciousness raised," as people used to say, to the ambiguities of meat-eating. And yet . . . hunger rose.

It is surely somewhere here that the *real* difficulty about the whole vexed meat-eating question lies. Not how we think abstractly about the rights of meat-eating, but how we actually feel when we eat meat. In that most evil of all films, the Goebbels-produced Nazi-era "documentary" *The Eternal Jew,* there's a bizarre, interminable sequence—obscenely heralded by a title page warning off "sensitive German viewers"—of kosher butchery, taken during the Polish invasion, in which a cow, its throat cut, is bled to death, poor beast, and the indifference of the bearded Jewish butchers to the suffering is a sign of their evil indecency. Because they are cruel to animals (let us bracket, both on the page, and in our minds, whether kosher butchery is truly crueler than any other kind) we can be cruel to *them:* they don't have the same feelings as the rest of us, either of empathy or of sensitivity. Exterminating them is not like exterminating people; it is like exterminating rats.

Of course, vegetarians are not Nazis—but there is a sense in which sensitivity to animals has nothing at all to do with any other ethical acquisition. People have, historically, as often used cruelty to animals as a justification for being cruel to people as they have as a reason for not being cruel to anything. See how they treat their horses, was one cry of the Mongols about their enemies. The path from sensitivity to the suffering of animals to sensitivity to the suffering of humans is, as a matter of plain fact, far from open or easy.

Our little dog, Butterscotch, lives for steak. It is the beginning and end of pleasure for her. Her nose quivers, her whole small fluffy body shakes, gripped by a primal hunger so intense that she can barely contain it. She smells steak and she does a sit, does another sit, tightening the first one—falls to the floor in a "down" and then does a head-down and a spin and a shake; her whole repertory of tricks, just to show how much she wants it and how eager she is to do anything she needs to do to get it. We slice it fine for her, and then watch her inhale it—well, she is a carnivore, a little wolf, not by sentiment but by genetics: isn't her hunger for meat some sign that eating it is, not compulsory certainly, but hard to call evil in any recognizable sense? An appetite implanted so deep in our natures seems less of a sin and more of a scar—something that we just *have,* as part of living in the world we live in with the heritage we share, and that we can only improve by being certain that we are not cruel in its pursuit.

I don't know; I shudder at the verdict of our descendants even as I recognize the carnivorousness of our animal natures. And I go on eating, and serving, steak.

In slicing the *pommes soufflées,* and readying the two Dutch ovens for their brief role as frying pots, I am aware that there is an element, what I believe could be called a "stark" element, of show, of carnival barkerishness, in the dish. This used to be part of the business of the chef—public amazement—which was then judged vulgar and largely banished. Or rather expelled to another world, to the nightly ribbon of spectacle. I wonder what *you* would make of cooks on cable television? What would you think—cook after cook, traveling and arguing and competing, making part of the public show things that were kept in the sanctity of the kitchen? Now, I am aware that for all that we have in common, you depended on servants a bit more than your writing quite likes to show. And nowhere more than in the *pommes soufflées* business—let's be candid, your airily summoning up a plate of them does not mean that you are about to go off to the kitchen, Elizabeth, and make them. It means either that your cook has been busy or that you are imagining them, as eaten in Paris. One thing that separates our time from yours most firmly: there are no cooks outside the kitchen in yours. You mention famous chefs from time to time, but they belong to the distant and remote past.

So I wonder how you would feel about our cable carnival of cooking? Every night, there are competitions, tours, chef against chef, young cook against old cook—thirty minutes head-to-head. We are supposed to be disapproving, of course, and to see this as a degradation of the art. And the idea of food shows on television is a paradox that Chesterton could not have imagined: food *watched,* food that no one can taste or smell or eat. To be honest, while my taste for recipe books is insatiable, my appetite for cable cooking shows is very limited. The ideas take so long to blossom, the preparations so long to prepare, that I get impatient.

But there's nothing really offensive or "off" about it: it celebrates, in however debased and diminished a form, an idea of expertise, of craft, which is the one thing that is vanishing from our world. Mario and the Iron Chefs are there because they have finish—they're good at what they do, rather than being freakishly who they are. Being good at what you do is so odd and rare a thing in life now that just showing someone being good at something is enough to hold several million people. Even the contest shows make at least a pretense at excellence: the viewer can't taste the food but Padma can, and the alarming sternness of the judgment at least simulates, pantomimes, the idea of something being at stake in the act of craft. (One can't imagine a *Top Artist* show because the standards of what is considered art and poetry are by now so essentially whimsical or arbitrary that no one could agree: being good at rhyme or drawing has only a tangential relation to being famous for being a poet or an artist.) At least, when a chef makes something, she is making something. It's either tasty or it isn't, and the taste rises from the practical mastery of a craft. This is surely the reason that people respond with such excitement even to things that seem to me tedious, like *Dancing with the Stars* or *American Idol*—the "cruelty" to the contestants isn't cruelty at all; it may be the only time many people in the audience have seen a craft standard enforced with craft severity: there really is and isn't a right way to tango, as there is a right way and wrong way to make *pommes soufflées.*

Oh, yes, the *pommes soufflées.* Well, I did them, ever so carefully, slicing and prefrying and then true frying . . . and they failed, totally and utterly. Not a single blossom or blister or even a hint of puffing and expanding. Obviously I had the width wrong, or the heat wrong, or the order wrong. There is a reason that French restaurants don't do them; they're too much trouble for too little reward. The reward is just the look, the puff, the hot air inside—the potato is still the same.

The infusion of air is always a sign of elegance, in your day as in ours. How many things in the kitchen involve simply beating in air: meringues, whipped cream, *pommes soufflées*, soufflés themselves. It is, perhaps, no accident that we call a book cover's blurb a "puff." We condemn hot air even as we eat it. Air is the forgotten medium of cooking.

Did I say they all failed? In truth, there was a single *pomme soufflé*—one slice had popped and blossomed amid the rest that had decided to remain potato chips. I looked at it and put it aside, and then fed it to the little dog.

Very best,
Adam

12

What Do We Write About
When We Write About Food?

RECENTLY, THERE WAS an exchange in the pages of *The Times Literary Supplement* about the presence, and the propriety, of recipes in novels, and I intend to settle the questions that have arisen there in the American way, right now, and for good. There are four kinds of food in books: food that is served by an author to characters who are not expected to taste it; food that is served by an author to characters in order to show who they are; food that an author cooks for characters in order to eat it with them; and, last (and most recent), food that an author cooks for characters but actually serves to the reader.

Most books that have food in them, including the classic nineteenth-century novels, have the first kind of food. In one Trollope novel after another, three meals a day, the parsons and politicians eat chops or steaks or mutton, but the dishes are essentially interchangeable, mere stops on the ribbon of narrative, signs of life and social transactions rather than specific pleasures: "Mr. Peregrine greatly enjoyed his chop" or "For Dr. Patterson, even the usual satisfaction he took in his beefsteak and porter was somewhat diminished by this thought"—such food provides space for a moment of reflection. The dishes are the foam peanuts in the packaging of classic narrative. There are moments in Trollope when what a character drinks matters—claret good or bad, porter or port—but his food is, in every sense, at the service of his story.

Next come the writers who dish up very particular food to their characters to show who they are. Proust is the second kind of writer, and Henry James is, too. Proust seems so full of food—crushed strawberries and madeleines, tisanes and champagne—that entire recipe books have been extracted from his texts. But he's not a greedy writer; that his people are eating lobster or veal matters to who they are and how they feel about who they are, but we are not meant to leave the page hungry. Proust will say that someone is eating a meal of gigot with sauce béarnaise, but he seldom says that the character had a delicious meal of gigot with sauce béarnaise—although he will extend his adjectives to the weather, or the view. He uses food as a sign of something else. (It's what social novelists, even mystically minded ones, always do: J. D. Salinger doesn't like food, either, but the fact that his characters are eating snails or Swiss-cheese sandwiches tells so much about them that it must be noted, and felt, like every other detail.)

The third kind of writer is so greedy that he goes on at length about the things his characters are eating, or are about to eat—serving it in front of us and then snatching it from our mouths. Ian Fleming is obsessed with food; gluttony, even more than lust, is the electric current of his hero's adventures. Newcomers to James Bond, imagining him to be the roughneck he has once again become in movies, will be startled to see how much time he spends in *Casino Royale* and the other early Bonds giving advice to his girls and his spy superiors on what to eat, with the author hovering over his shoulder as he examines the menu: the problem with caviar, Bond announces, is getting enough toast (not true); English cooking is the best in the world when it's good (certainly not true then); and rosé champagne goes perfectly with stone crabs (very true). His creator, one feels as the excitement builds, is not just itemizing the food, waiter-like, but actually sitting at the table and sharing it with him.

The fourth kind of writer, ever more numerous, presents on the page not just the result but the whole process—not just what people eat but how they make it, exactly how much garlic is chopped, and how, and when it is placed in the pan. Sometimes entire recipes are included in the text, a practice that links Kurt Vonnegut's *Deadeye Dick* to Nora Ephron's *Heartburn,* novels about the inadvertent mayhem that a man can inflict on a woman; in *Heartburn,* the recipes serve both as a joke about what a food writer writing a novel would write and as a joke on novel-writing itself by someone who anticipates that she will not be treated as a "real" novelist. These days, we have long cooking sequences in Ian McEwan; endless recipes in James Hamilton-Paterson; menus analyzed at length in John Lanchester; and detailed culinary scenes involving Robert B. Parker's bruiser of a detective, Spenser. Cooking is to our literature what sex was to the writing of the sixties and seventies, the thing worth stopping the story for to share, so to speak, with the reader.

Not long ago, I attempted to mimic some cooking as it is done in a number of relatively recent novels. I began, foolishly, with several recipes from Günter Grass's Nobel Prize–provoking *The Flounder,* the epic allegory of German history told through the endlessly repeated parable of an evil fish, a gullible man, a virtuous woman, and a lot of potatoes. The talking Flounder, being both the evil daemon and the central consciousness of the piece, has a natural class interest in flounders' not being eaten, so there is a shortage of fish recipes in *The Flounder.* (I was tempted by a detailed description of how to make stewed tripe, but who in my gang would eat stewed tripe?) There is one nice moment, though, when the eternal talking Flounder, who "knew all the recipes that had been used for cooking his fellows," mentions simmering the fish with white wine and capers. Well, from his mouth to our plate: I did just that, with a nice filet from the Citarella market, and, as suggested, added some sorrel. Then, learning in a later section what could be done with potatoes and mustard—the potato, with its false promise of cheap nutrition for all, is, I suppose, meant to represent the false hope of the Enlightenment in Germany, but the mustard surely could represent the saving genius of the Bavarian rococo—I made a gratin with mustard to accompany it. It was fine, though it reminded me of why it is that, at a moment when Spanish cooking is everywhere sanctified and even English cooking, for the first time, canonized, not many people are making a case that German cooking is much more than fish and potatoes and sauerbraten. Eating Günter Grass's flounder was actually like reading one of his novels: nutritious, but a little pale and starchy.

Great masters are not meant to offer small plates. My eye fell next on *School Days,* one of Robert B. Parker's excellent Spenser mysteries. Where John D. MacDonald's Travis McGee, Spenser's daddy in the genre, would occasionally throw an inch-thick T-bone on the grill of *The Busted Flush,* Spenser produces entire dishes, and we read about them bit by bit. (Nero Wolfe had a personal chef, and ate a lot, but it was mostly in the "the great detective dined on *quenelles de brochet*" line.) In *School Days,* Spenser, with his beloved Susan away at a psych seminar, and only the dog for company, makes a dish of cranberry beans, diced steak, and fresh corn, dressed with olive oil and cider vinegar.

The beans alone establish Spenser's credibility as a cook. "I shelled the beans from their long, red-and-cream pods and dropped them in boiling water and turned down the heat and let them simmer," he tells us. A devotion to shell beans, I have noticed, divides even amateur cooks from noncooks more absolutely than any other food, and they are, into the bargain, a perfect model of writing. Like sentences, shell beans are a great deal more trouble to produce than anyone who isn't producing them knows. You have to shell the beans, slipping open the pods with your thumbnail and then tugging the beautiful little prismatic buttons from their moorings—a process that, like writing, always takes much longer than you think it will. And then even the best shell beans, cleaned and simmered, are like sentences in that nobody actually appreciates them as much as they deserve to be appreciated. Shell beans are several steps more delicious, lighter and finer, than dried beans, let alone canned beans; but the sad truth is that nobody really cares beans about beans, and not many eaters can tell the fresh kind from the dried, or even the canned.

I carried on with the recipe: Spenser takes a small steak from the refrigerator and dices it, sautés it, and then mixes it with the beans and some corn. I did this, and, honestly, I don't think it's a good idea. Maybe I didn't do it right—there is a certain lack of specificity about what kind of steak he's using and just how long he keeps it in the pan—but I found that my steak dried out when it was diced and cooked, and, anyway, didn't have enough salty punch to play off against the floury blandness of the beans. Sausage, not steak, is what's called for here. As for the corn, well, even off-season corn is pretty tasty mixed with oil and vinegar, and makes a good combo with the shell beans. It's a nice dish, worth interrupting the murders for.

Still, you have to wonder how well the food fits in the book. The purpose of the scene, after all, is not to teach a recipe but to paint a mood—to show the lonely Spenser as somehow more modern, broader in interests and resources, than lonely city detectives in fiction often are. Down these mean streets walks a man with a recipe in his head. What the reader recalls, though, is not the setting but the dish. Should the food come off the page onto the plate quite so readily, overwhelming the atmosphere, and does this indicate that there is something subtly off, nonfunctional, about the presence of elaborate food-making in fiction?

Rising to a higher level of culinary ambition, I went on to

make, the following night, a fish-stew recipe, a kind of English bouillabaisse, from Ian McEwan's superb *Saturday:* Henry Perowne, the central character, a neurosurgeon, cooks this elaborate dish as he watches "monstrous and spectacular scenes" on television. Henry, though confessedly inexpert, is a convincing home cook; he admits that he belongs to the chuck-it-in school, the hearty school of throwing ingredients together in a pot—he likes the "relative imprecision and lack of discipline." In the passage I was following, he makes a tomato-and-fish stock for his stew, and, at the same time, starts prepping the rest. He "empties several dried red chillies from a pot and crushes them between his hands and lets the flakes fall with their seeds into the onions and garlic," before adding "pinches of saffron, some bay leaves, orange-peel gratings, oregano, five anchovy fillets, two tins of peeled tomatoes." Then he takes some mussels from a string bag, throws those, with the skeletons of three skates, into a stockpot, and tips some Sancerre into the tomato sauce. Meanwhile, he readies monkfish, slicing tails into chunks, a few more mussels, and, finally, some clams and prawns. All the while, he is watching on the mostly muted television the run-up to the Iraq war—marchers in London, Colin Powell at the U.N.—and brooding on life in our time.

McEwan is obviously painting a picture of *l'homme bourgeois* as he is today, his hands filled with fish, his mind with intimations of terror. (McEwan really is serving this dish to his readers; a revised version of the recipe is right there on his Web site.) It's a tribute to McEwan's powers of persuasion that the scene would never work that way in reality. You can't idly make a bouillabaisse while you brood on modern life any more than you can idly make a cassoulet; these are nerve-wracking concoctions. The mussels, which Henry drops into his stock straight from a string bag, need at a minimum to be spray-washed, and probably cleaned and checked for those obscene little beards they have. European mussels have fewer of these, it's true—more like soul patches. (Later on, Henry scrubs the mussels, but he seems to be doing it absentmindedly, and you can't do it absentmindedly.) The fish needs to be taken from its wrappings and washed; and then how fine do you chop the garlic, and are you sure the alcohol has boiled off from the wine? The "orange-peel gratings" are a story in themselves, since all the experts insist that you avoid getting any white pith in with them, and this is about as difficult as writing a villanelle. (It doesn't actually matter much, but they say that it does.) Worse than that, having crushed a "handful" of those little dried peppers between your fingers means that you have to wash your hands instantly, with soap, since nothing is more common among home cooks like Henry than wiping a tear from your eye while chopping the onions, your hand still contaminated by hot pepper, with horrific results.

While you are doing all this, I was reminded as I did it, you are thinking about the bouillabaisse, not about life in our time. Or, rather, you are not thinking about the bouillabaisse, or about anything: you are making the bouillabaisse. And here, I suspect, lies the difficulty with using cooking as the stock for the stream-of-consciousness stew. It is that the act of cooking is an escape from consciousness—the nearest thing that the nonspiritual modern man and woman have to Zen meditation; its effect is to reduce us to a state of absolute awareness, where we are here now of necessity. You can't cook with the news on and still listen to it, any more than you can write with the news on and still listen to it. You can cook with music, or talk radio, on, and drift in and out. What you can't do is think and cook, because cooking takes the place of thought. (You can daydream and cook, but you can't advance a chain of sustained reflections.)

The recipes in these books are not, of course, meant to be cooked; they have literary purposes, and one of them is to represent the background of thought. Every age finds an activity that can take place while a character is meditating; the activity surrounds and halos the meditation. In Victorian fiction, it is walking; the character takes a long walk from Little Tipping to Old Stornsbury and, on the way, decides to propose, convert, escape, or run for office. But the walk as meditational setting and back-drop came to an end with Joyce and Woolf, who made whole walking books. In recent American fiction, driving was recessive enough to do the job; in Updike and Ann Beattie, characters in cars are always doing the kind of thinking that Pip and Phineas Finn used to do on walks. Driving and walking, however, do seem to be natural "background" actions. But you cannot have characters thinking while cooking; the activity is not a place for thought but in place of thought.

We need these devices in books, because we do not, in life, think our thoughts over time. Since our real mental life is made in tiny flashes in the midst of our routines, we have to stretch it out, taffy-like, in literature to cover a span of time worthy of it. If we accurately represented our mental life as it takes place—sudden impulses on the way to the washroom, a spasm of neurons unleashed over coffee—no one would believe it. Consciousness is not a stream but a still lock that suddenly drops into little water-falls. The lengthy descriptions of cooking that we find in modern literature are a way of artfully representing, rather than actually reproducing, our mental life—a modeled illusion, rather than a snapshot of the thing.

So no matter how much cooking a novel contains, in the end it goes back to being a book, as all books will. Even cookbooks are finally more book than they are cook, and, more and more, we know it: for every novel that contains a recipe, there is now a recipe book meant to be read as a novel. When we read, in the great French chef Alain Ducasse's recent *Culinary Encyclopedia,* a recipe for Colonna-bacon-barded thrush breasts, with giblet can-apés, on a porcini-mushroom marmalade, we know that we are not seriously expected to cook this; rather, we are to admire, over and over, the literary skill, the metaphysical poetry, required to bring these improbable things together. You and I are not about

to cook thrush breasts with a porcini-mushroom marmalade—
Alain Ducasse is not about to cook them, either—any more than
we are about to throw ourselves under the train with Anna or
sleep with Madame Bovary.

The secret consolation may be that it works the other way
around as well. The space between imaginary food in books and
real food is the space where reading happens. The people we
encounter in novels are ultimately mere recipes, too—so many
eyes, so many bright teeth, so many repeated tics and characteriz-
ing mannerisms—and we accept that we cannot perfectly reproduce them, either. Our mental picture of Henry Perowne, like
our mental picture of Lady Glencora Palliser, is as hard-won as
the bouillabaisse from *Saturday*, as vague in critical aspects and as
likely to vary from maker to maker, from reader to reader. (The
characters in Flaubert are like the recipes in Escoffier; we are surprised to see how much is left out.) We read about Cabourg in
Proust, and are unprepared for what we find when we actually
get there. The act of reading is always a matter of a task begun
as much as of a message understood, something that begins on
a flat surface, counter or page, and then gets stirred and chopped
and blended until what we make, in the end, is a dish, or story,
all our own.

13

What Do We Imagine When We Imagine Food?

THERE ARE two schools of good writing about food: the mock-epic and the mystical microcosmic. The mock-epic (A. J. Liebling, Calvin Trillin, the French writer Robert Courtine, and any good restaurant critic) is essentially comic and treats the small ambitions of the greedy eater as though they were big and noble, spoofing the idea of the heroic while raising the minor subject to at least temporary greatness. The mystical microcosmic, of which Elizabeth David and M.F.K. Fisher and Elizabeth Pennell are the masters, is the more modern school, essentially poetic, and turns every remembered recipe into a meditation on hunger and the transience of its fulfillment.

The two styles can't be mixed. If we are reading, say, about Liebling's quest for the secret of how *rascasse* are used in bouillabaisse, we don't want to be stopped to consider the melancholy lives of the remote fishermen who seek them out. And if we are reading David's or Fisher's sad thoughts on the love that got away or the plate that time forgot, we would hate to find, on the next page, the writer handing out peppy stars in modish kitchens. (The same thing is true of sportswriting: we go to it for either W. C. Heinz's tears or Jim Murray's jokes, Gary Smith's epics or

Roy Blount Jr.'s yarns, which suggests that, with the minor arts, our approach is classical and depends on unity of tone.)

The two styles, as we've seen, lie all the way back there, in the two first food writers. Brillat-Savarin was the founder of the microcosmic school, and his genius lay in his smiling sincerity; His contemporary Grimod created the mock-epic; his genius lay in his bitter wit. Since their day those two styles have dominated the world of food. (Bitter wit is more fun than smiling sincerity, but hard to build a world on.)

So when we read books about food we struggle to decide which school we're reading. In *The Perfectionist: Life and Death in Haute Cuisine,* Rudolph Chelminski's biography of the doomed three-star chef Bernard Loiseau, for instance, the story of Loiseau's restless search for a way to transform cauliflower from a discouraging vegetable into a radiant side dish by caramelizing it, we smile at first, thinking ourselves in the presence of the old mock-epic. It is, after all, only caramelized cauliflower. As the search picks up momentum and intensity, however, and we learn how Loiseau began to blanch and strain and purée, we start to succumb to the grandeur of the quest and think the story is microcosmic. Why should the search for caramelized cauliflower be any less significant than Ad Reinhardt's search for the pure-black painting, or John Cage's for pure silence? But then when we read that Loiseau committed suicide after his caramelized cauliflower failed to impress his critics, we rebel again, in shock. It was, after all, only caramelized cauliflower.

Loiseau seems likely to become a mordant icon of the eternal war between critics and cooks. He has a moving story to tell, with universal implications: the downfall of the artist through perfectionism and paranoia. Loiseau suffered throughout his life from a too-late-identified bipolar disorder, a syndrome that ought to be known by its old French name, *folie circulaire.* It's a syndrome that can strike truck drivers and Zen monks as easily as cooks, so any general principles should be taken with caution.

Still, Loiseau, if not typical, is in many ways exemplary of the chef's dilemma.

Loiseau was a member of perhaps the last generation of artists who were true to an ideal and a practice that had begun in the nineteenth century. He learned to cook as an intern in the kitchen of the Frères Troisgros, near Lyon, where he mastered the terrifying discipline by chopping onions and filleting fish for twelve hours a day; he even learned to kill frogs by slapping their heads casually against the kitchen table. The Troisgros kitchen opened every door in those days, and in the early seventies Loiseau, with almost no other apprenticeship, made a name for himself doing simple country cooking at a glorified bistro just outside Paris. He was financed by a shrewd promoter named Claude Verger, who saw that elemental food could be popular and still presented to the critics as something new: a variant of nouvelle cuisine.

That it was simple and not genuinely new does not mean that it was without value; no one had been cooking that way with passion or conviction for a while. Calling plain cooking high cooking was in itself a radical act. Loiseau became a star, and, with money advanced by Verger, he bought La Côte d'Or, a famous old restaurant in the Burgundy town of Saulieu. In the dense, deep-eating days of gratins and casseroles, the place had once held three stars in the Michelin Red Guide; by sheer effort, Loiseau built it back up, and the reader cheers with him when he finally gets his three stars, in 1991.

The trouble was that there was no reason to go to Saulieu except to eat, and this made Loiseau particularly, even uniquely, vulnerable to the Guide and its system of stars and inspectors. The Guide no longer had an easy or organic relation to French cooking. The Red Guide grew up with the automobile, and with the idea of the long journey away from Paris that required several stops for lunches and dinners. By the 1980s, though, the new autoroutes and the high-speed trains (and the planes, racing over) had reduced the need for road stops. The Michelin inspectors, gloomy middle-aged men eating alone, used to be indistinguishable from the other gloomy middle-aged men eating alone, and their stars were a kind of summary of the opinions of all those tired traveling professionals. Now all that's left of this once self-evident system is the inspectors, dining alone and passing out stars. People do not drive by the restaurant and stop to eat; they drive to the restaurant and stop for a three-star meal. To be a destination is a difficult trade: it is nice to run a place where the food, in the famous phrase, is worth a journey; hard to keep it going when the only reason anyone makes the journey is to eat the food.

Loiseau was terrified of losing his stars, particularly when François Simon, of *Le Figaro*, hinted that La Côte d'Or was on its way down. The chef may have been paranoid in this, but he was hardly alone. All artists in all fields despise all critics all the time. (They may like the individual critic, but they despise his conviction that he has a right to criticize.) Still, there are levels of loathing, as there are circles in Hell. Writers at least recognize that the critic is a writer, and shares a table, if not an agent. Magicians, on the extreme edge, despair of those outside their circle ever knowing the difference between a trick that anyone can buy for six dollars and sleight of hand that only two people have learned in six years. Chefs are close to magicians in their certainty that their critics cannot tell the difference between something that takes time, thought, and talent and something that dazzles only by surprise, perversity, and snob appeal. But, even more than magicians, chefs depend on the good opinion of those whose opinions they cannot think are worth having—and the nature of Loiseau's cooking left him open to the exhaustion of critics.

Chelminski points out that food critics are even more inclined than other kinds to fatigue. Most food critics are sick of eating rich, expensive food and will do almost anything to have something new; a perfectly prepared veal chop (one of Loiseau's elemental specialties) first gets a smile, and then a yawn. But

Loiseau, his biographer admits, was at an edge of simplicity so extreme that it hinted at innocence. (Chelminski suggests that Loiseau's training was short on fundamentals; he was notorious among his staff for being unable to make even basic sauces.) Famous for the purity of his approach, Loiseau deglazed his pans with water instead of wine or even stock. It was admirably minimal, but it also tended to be oddly ascetic and depressing; the elemental and the elegant are sisters, but not twins. Loiseau had no hesitation about publishing a recipe for John Dory served with a purée made of boiled celery. (It seems so simple that one is convinced that it must be mysteriously great; I have made it, and it tastes like fish with boiled celery purée.)

Loiseau, it now seems, thrived briefly at a short, fundamentalist moment in the history of cooking, just between the Protestant Reformation of nouvelle cuisine and the rococo Counter-Reformation of today's *cuisine tendance* ("trendy cooking," though "speculative cooking" might be a better name), the kind of ostrich-tongue-with-rutabaga-foam-and-Jurassic-salt-on-a-stick cooking that unites Ferran Adrià, of elBulli; the Californian Thomas Keller, of the French Laundry; and New York's own Wylie Dufresne, of wd-50.

Yet Loiseau is hard not to love. He was, like everyone, a casualty of history and his own demons; but he was also, as Chelminski insists, a perfectionist, for whom the disapproval of a single diner was almost impossible to accept, which is what makes his story heartbreaking and instantly understandable. "Why didn't he like it?" he would moan inconsolably when one of a hundred diners sent a dish back unfinished. The chef's life is a long struggle with the reality that tastes differ, and tastes change. The mutability of taste is a truth chefs live with every night.

And the Loiseau example suggests that the divide between the mock-epic and the microcosmic schools expresses an even simpler divide between the way critics and cooks experience food. The diner experiences it as a form of comedy and the cook experiences it as a form of work. (The cook's recompense for not having fun—for those hours and hours of life spent chopping onions—is a sense of soul and of significance.) One goes for pleasure and believes in his right to mock and have fun; the other cooks in desperate exhaustion and believes in his right to a livelihood.

Ruth Reichl's *Garlic and Sapphires: The Secret Life of a Critic in Disguise,* a memoir of her time in the hottest of critical hot seats in America, that of restaurant critic of *The New York Times,* tells the story from the other side of the mirror. Her book would make a terrific romantic comedy, if Lubitsch or Billy Wilder were alive or if Nora Ephron wanted to make it. Reichl, in order to conceal her identity from the restaurant people who were desperate for her good opinion, dined in disguise throughout her five years at the *Times,* not merely wearing wigs and dark glasses but actually creating and inhabiting whole alternative characters: a chorine called Chloe, a sad *Glass Menagerie*–type lady called Molly, and even a motherly type, homey and sensible. A Method critic, she came to live these characters: they wrote the reviews. In the movie of her life, of course, the hard-eating, Falstaffian R. W. Apple, Jr., character would hate her in her fussy office identity as a "nouvelle" eater, and fall for her in one of her disguises in the restaurant. (There is even a wisecracking, snooty but winning friend—obviously the Stockard Channing role—who has to be converted to the merits of sushi.)

What makes Reichl's book genuinely touching is that—in a plangent complication—she sees herself first of all as a cook, and seems to identify secretly with her targets. Compelled by admirable maternal instincts, within a two-career marriage, to take her son from one overpriced, overwrought restaurant meal to another, she convincingly suggests that the restaurant critic's life is an ordeal; the recipes she inserts in the text (leg of lamb, *matzo brei*) seem to be intended as oases of sense in the midst of all this madness, and as signs of her real identity, as a cook.

At the same time, the book is wonderfully revealing about the double consciousness of the critic. Although pain-giving herself (and she likes to read "delightful" pans of restaurants), she is sensitive about criticism of her own criticism, and spends time collating phone messages for and against, walking the streets with anxiety when her first review comes out as she waits to hear what the bosses think. (Critics never allow these two parts of their brain to communicate, or stop to think that the pain you take, as the Beatles might say, is equal to the pain you make.) The back-and-forth between the soulful stuff that she writes about her family and the sometimes surprisingly catty stuff that she writes about her working life (she is not particularly kind about her editors at the *Times*) is conscious, certainly, but also deeply felt. You think, She really didn't like the gig.

There is a moment when, after she reviews Le Cirque, she walks back to her childhood neighborhood, reconnecting with what actually made food into a significant thing for her. She clearly feels that there is something ignoble, or at least remote from her original infatuation, in sending expense-account diners off to this or that French temple. This is the lesson critics learn the hard way, and we are as relieved as she is when she is at last set free and gets a job as editor of the magazine *Gourmet*. She is tired, we know, of eating in disguise, when what she really wants is to be cooking for her family out in the open.

Reichl, after all her experience, compares the restaurant world of New York to a theater, with the diners and critics merely players in it. But everything can be described in terms of performance and theatricality; all the world's a stage. Surely it is identity politics, rather than just playacting, that is at stake in costly dining out. All those people waiting in line at Le Cirque are not waiting for their selves to be lost or exchanged; they are waiting to be affirmed, even enhanced, and they do it even at the risk of humiliation. Not "Enter and become another!" but "You belong here" is what we want the maître d' to tell us. (And the illusion that we want the chef to give us is not "I work for you" but "I feed you from love.")

This affirmation, it seems, is easier to get than we might think. Steven A. Shaw is identified by his publishers as a former attorney who began a second career as a food and restaurant critic in 1997. He has a book called *Turning the Tables: Restaurants from the Inside Out,* which attempts to show you how not to be intimidated or overwhelmed when dining out: he wants you to be an expert at eating in restaurants, even as the author is an expert on eating in restaurants. This seems a queer expertise, a self-evident specialization, but he does give much sound, neighborly advice on getting reservations (just humble yourself to the person who answers the phone, and someday the table, like your prince, will come) and some sane if fairly obvious counsel: "Understanding one's own preferences and needs, as well as those of your dining companions, is foundational to making good restaurant choices."

He is briskly tough, though, and quite courageous in his assaults on the *Times'* reviewing. The whole elaborate, boastful rigmarole of disinterestedness and disguise celebrated in Reichl's book he sees not as honest but as ignorant and provincial, common sense clouded over by fear—as though restaurants were there to scam you. He insists that the food in the kitchen is, of necessity, the food that gets served to everyone, critic or yokel (and the few exceptions are those restaurants where contempt for the paying customers is apparently part of the charm, as at Le Cirque). There is no more need for the elaborate masks of the restaurant critic than there is for the art critic Robert Hughes to go to a museum in a Groucho Marx nose and glasses. A good critic can't be fooled. The best that the critic can hope for is to be treated as a friend of the house, but all you have to do to become a friend of the house, Shaw says, is to be one. Restaurants are businesses before they are anything else. Dine twice a week at Le Bernardin, the thought is, and you will magically have the table you want at Le Bernardin. This is only partly true; the known critic gets sent out far more plates and extras and desserts than you or I do, and often far more than he knows what to do with. (I once ate with a very fine chef who had the habit of sending out extra plates to friends at his own place. When the chef at the place where we were eating kept sending out extra plates to him, he said, finally, "You know, it never occurred to me before how annoying this is. You're forcing people to eat things they weren't in the mood for and then to make a big show of appreciating them.")

Shaw, it emerges, is a rare thing, a food writer who identifies not with cook or critic but with the restaurant owner, whose struggles and exasperations he admires and sympathizes with. (Please call to cancel that reservation, he urges.) He wishes that restaurant critics, instead of skulking around cross-dressing and pretending to be called Marmeluke, would, like critics in other fields, be "champions of excellence who promote the best . . . while exposing the worst." But, of course, all those other critics, though rarely dressed up in wigs and makeup (or dressed at all, for that matter), are notoriously irascible, tendentious, bad-tempered observers who like nothing more than settling old scores, indulging eccentric prejudices, and using someone else's table or text as an occasion to riff on their own obsessions. Critics cannot be made responsible any more than chefs can be made calm; it is the occupational disease. The real use for the food critic's disguises, anyway, one suspects, is not as a form of espionage but as a form of armor: it is not we who are protected from getting a false impression but the critic who is protected from violating the most primal of all taboos—being publicly ungrateful to someone who has shared his food with you. (If it wasn't really you, then you weren't really ungrateful.)

From these practical essentials, it is a pleasure to move to the world of encyclopedic knowledge. The encyclopedia form, of brief and then longer bursts of pure weird data, only just touched by the spry hand of commentary, is irresistible, and alphabetical organization, being both hyperorderly and completely random, is irresistible, too. In the extraordinary new *Oxford Encyclopedia of Food and Drink in America,* edited by Andrew F. Smith, the dour history of Pizza Hut abides near the basic conundrum of Plates, which nestles beside the joys of Plums, while a neat, disabused bit on the Politics of Food in America gives way to the fun of Pomegranates and Popcorn, before the social historian resumes his seat with a history of Popeye's Chicken & Biscuits. Anyone who can put it down is unburdened by curiosity about anything. Through its countless entries, two stories emerge. First, of the overwhelming abundance of the American larder, and how capitalism has struggled to enlarge and exploit it, and, second, of how the Protestant tradition of making people feel guilty about eating well—expressed in fad diets, health scares, and so on—has been balanced by the Protestant tradition of making people feel guilty for not eating well, expressed in cooking lessons, recipe books, and the growth of a huge industry of food writing meant for home cooks. One has only to compare Ducasse's *Culinary Encyclopedia* to see what can be made elsewhere of the same idea. Ducasse's encyclopedia consists not of entries on food but of pictures of and recipes for good things to eat. Under "P," we get a picture of simmered suckling-pig chops and feet with porcini-mushroom polenta in a sage sauce, and the recipe. Even for a good cook the dishes are essentially unrealizable, but that does not alter their encyclopedic significance: images of Heaven are painted to encourage you to go there, not to help you build it in your backyard. At the opposite pole lies Denise Gigante's *Taste: A Literary History,* which takes food and eating as a metaphor for Western experience. Gigante's is the kind of book that one can mock with ease and imitate at peril: "If we approach Wordsworth's concept of feeding through the mechanics of assimilation, as described in Romantic *Naturphilosophie,* we find that the feeding mind naturally exists in a precarious state of tension with its own abjected matter," and so on. But it makes an arresting point: the model of food as a metaphor for pleasure is balanced uneasily between the mouth and the anus, between taste that urges us on and the excrement ("abjected matter") that food becomes. The larger argument is that the bourgeois age of the restaurant was born of (or accompanied by; it is sometimes hard to be sure which) an aesthetic shift, vast in scope and incarnated by the poets, in which the old attempt to banish excrement from the discourse of appetite by emphasizing the purity of the eater was overtaken by an aesthetic in which the reality of digestion was accepted and made part of the acceptable way in which people thought and talked about life. Appetite need be neither indulged nor suppressed—it could be modified, by that very thing called "taste." Gigante has a nice section on Charles Lamb in which she shows how, in his famous essay on roasted pig, he invented a comic but still largely melancholic, elegiac tone with which to write about eating.

Gigante is surely right that eating, along with seeing, provides the most universal of all metaphors of value: along with the sensations of light and dark, which properly belong to painting, the perception of sweet and bitter is the most natural of all natural metaphors. The metaphors of taste are so basic that they imbue and infiltrate our entire experience, and we no longer think of them as metaphors.

With no other crafted thing is the line between sensation and meaning quite so quickly crossed, quite so easily extended from something felt to something known, as with food. The tongue has no sooner said "Sweet" than the heart says "Home!" All art, it has been said, aspires to the condition of music. But we want some of our art to aspire to the condition of background music. What makes Mozart, Vivaldi, the Beatles, essential to our lives? Is it the hours we spend with scores on our knees, listening in the dark? Or the hours and hours and hours we spend with them just on, wrapped around our lives—giving them some emotion to organize that they, miraculously, do? What makes van Gogh's stars and cypresses or Botticelli's faces so dear to our existence: the minutes we spend footsore, staring at them on a once-in-a-lifetime trip, or the glimpses on posters and in books and postcards that fill the corners of our eyes and lives? Good cooking is beloved because, when it is good enough, it gives more immediate pleasure and then recedes more rapidly, more gracefully, into the metaphoric middle distance than any other cultural thing, letting us arrange our lives, at least for one night, around it. The metaphors of food are so closely tied to our sensations that they must be elevated to ring out. That would explain why good food writing, by cook or critic, has been so expansive in theme. This largeness of vision ("I write of hunger," Fisher said flatly, when tasked with writing about food) seems to have become harder to achieve, perhaps because the subject has become so specialized.

There is too much food in most food writing now—too much food and too little that goes further. When Liebling and Fisher wrote, they gestured from plate and glass to something bigger, outside the dining room—to France, or to appetite itself—and the gesture carried instantly, because there was little else in the room to absorb it. These days, the old twin circles (the family around the table, the cosmos beyond) have been supplemented by so many other circles of attitude that the writer points from the plate to—another writer. Like so many other subjects, food writing is constricted within these ever-tighter circles of opinion, when what we want from it is ever-broadening metaphors of common life. Metaphor is social and shares the table with the objects it intertwines and the attitudes it reconciles. Opinion, like the Michelin inspector, dines alone.

14

E-MAIL TO ELIZABETH PENNELL:
Rice, Milk, Sugar

Dear Liz:

All these recipes! All this time. I was feeling a bit, well,
unmanned, reduced, by the practice of writing down recipes,
no matter how delicious they might seem or how much one
could defend the practice—insufficiently testicular, to use the
word with which Lane Coutell offends Franny Glass in *Franny
and Zooey*—and so I bought Keith Richards' autobiography,
wittily entitled *Life*, to read. I am a keen Stones fan, who begins
each day with a piece of "Get Yer Ya-Ya's Out," but . . . could
I explain British R & B to you, Elizabeth, modern woman you
may be, but still a woman of the nineteenth century? A defining feature of my time, and your adopted country, it seems to
escape prediction and explanation. You see, Elizabeth, in about
fifty years, poorer English boys from the London suburbs—the
ones with the lunatic asylums—will listen to recordings of
American Negroes, and try to imitate them as closely as they
can, and these imitations, heavily amplified, will become the
most popular music in the world. And then they will move right
around the corner from you; Keith's home, through his druggy

London years, will be in Cheyne Walk, the very heart of the Chelsea-Whistler country!

Oh. Rather like . . . rather like minstrel music? I hear you ask. Well, yes and no, I reply—yes, in that they're imitating the sound, no, because it's serious and sexual and admiring. Anyway, I keep an electric guitar tuned to an "open G," Keith's favorite, and strum through it, searching for those voicings, the dumb revelation that most of what seems mysterious and beautiful— from Stones riffs to béarnaise sauce—is just a matter of breaking it down and learning the technique. The tuning matters even more than the technique, and I wonder if that isn't true of cooking as well. The tuning is just the base of what you do—the eggs you buy, the fishmonger, the thing itself—and with every good cook I've known, the sound is like that: a good tuning and a resonant drone, a fine fish and a favorite spice.

In any case, I thought to myself, well, Keith Richards, *there's* the man, be more like him; utterly forgiven, no matter what he says or does—women are all bitches, and gay people are poofters, and no one is indignant or offended, because we all make up the rules by which we are to be judged in advance. Declare yourself irresponsible when you begin to act, and all will be forgiven when you are. In this case, the book, crafted as a celebration of living on the edge, is in fact on every page a testimonial to the privileges of money and fame. Each time poor Keith is about to be arrested for drug possession (of which he is, like it or not, always guilty), he is saved by a lawyer or hyperwealthy fan (or the father of a groupie) who intervenes on his behalf. . . . Well, okay. He's still a wonderful guitarist. (The funniest and most telling remark in the book concerns his band-mate Ronnie Wood. After detailing Wood's many long periods of crack addiction, and his many efforts in rehab to get free from them, Keith concludes, "To be honest, it didn't make much difference. He was about the same both ways." Thus the epitaph on all artistic addictions.)

But after all the heroin and the cocaine and the general sense of a man nodding off in space, what really gets Keith alight, what does he end up caring about most? Yes, he devotes a few glancing evocative paragraphs to guitar playing, the technique of the blues, a few words to warn against freebasing. But what is the *one thing* that he offers in carefully itemized detail? The one thing that he offers with real zing and passion? His recipes! His favorite food! His own ways of making shepherd's pie and bangers and mash—which he reproduces right there in the book alongside his tales of scoring heroin on the Riviera. How you should get bangers made fresh—presumably a challenge in Connecticut, where he lives, though God knows there's probably a chic pork store in Greenwich by now—and then, interesting point, this, that you should put the sausages cold into the frying pan, and then slowly turn up the heat. Rather an English approach, but still, okay, and there's something nice about the way he implies his mashed potatoes but doesn't feel it necessary to *explain* his mashed potatoes. His shepherd's pie, ground meat and more of those mashed potatoes, sounds very good—and, as a true food lover will, he insists that the key moment is the moment when you plunge the knife into the shepherd's pie. The aroma, not the dish, fulfills the appetite. So the attempt to run away from food to something more obviously *male,* rock and roll, leads us inevitably and inescapably . . . back to food. If Keith writes down recipes for his readers, we can *all* write down recipes. And with it share the strong, intelligent realization that it is the first cut of the shepherd's pie that makes the pie—that is the *point* of the pie.

And then—there is a connection here, trust me—the point that Keith makes about his distinctive open-G tuning is that it's a drone tuning, a folk tuning—that one steady note, the G, buzzing in the background even as the rest of the chords mark the changes. (And he makes the musically alert point that Vivaldi and Mozart write this way, too, in reverse, with the steady unchanging note up in the treble.) Would you agree with me that the folk tuning of food, the open-G tuning, is rice pudding? Everywhere you go in the food world, there is a rice pudding playing somewhere in the background, droning a little sweet and nubbly number behind everything more ambitious that goes on. If you go out for Indian food, you can rely on a rice pudding; if you go for Italian, or Greek, there is at least a pudding made with rice. In every culture and every country, as Elisabeth Luard's lovely book *Sacred Food* demonstrates, some mix of rice and milk (or coconut milk) and vanilla (or cardamom) and sugar (or honey) is the drone sound of the table. And this sweet, this pudding, is almost always part of rites of passage, of weddings and christenings and funerals, gifts to the gods and rites of the elders. There seems to be something close to a natural magnetism between rice and ritual, most familiar to us in the habit of throwing rice at weddings (and leading to Woody Allen's perfect one-liner about the wedding where the bride was pregnant and everyone threw puffed rice). And what's more, just as Keith says about open-G tuning—that it lets you add stray extra notes to the chords, so that in every G there's a touch of A; in every B dominant seventh, a little hint of E minor—is true of pudding-making, too. A certain sloppy elegance is necessary in both rock guitar and rice desserts.

I make three rice puddings, and each one has a savor and meaning particular to itself. The first and in some ways the simplest, and in some ways my favorite, is the baked-custard rice pudding my mother used to make. I'm not sure where she learned it—and I know that I could answer that question with a phone call, but somehow making that phone call turns recollection into an interview—but it's simple and perfect. You take two cups of cooked rice, left over from the night before, most often (and I often don't oversalt the rice so that it works for the next-day pudding), put it in an ovenproof dish, and then make a simple custard alongside—say, six cups of milk, five eggs, two-thirds of a cup of sugar—which you beat together and heat until it's almost scalded but not yet thickened. Then you just pour it over the rice, add some black raisins, and bake for about an hour at around 350°. Oh, and sprinkle some cinnamon on top when you put it in. You take it out when a knife comes out almost dry. (Almost dry—it's one of those cooking terms, like "about to boil," that are unknowable regions that everyone is thought to know.) The thing that I think is nicest about this pudding is what the kids don't like: the rice and raisins settle down sweetly on the bottom of the pudding cup, while the rich but simple custard sits on top. It's really a two-layer pudding, a sort of wholesome *pousse-café*. I love this effect, but it is, I will admit, antipudding in conception, since a platonic pudding is one in which everything is evenly mixed. For children, the promise of a pudding is that there will be no unpleasant surprises.

So the second pudding I make, most often with Olivia, is one that solves this problem by mixing things all together and smooth. I add Indian spices, too. You just make your rice on the stovetop with coconut milk instead of water, and then you make a simple crème anglaise, a stovetop custard: six egg yolks, four cups of milk, into which you place four to eight crushed cardamom pods. You mix the coconut rice into the cardamom custard, sprinkle on cinnamon, and let it cool.

My trouble with this one is that whenever I make a crème anglaise it never gets quite custardy enough. My friend Peter Hoffman suggested working with a candy thermometer, so that I'll know when it's at 165°. That helps, though not always and not enough. The curdles come. So I add to the custard . . . a bit of liquefied cornstarch. That *always* works. Cornstarch and gelatin, the two thickeners of an earlier age, have more going for them than we quite allow. Cornstarch is also, along with Karo syrup and condensed milk, one of the three bashful but beautiful sweet ingredients. What can improve on a pecan pie made with Karo dark syrup, or on a chocolate fudge sauce made with its lighter brother? And is there anything better than a key lime pie made with condensed milk and a graham-cracker crust? And a butterscotch pudding made with cornstarch and burnt brown sugar has a depth of flavor that few Sauternes can equal. Sweet is simple, emotionally and practically.

More than any dessert I know—more than any soufflé, or molten cake—this rice pudding seems to delight the crowds, and what's more, it appears to be sophisticated work. I suppose the blend of cardamom and coconut gives a misleading impression of premeditation. (Obviously, this would not be the case in India.)

My third rice pudding hails from Paris, and is a variant of the *riz au lait* that is such a standard dessert there. It isn't quite like Greek-coffee-shop rice pudding, that New York staple, which is just a mix of rice and milk and sugar and vanilla, with, let it be said, cornstarch added. This one does something a little more ingenious than most recipes, which are really just marriages of milk and rice cooked slowly so that the rice soaks up the milk and the natural starch in the rice does the work of thickening. In this one, you make that kind of *riz au lait*—you know, Elizabeth, it's so simple that it's embarrassing to reci-petize it; you just make sweet milky rice by simmering them together. The only trick is not to let it get *too* dry. Then you beat by hand a cup and a half of cream till it's whipped but not quite in that stiff form, and you blend the sweet rice in with the whipped cream and then—this is important—pour it into a narrowish mold and let it refrigerate for quite a while, so that it stiffens up even more.

And once again, it suggests the magic of rice pudding: it overwhelms people, delights them, makes them smile and feel part of some peasant ritual, some rite of passage, even if the ceremony is only a midweek dinner. This is especially true if you serve either the Indian or the French rice pudding with little pots of extras: cherry jam, or dried apricots poached in white wine, something nice. It gives the whole thing a sense of unearned splendor, like listening to Keith play the opening riff of "Start Me Up" and then realizing that it's just a bar chord and a simple minor seventh shape, up and down the neck of the guitar, simplicity itself, with the recklessness of true simplicity.

Why does rice pudding, in any of its forms, have this ritual resonance? The answer, I think, lies simply in the slowness of its achievement. Eggs are little miracles; one minute slime, the next a meal. Meats are primal. But a rice pudding develops in slow and gradual stages—not even stages, *phases,* a slow and gradual field, passing from inedible hard grains and unpalatable raw eggs and milk to some combined, involved, semisoupy, semicereal, sweet and starchy but both at once delight. Rice pudding is like life: it's hard at first, gradually thickens, and ends well enough to make you wish you could have it again. No wonder we use it to mark life passages.

Yet I know, know deep down, that Keith would like these puddings. And your friend Whistler? Ah, Whistler would best like the baked one my mother does, which would remind him of his student days at West Point, of his youth in America, of his mother, too—who, we know, sits in her chair, patiently, while her brilliant boy paints her portrait, and thinks of what she will cook for him when he is done at last.

All best,
Adam

PART IV

Leaving the Table

THE SAVORY, serious part of the meal is over, and the talk is settling, and then—what happens? The sweet comes out, which some of the diners (the women, as it happens, most often) refuse to eat, and others relish. And there is a last drink, perhaps, and at home people begin to look at their watches (and the hosts longingly at the door), while in the restaurant the weary waiters begin to stack tables and pointedly if politely ask if you will be wanting anything more. At that moment, the bill to pay, the thanks to be offered ("It was absolutely wonderful!"—the degree of hysterical affirmation usually in direct reverse proportion to the degree of pleasure really taken), some sense of summary, of finish, even, perhaps, of a moral, is sought by those who came to the table. They want, it seems, something to take home....

15

Paris at Last

I WORRY about French food in the new age of spices and world cooking, as one might worry about English damp in the age of global warming, or about Canadian civility under the stress of imported talk radio. Something that one just took for granted as a fixed feature of the world suddenly seems fragile and fugitive, even ailing—even, perhaps, on its way out.

Having written about the crisis in French food early on, I suppose I always secretly assumed that French cooking would snap right out of it, the way that North American ice hockey did under the stress of Russian competition. The internal resources of France for cooking were so deep-seated, so powerfully entrenched, so much a part of the logic and wit of French life, that the narrowness and stultified repetition that had overcome so much French cooking seemed sure to end simply with a renewed act of will. Since no one can be more willful than a French chef, it seemed to me merely a matter of time and timing before the inevitable opening-out would take place. A new Robuchon, a next generation Ducasse would seize, say, on North African spices as Carême had once seized on the herbs of Provence—and French cooking would be reborn.

Yet though I would still rather eat in Paris than anywhere else in the world—eating, once again, is a social act before it is a purely sensory one; it calls on our moral taste more than our measuring tongue, and my own moral taste still leads me back inexorably to the wit and intelligence of French civilization—I recognize that the rebirth has not happened, that the crisis I identified, only half-playfully, a decade or more ago is more entrenched now than it was then, and that fewer and fewer people who care about cooking now think of France as first among all others.

And still we go on searching for signs of life. New generations of bistros open, and though they seem more tense than tempting—the demands of French labor laws often lead to the smaller restaurants' being staffed by an overstressed spouse and an overworked staff—I try them, and cheer. New geniuses are announced and sometimes even new guides are published, and of all of these the most "mediatized," as the French say, and at the same time the most puzzling, is certainly the food guide published by the group that calls itself, with deliberate insolence, Le Fooding. (The insolence lies in using an English word.)

I suppose I would have an easier time deciding if Le Fooding is going to be able to accomplish all that it has set out to accomplish—which is nothing less than to do the whole of the job that needs to be done, to save the preeminence of French cuisine from going the way of the Roman Empire, the five-act tragedy, and the ocean liner—if I had an easier time defining what it is and what its principles at bottom truly *are*. That it is a phenomenon is beyond dispute, its success having reached the point where the French daily *Figaro* announced, last summer, that French food is now divided into two families, each with its own public and cultural identity: "On the one side, Michelin, with its century of cultural expertise; on the other the Fooding guide, born ten years ago in an attempt to break the codes and finally offer real change to a gastronomy that its authors judge to be outdated."

Yet what, exactly, the new family stands for can be hard to

say. At some moments, Le Fooding seems earnest, in the manner of the slow-food movement; at others, it is merely festive, a good-time gang; at still others, it appears determined to wrench the entire culture of good food in France from its historic place, on the nationalist right, to a new home, in the libertarian center. To spend a few months studying its founders and their ideas is to get pretty much the same feeling you get when, studying French history, you have to take up the story of Jansenism at Port-Royal in the seventeenth century: all you can really figure out is that it's important, that it's a heresy, and that it's hard to follow.

The Fooding restaurant guide is the most obvious of the group's activities. Since its founding, in 2000, by Alexandre Cammas and Emmanuel Rubin, two gastronomic journalists exasperated by the conformity and conservatism of French food culture, Le Fooding has published, from its Right Bank offices, a handsome, atypically larksome, and unusually honest annual encyclopedia of the restaurants and bistros of both Paris and the provinces. (The guide boasts on its cover that its writers pay their own checks and can prove it—not a thing universally true of French food guides.) But the guide is, in a sense, merely the word, not the act, of the enterprise. The movement, which has been reinforced over the years by a constantly changing team of other Fooding-istes, also sponsors mass picnics—"Foodings"!—at which three-star French chefs, long separated from their diners by a kitchen door and centuries of decorum, offer good food in casual, high-spirited settings. These Foodings take place all over France; the atmosphere is somewhere between a buffet dinner and the Woodstock festival.

Le Fooding is in part a move to *épater la bourgeoisie*—it was at a Fooding event that the young chef Petter Nilsson famously assembled a plate of vegetables that symbolized the world's religions, with a giant *frite* in the shape of a cross on top—but it has also been accused, by left-wing journalists, of representing the bourgeoisie; the populist left-wing magazine *Marianne* charged that it was a kind of cosmopolitan fifth column in the continuing modern assault on French values, and Emmanuel Rubin left the movement last year, disillusioned by what he considered its loss of moral mission.

I first heard about Le Fooding in an e-mail from Raphaël Glucksmann, the filmmaker and human-rights activist (and the son of the philosopher André Glucksmann). "For once, I'm not writing on behalf of the Chechens, the Rwandans, or the Georgians," he explained cheerfully, and then urged me to meet with his friend Zoé Reyners, who was coming to New York as a kind of avant-garde of the Fooding movement here. Zoé turned out to be an exquisite, nervous blonde in white linen, with a distinct resemblance to the young Brigitte Fossey, and she explained that Le Fooding was planning to come to New York for its first American event, a marriage of art, food, and festival that would be called Le Fooding d'Amour and would take place on the grounds of P.S. 1 in Queens, creating a kind of Lafayette-Washington moment. The best of the new generation of French chefs were flying in to meet the best of the new generation of Americans and cook alongside them. She gave me a copy of the latest Fooding guide, which was illustrated by the young cartoonists who bring so much life these days to French journalism. The cover showed King Kong ripping the dome from a Haussmannian restaurant palace with a look of utter satisfaction as he eats the bourgeois diners inside with an enormous silver spoon. The tone of the reviewing had a jocose quality quite new in France: the section on three-star-style temples was called "Fais-Moi Mal!"—literally, "Make Me Ache!" or, idiomatically, "Hurt Me!" Zoé asked if I'd like to meet Alexandre Cammas, who was arriving in New York the following month for an extended reconnaissance of the new world. "He will be taking a house in Brooklyn, with his family, in order to lay the groundwork for American Fooding," she said.

I met Alexandre, with Zoé, in Bryant Park; he turned out to be the Danton of the Fooding movement, one of those passionately articulate young Frenchmen who speak with the relentless eloquence of French letters and philosophy, answering each rhetorical question as they raise it. "Fooding?" he said. "I was writing for the magazine *Nova,* and I needed a rhyme for the title of a piece." We had now settled on a bench. "I intended the word as a mélange of 'food' and 'feeling'—and I like the provocation of using an English word within the context of French cuisine," he explained. "I was already a food writer—I had been at *Libération* for a while—and this was in 1999, a time when restaurants in France were already beginning to move, to change. There was a new element of design, a new element of casual yet serious food. The old choice between *la cuisine de bistrot* and *la grande cuisine française* was ending.

"I wasn't, in the beginning, trying to do anything except characterize a little phenomenon—but I found it growing, in response to a new need." He cleared his throat and leaned forward, like one who needs to resolve complexities that his innocent listener hasn't even grasped yet. "What does it mean, the Fooding movement?" he went on. "Food and feeling—that's the heart of it. But with what practical effect? 'Feeling' in the sense that we mean to be part of *le goût de son temps*—the taste of one's time, though 'taste' in English is too weak a word. 'Fooding' means to eat and drink with feeling—to recognize that one eats with the nose, the eyes, and the mouth, with everything that makes us human! At the time we began, French culinary journalism was narrowly focused on the cooking of the kidneys, the tenderness of the poularde. What was on the plate was all that counted! But who lives that way? Who eats that way? We wanted cooks who cooked with the whole of their selves and souls, not technicians of the table. French cuisine was caught in a museum culture: the dictatorship of a fossilized idea of gastronomy. And this dictatorship has been enforced by tourism: you have tourists packing in to experience gastronomy in a kind of perpetual museum of edification. We wanted to be outside that, *sur le pont,* on the bridge, in front, defining everything that is new. We wanted to escape foie gras, *volaille de Bresse,* all the clichés."

He caught himself, bad-mouthing foie gras being a bit like bad-mouthing the Communion wafer: "Not that we have anything against it—we adore foie gras, and who doesn't love *poulet de Bresse?* But all this style that had been mechanically copied over and over—it's not living cuisine. In a living cuisine, things move and mix together, and that's what makes the cuisine of tomorrow. The classic French cuisine was dying. Everyone knew it outside of France, but it had to be said within. And it had to be said with joy—not as something to mourn but as something to celebrate, the beginning of a new taste of one's time."

Alexandre and Zoé went on to explain that the movement first made its mark with the publication of the guide, which immediately became notorious for ignoring some great names, like the restaurateur Guy Savoy, and honoring such masters as Alain Ducasse for their casual fusion places rather than for their grand restaurants. "We left out Guy Savoy not because he is not a fine cook but because he was adding nothing new," Alexandre explained. "We want food to be a series of provocations, not mechanical pleasures. Food must belong to its time."

I asked Zoé and Alexandre whom they would include on their list of Fooding chefs in Paris, and wondered if I might have lunch at a Fooding restaurant with a Fooding guru the next time I was over. Zoé mentioned a few places, including Stéphane Jégo's L'Ami Jean, a small Basque bistro in the Seventh Arrondissement; Yves Camdeborde's Le Comptoir, a twenty-seat dining room in the Hôtel Relais Saint-Germain; and Bruno Doucet's La Régalade, a bistro out near the Porte de Châtillon.

Both Zoé and Alexandre had the warm glow of revolutionary sectarians in their eyes, and, having shared their fond exasperation with the stasis of French cooking, I was inspired. At the same time, their desire for a head-to-toe, well-articulated renewal of French cuisine, complete with a guide and an advance guard of agitators, seemed a peculiarly calculated way of achieving increased spontaneity. The systematic, thought-through approach to a renaissance in casualness might itself be a symptom of the problem, it occurred to me, as though they were saying to one another, If only we could persuade our countrymen to stop being so entirely French, we could persuade them to be entirely French.

When I next got to Paris, later that summer, I realized that I had heard some of this before: American critics had been complaining for a while that French cooking, which had led the world in the idea that food might be art, had become stereotyped, unreal, and remote from life, and the complaint had at moments echoed in France. I had been one of these critics, and not the quietest or most decorous, voicing the complaint myself at length in an essay back in the nineties, to the anger of some in France and the pained acceptance of many others. (The critic Michael Steinberger had more recently gotten a good book out of the same theme.)

The grounds of the complaint, as I had made it once, and others since, wasn't just against French food, which was still as good as ever, but against the stasis in French cooking. Italian cooking, in particular, had established itself as the base, the longed-for country, the dominant style. In England, Italy had cleared all before it, become what France had been a century before, when Elizabeth Pennell took the greatness of French cooking for granted, and spaghetti had been sneaked in as a strange exotic possibility. Ruth Rogers and Rose Gray had, at the River Café in London, created a kind of satellite version of Italy which some of us thought as good as anything in the Old Country. More important, they had made Italian cooking—expressed strictly in English, without any of the patina of the *moda antico*—the natural language of the English cook. In America, Italian cooking, under the more temperamental presence of Marcella Hazan, still had something Old World to it, was "spoken" with an accent—Italian restaurants still had Italian waiters—but it was what men with expense accounts wanted for lunch and what women with children cooked for dinner. The grammar of French cooking itself—a lump of protein sautéed in a pan, the pan cleansed by a liquid, the liquid reduced to a sauce—which had been so radically new only a century before, now seemed tired on your plate and lethal to your heart. In its place, a variety of techniques, some old and Asian, some new and Catalonian, had taken their place: the grilled fish with a relish, the sweet-savory quick cook and slow simmer, based on curries and stir-fries, had become dominant. A kind of West Coast offense (short gains with quick slants) had taken over cooking—lots of small, intensely flavored plates instead of one big rich main. We live in a tapas civilization—quick-hitting bursts of information and gossip and malice—and a veal chop with butter and mustard sauce or a filet of beef with pastry and peppercorns suddenly seemed as dated as the four-hundred-page novel brooding on a single woman's plight.

As always in life, you voice a complaint against your beloved only to regret it later. "A Lover's Complaint" is the title of the first love poem, not the last. In New York, the empire of the French restaurant, which in my first years there had stretched from Le Lavandou, on East Sixty-first Street, to Le Périgord, on East Fifty-second, one long imperial highway stretching across the Upper East Side, had been reduced to a single restaurant. On birthdays we went to La Grenouille for the old food—cheese soufflés and Dover sole with white sauce and filet of beef with those green peppercorns—and cherished the last refuge of the red banquette and the towering bouquet. There was still good brasserie food around—the simple country-based food that had itself been fast food in France a century before, grilled chicken and choucroute, which is just franks and beans. *That* you could find all over. But I longed for another kind of French meal: that veal chop with mustard sauce, a purée of endives and a small potato gratin, a sharp salad with a smooth and tangy goat cheese and then a bright and supple apricot soufflé. A *foie de veau* with raisins and mustard-tarragon butter, and an endive salad and *île flottante* and profiteroles. Lobster à l'Américaine, *sole à la neige, poulet à la normande.* You didn't find them much even in Paris, for while there might be stasis in French food, it was stasis that had frozen the high end and the lower end while leaving out the middle. The *cuisine bourgeois* was passing even as the old bourgeois themselves were. City food for city people. Food for twilight times. You couldn't find that anymore.

Not long ago, I had coffee with Benedict Beauge, a French writer who occupied the necessary ground between history and food writing. "We no longer have a crisis of French food," he said with the bright gloom, the Epicurean skepticism, of the French food lover. "Now we have a crisis of the French restaurant." He meant, I discovered, that the best new cooks in France—Guy Martin at Le Grand Véfour, Passard, Pierre Gagnaire at his own restaurant—were as good as anyone, having absorbed the lessons of the Spanish with a greater aplomb, but their places were still rooted in the old Michelin system: three-star temples, fit for a voyage. There was a kind of permanent misfit between the cooking talent and the culinary temple. The idea of "worth a voyage" expresses its nineteenth-century nature. We now think of food being worth a revelation. And revelations, we know, happen in eccentric places, caves and chapels.

I was moved enough by memories of the old classic New York French restaurants—all those stuffed chicken breasts and tiny copper serving pots, all those waiters, by turns obsequious and imperious, all that puff pastry and red velvet upholstery—that I thought to salute them, or elegize them internally, at least, by being present for the last lunch at La Côte Basque. The classic, famous old restaurant was closing on March 7, 2004, as its chef-proprietor, Jean-Jacques Rachou, neared seventy. Along with the deaths of Lutèce and Gage & Tollner, the event marked the end of something or other, at a time of who knows what—but it needed to be observed.

The Côte Basque that ended was not the Côte Basque that began. That one, familiar to readers of Truman Capote (who set a gossipy story there), was actually one block over, east of Fifth Avenue, in the space that became a Disney Store. The entire operation—the tables, the banquettes, and the murals of the Basque coast by Bernard Lamotte that gave the place its name—was dislodged in 1995, and replanted more or less successfully in the new space farther west.

Historians, or, at least, chroniclers of the New York restaurant world, will also recall that the original Côte Basque was intended, rather defiantly, not to be what it ended up being—a temple of haute cuisine. It was Henri Soulé's second restaurant, the "relaxed," ostensibly bistro-ish alternative to his Le Pavillon, which was itself a relic of the 1939 World's Fair. As Joseph Wechsberg explained in *The New Yorker* some forty years ago, the Pavillon was the first restaurant in New York to be emphatically and uncompromisingly major—three-star cooking, as they did it in Paris—and La Côte Basque was the first to be major in a minor way. (Reading Wechsberg now, one is struck by how tired the food sounds, much of it made earlier in the day and presented as a *buffet froid*, to be admired as people entered the restaurant.) La Côte Basque, however, became the fashionable place, on the universal principle that whatever is defined in advance as exclusive is uninteresting, while whatever is defined in advance as informal can have an overlay of exclusivity bestowed upon it. La Côte Basque, which stumbled after Soulé's death, was revived in the early eighties by Jean-Jacques Rachou, who had earlier created what was for a spell one of the best places in New York, Le Lavandou. Rachou was the master of a brief rococo interregnum. (This had to be a food-magazine cover line back then: "The Rococo Interregnum.") His chicken was still stuffed; his fish still imported; and if he met a tournedos he greeted it with a slice of foie gras and a truffle sauce. He was mostly famous for the free-form inventiveness of his plates, which often looked, one critic wrote, if memory serves, "like the flags of some effete nation." The style had its moment, and the restaurant got a cheerful second life, which is now over. There is a second life for institutions when people in their twenties arrive; and another second life when people in their fifties return—the second sort of second life was the kind that La Côte Basque had.

And yet, looking around the room at the red-faced and the silver-haired, the soon-to-be-thrombotic and the recently revalved, the women who still tied their scarves to their bags in the manner of Babe Paley, and men who still dressed in trim gray suits in the manner of her husband, one realized that it was the restaurant's thorough and even comic Frenchness that had made it so entirely New York. The banquettes, the lovely red-and-white-striped awning above the bar, the flow of penguined waiters, and above all those murals, showing Basque harbor scenes—no truly French place could be so resolutely French, any more than a truly New York restaurant would ever do itself up in pigeons and water towers. The colors, the open brushwork, and the sea beyond—all of which were intended, in 1962, to make you feel as if you had been transported to southwest France in 1905—now made you feel, one last time, as if you had been transported to New York in 1962. The Gotham Bar and Grill could be anywhere; La Côte Basque could only be in New York City.

And the food? It was okay, yet weirdly disconnected. What I had wanted, but not what I had dreamed of. Things were roasted crisp and sautéed crisper, the truffles were black and the Madeira sauce gleaming, and it was all done with the rich and, if truth be told, slightly sick-making flavor of the old-style cooking, of the kind Levin and Tynan had known. Had our palate changed, or had the cooking changed? More the first than the second, surely. The cobbler must stick to his last, but the chef must stick to his customers, and one generation's delights are the next generation's curiosities. At lunch, someone said, apropos of Capote, that taste is the last thing that passes after talent is gone—it is the most mysterious of gifts, the one thing that lasts, and yet the one that always changes. It seemed a sufficiently elegiac thought to take back home, along with the memory of lunch.

So France is gone, France has fled, what was once an empire is like Byzantium just before the Turks won for good—merely a citadel. Yet the Italian empire exists and flourishes. Why the New World over the Old World is easy to understand. But why Italy over France? Perhaps because what Italy represents in the American, or at least the New York mind, is the *easy* Old World. Olive trees and cheap red wine, pasta and garlic, tomatoes cooked down and cheese scraped off—it all feels accessible, where French cooking, even as it dates, has some evident degree of difficulty about it. The simple acts of French country food—separating eggs, making crème anglaise, beating egg whites, reducing sauces, making liaisons of a sauce and a thickener, even one as plain as flour and butter—are hard or, anyway, harder. Even the peasant dishes can wear you out; even cassoulet is *complicated*. There was a time, now passed, when the difficulty was itself an attraction. "Mastering" the art of French cooking was the point, and mastery is something different from merely making. We make Italian food; we master French. (And we muddle through with American and Greek and the rest.) We like *results*.

But there is also something ever more insular about French cooking itself, and that can't be denied. To read, for instance, the most ambitious recent books about French food is to note a puzzling inability to see beyond France, even in defense or counterattack. *Cooking: The Quintessential Art,* for instance, by Hervé This and Pierre Gagnaire, is an attempt to revive the old eighteenth-century form of a romantic educational dialogue, in this case between two characters called Jean and Hélène, who flirt, in a cerebral way, as they talk about the meanings of food. The principle of "natural" tastes is explored and rejected, narrative in cooking is considered ("I'm not always sure how to 'read'—that is, eat—dishes that consist of several elements," Jean confesses), and the complexities of color and taste laid out (we describe red wine with dark adjectives; white with lighter ones).

But though the wonderfully named This advertises himself, not without reason, as one of the founders of molecular cuisine—he is, in fact, the first, or among the first, to use the term, and his discoveries include the Tesla-like use of an electrical field to smoke salmon—the national question is never raised anywhere in their book. Ferran Adrià and his brother Albert of elBulli, the prime Spanish magicians, if not the first inventors, of molecular cuisine, make no appearance in the book at all, as exemplars or enemies, and Gagnaire—a great cook, to be sure—is uncritically accepted as defining the totality of the new cooking. The dominance of French cooking is simply asserted; the references to history are all narrowly French—Carême and Curnonsky—and even the world's sense that French cooking is in crisis cannot penetrate the small hard shell of complacency. It reminds the reader of the statues in the Luxembourg Gardens, where Branly's pedestal advertises him as the inventor of radio, and Lamarck's as the father of evolution. Neither claim is entirely false, but both are a bit enclosed.

I had a doubled sense of this when I went to an epic French dinner in the company of Beauge. The Beard Foundation in New York had assembled three of the great chefs of France to cook together a single celebratory dinner. The three were Joël Robuchon, Alain Ducasse, and Guy Savoy—but it was well understood by all involved that, as fine a cook and restaurateur as Savoy is, he was very much a kind of Jordan placed between the Egypt of Ducasse

and the Israel of Robuchon. Two grand masters of French cooking, the greatest since the heyday of Paul Bocuse, they were
legendary for having, if not disdain, then at least a glossy indifference toward each other—not so much diva-ish as duke-like in
its rivalry. Beauge is a self-conscious follower of Brillat-Savarin,
about whom he has written the entry in the soon-to-appear
revised encyclopedia of French food, and whom he recognizes,
as not enough do, as the great liberal of gastronomy—the man
who carved a progressive path. We agreed that one problem in
French food, buried for a long time, to be sure, was the rich but
reactionary tradition of Grimod de La Reynière. It made French
cooking narrowly French, denying its mixed-up cosmopolitan
basis, and turned France toward undue navel gazing. We are paying the price for the national narcissism now, which is, always, not
the end of fascination with oneself, but the growing indifference
of everyone else.

The lineup of wines was excellent, and we began with a Robuchon dish: potatoes with white truffle. We tasted it.

"Yes, this is delicious. But"—Benedict's brow furrowed—"how
could it *not* be delicious? If we are to root for white truffles and
boiled potatoes? . . ." We stopped for a pull on a glass of Ries-
ling. Benedict, in a red tie (I had gone tieless, as a little gesture of
independence, I suppose), looked at my collar gravely. "I did not
know the codes," he said, "or what degree of idiosyncrasy one
could show without spilling over into impertinence."

Not long before, Guy Savoy had said, "There is no way that this
dinner could happen in Paris. There is no way." The implication
was, it didn't need to be said, that in Paris the competitive pres-
sures would have just been too intense. "Ducasse is an emperor, a
CEO of cuisine—omnipresent, omnismart, all-seeing . . . Robuchon is a man of the kitchen, a man devoted to technique and
style. They have no rivalry, merely a division of labors," one of
their supporters who had come from France announced. This
view of the two of them is not entirely wrong—it has been a long

time since either has been cooking in a kitchen every night—but it does not, perhaps, define the other problem, which is that in Paris they are *"marques,"* brands, before they are cooks, and the difficulty in bringing them together is less the difficulty of having two sopranos singing side by side than it is the difficulty of making a blend of Pepsi and Coke, or, if that is too plebeian, of Chanel No. 5 and Lanvin's Arpège. You could do it, of course, but it would not exactly be an advance, or an adventure, just an oddity of the evening. Each has a style so distinct that they can only be left alone.

The next plate was by Guy Savoy, one of his classics: an artichoke soup with black truffle and a brioche. (I was so hungry that I ate the brioche first.) "This is a classic plate," Benedict said seriously. "But it is not quite as perfect as it is at his place, where the quality of the bouillon is better. Still—it is beyond complaint." And it was, too: pungent and rich by turns. However, we had had two plates, and one turned on white truffles and the next on black, and though doubtless Ferran Adrià and René Redzepi use truffles when they want to, in neither's cooking is the truffle ever the point, the climax, the concluding phrase.

All the wines—save one good Oregon Pinot Noir—were French, and they kept the evening going. "Except explain to me," Benedict said, "why in America I am always served red wines that are ten degrees too hot, and white wines that are ten degrees too cold?" It was true: red wines, even Burgundies, in America tend not to be served at *cave* temperatures but at room temperatures, and they get soupy and too obviously alcoholic tasting, instead of being neatly gripped by the proper bouquet of smoke and dried fruits, in the process. "It is part of the predicament—the meaning of room temperature has changed so much from the nineteenth century," he commented. We agreed that we liked our champagne, at least nonvintage champagne, very cold indeed, and we began to talk about the best champagnes we had drunk.

Benedict furrowed his brow again. "Well, a great Salon. Or

perhaps a Winston Churchill Pol Roger." This was the great prime minister's favorite, and, despite the recent vintage of its name, it really is great. (Though, to be sure, most of the *grandes marques* of champagne—Dom Pérignon and Grand Siècle and so on—despite the antiqued bottles they often come in, are actually quite new, in the wine scheme of things, usually dating from after the Second World War.)

"I recall," he said, "I recall a plate that one of the Troisgros brothers prepared for me once to go along with a bottle of the Churchill cuvée. He took a plate of scallops, *coquilles Saint-Jacques,* and then minced them, and turned them into a gently adhering ball, with raw black truffles adhering to the outside!" His excitement was manifest and contagious; he turned toward me as he spoke. "Then he poured a boiling, a truly boiling, reduction of asparagus! My God! It was served with a white Hermitage. My God! Perhaps it was the single best thing I've ever eaten."

He shook his head, and I sensed the mix of remembered delight, nostalgia, and continuing sense of impasse that such memories would set off in a great French eater in this day. It was great, it was simple—too simple, probably, to be kept on a three-star menu—and it . . . led nowhere. It was an announcement about ingredients, produce, more than it was a new idea about cooking. Delicious, but not driven. It wasn't that it was too simple to be praised; it's that it was too elemental to become essential. Boiling broth and raw scallops was, in the day of complex illusionistic desserts and freeze-dried foams, like a beautiful tune played on a recorder: it might be more beautiful than anything made in an Auto-Tune mix, but you couldn't really call it modern.

There was a fancy, heavy grilled aubergine by Ducasse, which seemed to both of us typical of Ducasse's cooking: complex in statement and lacking in point. The main course, prepared—"prepared," of course, more by decree than work—by the New York interloper Jean-Georges Vongerichten, was a rack of lamb with a hyper-hot sweet-and-sour Chinese glaze. We agreed that it was good, but so essentially Asian that it didn't point a new way as much as surrender the field.

"There are no new restaurateurs in Paris," Benedict concluded gloomily. "We have star chefs in three-star temples, each sunning himself in the light of his own name—but it is a food spectacle, not a food culture." Not a food scene, I thought, and I explained to him what I meant, a little laboriously. "No real magazines, no real food plates . . . no wonder the next generation looks outside France for the future." He shrugged. "Did I tell you about the butter I had in Montenegro? Serbian butter!"

No American or British eater would eat with such philosophical aplomb, with such innocent, unwatchful enthusiasm or with such an unfussy, reliable, vigilant feeling for all the details, long ago acquired—the temperature of a wine, the taste of a butter, the placement of a plate. It was not the dreary fussing to get it "right" of the anxious new eater—that nose-sniffing, brow-creasing, glass-swirling show—but a wry French sense of order and irony. French civilization has a taste for excessive order, and then an ironic sense about its own taste. (Italians have the ironic sense and Germans the excessive order, but neither has both together.)

French food persisted as a civilization after it was finished as a form. I loved the civilization so much that I would take it, so to speak, on an empty plate. But I would rather have the form and the civilization to go with it, and don't see why we can't. But Benedict knew that Brillat-Savarin's tradition was being endangered by its own heirs, and when he talked about the best butter, he talked about a table in Montenegro. Without his saying so, it was plain to me, by the lift of an eyebrow and a benevolent shrug of the shoulder, that he regarded the Fooding folks as a bit silly and self-promoting—but it was also plain (by the droop of the eye and a sigh of the mind) that he knew that what they said was mostly true.

The ongoing insularity of French food, however defensive it may make a Francophile, is the real target of the Fooding movement. Their program is largely negative; what we don't want is more of this, or This. What they do want is . . . whatever else there may be.

Doing some research in the French papers, I discovered the same puzzlement that I had had about Le Fooding. One magazine interviewer commented to Cammas and Rubin, "I don't see what, exactly, in Le Fooding is revolutionary or even original—you're searching for good little restaurants that aren't too expensive. Where's the novelty in that?" For that matter, a similar complaint about the conservatism of French cooking was at the heart of the nouvelle-cuisine revolution back in the seventies; its version of the Fooding guide was the Gault Millau guide of Henri Gault and Christian Millau.

Nor were the cooks who were being touted by Le Fooding for challenging the paradigm in any real way revolutionary. Le Comptoir, La Régalade—perfectly nice places, but not wildly imaginative. And, anyway, it seemed to me, back in Paris for July, that the new crisis in cooking looked about the same as the old—wonderful food, wonderful rooms, all passé by New York or London standards—and, surely, if the same crisis continues for decades it is no longer a crisis but merely a condition. It was a cheering thought. The real absence in France was not of good food but of what might be called think food—places like elBulli, or like Fergus Henderson's St. John, where the food is devoted to an idea, whether of molecular transformations or of whole-beast eating. And, past a certain point, I realized that the absence of think food was not an absence that truly, in my heart, I regretted. Not everything has to evolve. There are enough ideas in life without having them all on your plate.

Nonetheless, I decided to continue my research. Another member of the Fooding team, Marine Bidaud, met me for lunch at

L'Ami Jean, on a quiet side street near the Eiffel Tower. Where
Zoé had been an embodiment of fifties French beauty, elegant
and tense, Marine was more in the line of the young Bardot. She
coolly explained that her values derived from her upbringing in
the South of France, where her family still gathered around the
table, and that she loved L'Ami Jean because it put her in mind of
that tradition. She turned out to be an ex–art historian, who had
done research on, among other things, Courbet's great gyneco-
logical picture *The Origin of the World.* I picked at the charcuterie
as we spoke. (I mention the glamour of the Fooding officials only
because it is so atypical of the old French dispensation. Gourmands in the past were always middle-aged men with napkins
tucked under their chins, or perhaps insolent thirty-somethings,
like Gault and Millau, and never beautiful young women—or
men either, for that matter. I pressed Alexandre about the astonishing glamour of the Fooding-istes, and he admitted that it was
somewhat purposeful to have a staff that gave eating a more
alluring aura than was always the norm in France.)

Stéphane Jégo, the chef at L'Ami Jean, had a black eye that
day—the prize of a rugby fight—but his food was wonderful,
varied and intelligent, and full of southwestern folk charm:
slow-cooked veal shin, tender without being mushy and comforting without being dull; the usual foie gras, but here more buttery than bland; and the best rice-pudding dessert I have ever had,
complete with black-cherry confit. I hadn't had a better meal in
Paris in a long time. But was it a new frontier? Could you build
a revolution on rice pudding, even great rice pudding? "We need
to change, we need to move," Marine said, but the movement
seemed to be movement within the same familiar thing.

Change we can eat . . . The Western world has been filled with
food-reform movements in the past twenty years. Slow food, the
Edible Schoolyard, the various vegetarian and ethical movements
sprung by the likes of Peter Singer—in no other time would a
highly regarded young novelist like Jonathan Safran Foer view
a book about the anti–animal eating movement as a necessary

extension of his oeuvre, the way a novelist in the sixties might have felt obliged to write a book about the antiwar movement. This proves, depending on your point of view, either that the reform of food has become essential to the reform of life or that, failing in the reform of life, we reform our food instead. Yet all these movements—vegan and whole beast, localist and seasonalist—share a sense that the industrialized, Americanized food economy is destructive of small-scale, European, traditional, farm-based eating.

What distinguishes Le Fooding, I was beginning to understand, was that it is, in effect, *against* an overly European, tradition-minded approach to food. Slow is the last thing it wants French cooking to be, French cooking being slow enough already. The goal of the Fooding movement is to break down French snobbery, in the form of its hidebound, hypersensitive discrimination, while the goal of the slow-food movement, though not put quite this way, is to build up American hidebound hyperdiscrimination. Fooding is a form of culinary futurism: it wants the table to move as fast as modern life. (And, indeed, the Italian futurists were obsessed with food, and wrote their own cookbook.) The Fooding guide is open to pizzerias; Alexandre says that it is even open to fast food, in the right time and the right place. Although McDonald's and the like are not included in the guide, Alexandre has admitted to a certain affection for the Chipotle Mexican Grill, and can recall a welcome meal at a McDonald's in the Carpathian Mountains.

When I pressed Alexandre about the difference between the nouvelle-cuisine revolution in the seventies and the Fooding revolution, he had no difficulty defining it. "Nouvelle cuisine manifested itself in terms of rules," he said. "Its practitioners rejected the old rules but had rules of their own: instead of too much butter, no butter at all. They replaced the norms with other norms. We're for liberty, for the end of categories—a good meal is a rich experience, of any sort. They said no butter. We say no rules! No

rules save excellence." He looked grave. "And another thing. Nouvelle cuisine was largely cut off from the changes in the society
going on around it. It was a palace revolution. We want a cuisine
of this time that is in harmony with this time. The philosophy
of food in France has always bent toward the right, sometimes
the extreme right—Christian Millau and Henri Gault both came
from right-wing backgrounds. I find that the posture of Le Fooding can be replayed in politics, but in a different key. Not Sarkozy,
but Cohn-Bendit. A new openness. An end to false boundaries
between peoples, as between brasseries, bistros, grand restaurants, and the like. All that matters is talent."

In America and England, you are what you think about eating.
Tell me where you stand on Michelle Obama's organic White
House garden and (with the exception of a handful of "Crunchy
Cons" and another handful of grumpy left-wing nostalgists for
whiskey and cigarettes) I can tell what the rest of your politics are.
People who are in favor of a new approach to food—even if that
approach involves a return to heritage breeds and discarded farming methods—are in favor of a new approach to social life. But in
France the philosophy of food does not break on such neat party
lines. In France, the diehards for the traditional national cuisine
tend to write for leftish magazines and newspapers, like *Marianne*
and *Libération,* while those most open to innovation from the
exotic tend to be found in the pages of the center-right *Le Point*
and *Le Figaro.* An organic garden at the Elysée Palace might be a
sign of surging nationalism, or of pluralist internationalism . . .
it would be hard to know which in advance. Alexandre, who says
that he now regrets his vote for the centrist François Bayrou in
the last presidential election, cannot, as a rule, count on a reliable
base of supporters, which may be why Le Fooding constantly
needs to whip up new enthusiasts at its events. The politics of
food in France cut haphazardly and unpredictably across party
lines and allegiances; tell me what you think about eating, and I
will tell you only that you are French.

And yet there was enough intuitive enthusiasm to bring a handful of those new-old French cooks to P.S. 1, for Le Fooding d'Amour. Organized by a new executive at Le Fooding named Anna Polonsky, a young Anouk Aimée as rendered by Modigliani, it had induced Yves Camdeborde and Stéphane Jégo, the twin princes of the French movement, to make the trip, and several fashionable New York cooks—among them Lee Hanson, of Minetta Tavern, and David Chang, of Momofuku—came, too. There was a belly dancer, and wandering musicians, and long lines at the food tables; Stéphane Jégo's slow-cooked lamb, braised for twenty-four hours, was, like his Paris veal shin, particularly memorable, as, in another way, were the mini burgers from Minetta.

I sought out Yves Camdeborde, and he spoke intently about his commitment to Fooding as a movement. "If we don't do this, we're against the wall," he began. "The Michelin Guide approach is dead. I worked at the *grandes maisons,* at the Crillon. They look at the rug, and they measure the chandeliers. We'll go right into a wall if we continue this way. What can it mean? Two stars? Three stars? Who cares?" His tone was not angry, or indignant. He simply looked over at the tables of the American chefs, passing out mini burgers as lines grew ever longer. "It's more than a bistro movement. People say, Bistro, bistro, bistro. But what I do is not bistro—it's *aubergiste.*" He looked at me keenly, to make sure I followed the distinction: an *auberge* is a rural inn. "I'm a kind of urban *aubergiste.* It's a cuisine of complexity and high quality—high cooking without pretension. Slow food—slow food is about defending the traditions, the *terroirs,* the quality of products. It's about producers. This movement is about consumers: about remaking the clientele. It's a way of increasing the spontaneity of things."

As Camdeborde said that, I suddenly saw the right analogy: Le Fooding was to cooking what the New Wave was to French cinema. The hidden goal was to Americanize French food without becoming American, just as the New Wave, back in the fifties and sixties, was about taking in Hollywood virtues without being Hollywoodized—taking in some of the energy and optimism and informality that the French still associate with American movies while reimagining them as something distinctly French. It had a similar cast of characters, with Cammas as André Bazin, the propagandist; Rubin as the anathematized Eric Rohmer; Jégo as Truffaut, the humanist-revolutionary; and Camdeborde as Godard, the serious radical. Like the New Wave filmmakers, these chefs had a vague sense of what they wanted, combined with a vigorous determination to achieve it, whatever the hell it was. Both were movements to remake French audiences in the light of American attitudes—to refashion their expectations as much as to create a new kind of object. The idea was that we had to change taste in order to change art. Appreciating old movies in a new way was as much a part of the legacy of the New Wave as making new ones. Eating with a new attitude was as important to Le Fooding as actually eating something new. The creative act in cooking was to change the style of criticism.

The morning after the Fooding event in Queens, I submitted this analogy to Alexandre during a walk, and he allowed that there might be something in it. He was shining with delight at the success of the launch, and was already making plans for new campaigns in France and America. He told me that he had begun work on a *bande dessinée*—France is a place where the adult comic book is a major vehicle for communicating information and emotion—that would expose the history of clandestine right-wing propaganda in French food writing. (It's true that French food writing has tended to be reactionary; the most famous French food writer of the past century, Robert Courtine, was revealed to have been an active anti-Semitic collaborator with the Vichy regime.) Alexandre goes further. Even Brillat-Savarin's far more liberal and famous definition of gastronomy's aim—to regulate and fix limits for appetite—is, he thinks, touched by a panicky need for control. "Think how we would feel if we used the same words for the study of sex!" he exclaimed. "To regulate and fix the limits of it! Our role is to work against that tradition: to open minds, to reveal history, to change views. It should be a movement of the young."

The most recent Fooding guide is in a way the most provocative. Nearly all the Michelin three-star restaurants have been dropped completely, there are passages in English, and, most important, a couple of new chefs have been identified who can fairly be called revolutionary: Adeline Grattard, of Yam'Tcha, on the Rue Sauval, who has invented a Sino-French fusion cuisine rooted largely in steaming and teas; and, still more revolutionary, Gregory Marchand, a young Frenchman who trained in New York and London—an unthinkable notion twenty years ago—and whose restaurant, on the Rue du Nil, is actually called Frenchie. The next Fooding event in New York, promised for September, would be, instead of once again a Franco-American conversation, a match, even a confrontation, between San Francisco and New York chefs. "We don't want to be narrowly identified as a 'Franco-Français' movement, just bringing French chefs to America," Anna confided recently. "Then we might as well be part of the French cultural ministry."

Alexandre is particularly glad to be coming back to New York. "I grew up watching American movies," he said the morning after the Fooding event in Queens. "America still feels so young to me. I love New York. I still see things like Momofuku that are entirely of New York. Can we make that kind of place in France?" He mused for a moment, and then brightened.

"Do you know a film I love?" he asked. "*Tarzan's New York Adventure*. Do you know it? With Johnny Weissmuller? And that scene when he leaps from the Brooklyn Bridge?" His hand moved through the air, Tarzan jumping from the bridge. "I love that moment. It's an important moment for me. It seems so, so romantic."

16

E-MAIL TO ELIZABETH PENNELL:
Salmon, Broccoli, Repentance

Dear Mrs. Pennell:

Tonight I shall make my repentance meal, my remorse meal: salmon and broccoli with brown rice. It's the one meal I do when I am feeling guilty about all else I've been doing. For of course, despite all my brave talk about the relativity of taste, for all that I can reference the whirligig of fashion and the inevitability of alterations in likings, the truth is that I am as much a captive of my time's tastes and taboos as anyone. I make cream sauces, but I feel rotten about them afterward. Guilt rises in my craw as I contemplate a beefsteak, whatever brave things I may say about the scavenger ethic, and so I believe in the holy-healthy trinity of wild salmon and organic broccoli and brown rice. It is a plate that tastes like forgotten virtue. It is the right dinner for a moment of shame.

And all this remorse, this penitence, this doubt, is directed, or occasioned, anyway, by what now seems to be my misguided romance with *you*, Elizabeth. The bad habit of the strategist is to go one bridge too far, and the worst vice of the overeducated is to read one book too many. It is a form of hubris: wiser to

find something good, enjoy it, and not contaminate it by searching too much further. Do not discover Carlyle's politics, or Scott
Fitzgerald's parenting, or Philip Larkin's taste in porn. It will
screw you up to no good purpose, and diminish the writer without adding to your understanding. I know this, and should have
quit while I was ahead.

You see, I found the book you wrote upon your return to
Philadelphia in 1904. It was full of life. Like me, you have and
keep a warm appreciation of the beauty of old Philadelphia—its
grid, so neatly laid out in inward-looking streets and squares
with none of the relentlessness (nor the dynamism) of New
York's less perfectly ordered plan. The Schuylkill city's spa-
ciousness, its slight air of eighteenth-century clarity and
red-brick virtue. You love all that, too, and I read all that with
pleasure.

And then I found within your book a line of stark, vigorous bigotry directed not just at the undeserving but
at—well, directly at *me,* or, rather, at my not-so-distant
great-grandparents, who were among the Russian Jews who
had since your youth taken over the center city of Philadelphia.
And what possessed you was not mere social bigotry, but real
animus. "I cannot understand, and no one can explain to me,
why the Russian Jew has been allowed to push his way in [to
the city]," you write. "I have heard all about his virtues; nobody
need remind me of them; I know that he is carrying off everything at the University so that rich Jews can begin to think in
turn that they should in return make it a gift or a bequest, as no
rich Jew has yet, I believe. I know that the young Philadelphian
must give up his sports and his gaieties if he is to compete with
the young Russian Jew who never allows himself any recreation
on the road to success—I might add the fact that the Russian
Jew has mastered, in a very short time, the possibilities of bank-
ruptcy and arson."

What particularly offends you is the presence of Russian Jews, like my great-grandparents, on the legendary inner, tree-named streets of the city, Chestnut, Walnut, Spruce, and Pine. "The tragedy is that the Russian Jew should have descended upon just this section, should now, not so much dispute it with him [the old Philadelphians] as oust him from it—the Russian Jew, a Jew by religion but not by race, who has been found impossible in every country on the continent of Europe onto which he has drifted, so impossible that when that country is Holland that the Jews who have been there for centuries collect among themselves the money to send him post-haste on to England and America. . . ." More, and then more, the old and usual ugliness, and with the usual much-rehearsed and patently insincere exceptions: The old, original Jews of Philadelphia were all right in their place.

This is, of course, in one way the standard anti-Semitism of your place and time and circumstance. Henry James shared it, and for the same reasons, and expressed it in almost exactly the same way: the Jews who had filled the Lower East Side seemed to him as remote from his ideas of Americanness as the Russian Jews on Spruce Street seem to you. I know that. I can tell myself what is true, that this bigotry was the bigotry of your people and your time, to be found in Henry Adams, too, and for the same reason: like Henry James, he had grown up in one America, and found himself in what seemed to be another one, very different and disconcerting. These are the standard-issue attitudes of the Old Americans of the East Coast cities confronted with the new immigrants, and they go on to this day, when the Old Americans are often the descendants of the original obnoxious immigrants.

Still, I take this to heart. My great-grandparents moved around town, as it happens, but we ended up on Locust Street—just a few blocks away from Chestnut and right by Walnut, and I spent my quite "assimilated" but still distinctly literary-Jewish-intellectual boyhood riding and racing on

Spruce and Pine. So I felt, reading these words by you, as blue and betrayed as if I had found my wife in flagrante with another man—and a young, blond SS officer at that. And I have since discovered, what is harder to accept, that this was not a passing bigotry in an otherwise openminded life, but a recurrent theme of yours: your husband, Joseph Pennell, in particular, was an obsessed anti-Semite in a time not short on them, who wrote and illustrated a long book about the hideousness of Russian Jews, serialized, bizarrely, in *The Pall Mall Gazette.*

We have, of course, been here before. My beloved Chesterton had a true program (a word that sits in sinister poise with "pogrom") for Jewish expulsion from England. With an effort of will, one can see, if not sympathize with, the shock of Old Americans at the newcomers—a prejudice not entirely unknown to the Jews who, having been here for a century, now see their "own" neighborhoods and landmarks disappear under the pressure of Muslims and West Indians. But there it is. You hate my kind, in the place where my kind went, in exactly the street where not just my kind but my family lived.

Can we eat in peace knowing you despised my grandparents? Must I put a stopper on our relations? Should I end these e-mails, this imaginary conversation? One part of me thinks I should: the only meal I truly regret in my life was a tray of hors d'oeuvres passed around at (the very elderly and deaf) Diana Mitford's place when she came back to an apartment in Paris from her long life with Oswald Mosley in Versailles. I plead ignorance—her children were lovely people, and my friends, and I did not know then just how Hitlerite she had been, or I would have stayed away. One of the strange sad truths about the gastronomic tradition since Grimod is that good food writing has always bent right, and often toward the extreme right. One had already gone through this pain with Robert Courtine, the great food writer of *Le Monde,* when it was revealed after his death that he was not

merely an anti-Semite but an active collaborationist—and that
this might have been so, must have been so, one sees retrospec-
tively in the contempt for all but France and anything but French
cooking that runs through his work.

In a way, a bitter way, I should be grateful for this discovery,
for it raises the central point of these pages, the key issue, the
one big thing too easily avoided: how much can the table *truly*
reconcile—how sweetly can, or should, the rituals of social
life reconcile us to our opposites? It is sentimental, surely, to
pretend that the ugliness of life escapes the table; we rightly
condemn the French intellectuals and artists who made too
easy a social peace with their occupiers. But is it unrealistic
to wish that some reconciliation of opposites might yet take
place there? It's a hope, at least. Very different people do dine
together, or try to. We think about Dr. Johnson, greatest of
religious conservatives, reconciled over a good dinner in 1776
with John Wilkes, greatest of libertine libertarians, through
the good offices of James Boswell, and we recognize that some
of the sanity of British political life, compared with French, is
owed to such primal acts of sociability. We can't wish away differences, but we can hope for an end to hostilities. Disdain for
others is part of life; learning to dissimulate it through manners is as good a cure as we can hope for. While we wait for the
reign of Universal Love, we can at least share the premise of the
Common Table.

After all, the good angel I have on my other hand, Jacques
Decour—whose letter began this book—was, for all his
heroism, a committed and unrepentant communist, which
means, in plain French, a Stalinist, albeit one of enormous
courage and humanity. And now, on my other, an anti-
Semite . . . upend the table or keep it set and hope for pleasure
to uplift our hearts? We write glossily of the continuities of the
table, but this is the perpetual fragility of its concord, which
breaks on bigotries and false beliefs that can't be wished away.

But that they can't be wished away doesn't mean that they might not yet be reconciled. Good things do happen when people sit down for dinner. That's itself a faith. Obviously, we don't want to sit down to dinner with Nazis, and we rightly condemn those French artists who did. But we do want to sit down to dinner with people *before* they become Nazis, if it might help keep them from becoming so. It is not wrong to hope that the revelation of a common human touch, a common taste, shared and relished, can become itself an argument for humanity. We disapprove, and rightly, of those who sat down with their occupiers, but we smile, and often, at the countless travelers' tales of violence averted by bread and salt and beer.

The answer, I think, is that there isn't one. We try to reconcile as many kinds as we can, and when we can't, we can't. We tolerate all that's tolerable, eat with whom we can, draw lines as we have to, accept as much as we're able. Liberal tolerance is an injunction urging efforts, not an instruction manual making rules. It says, Do your best with as many as you can until the very last moment when you can't anymore. And how will you know when you can't? Why, by the feeling in your stomach.

> . . . behold the mutually hostile
> Mouth and eyes of a sinner married
> At the first bite by a smile.

So I quoted Auden, back at the beginning of this book, in the epigraph I intended only as a benediction. Now, under the pressure of finding out some more of who you really were, or thought, Mrs. Pennell, I think harder, and now I'm inclined to believe that Auden thought the mouth and eyes were hostile because the mouth always seeks pleasure and the eyes always make judgments. Reconciling the two, our molars and our morals, is what a great meal does—but it can only do it for a moment. Then we are back in the real world of mixed emotions and dubious alliances, where those who share our pleasures are rarely those who please our minds. Brillat-Savarin, whom you called the Master, thought that the rituals of the French table were soft power for decent liberals like himself, but though soft power is power it is still always soft. Would you have taken the trouble, seen a wiser way, with better company and a larger view? I don't know. But, having summoned you back to life I am surely allowed to hope you would have. I wish I could have tried.

Wild salmon, broccoli, and brown rice. Delicious without being indulgent, good to eat while having some tang of austerity, of firm assertion, about it, I shall make this meal tonight. Cleansing, somehow. A kosher meal, come to think of it!— though, given your obsessions, this is a thought that probably occurred to you before it occurred to me. Come over in spirit and I will cook you all of these things. Salmon, and broccoli purée and perhaps lentils and brown rice, the simple penitent foods. I cannot exactly forgive you. But I can still feed you. Four minutes on one side, three on the other. Salmon should be done in a cast-iron pan. Broccoli is best steamed for eight minutes. Brown rice just takes time.

A Gopnik, of Locust Street

17

Endings

JUST A YEAR AGO, I gave up sweets. I was in a restaurant in San Francisco, and, for the first time that I can recall, when the waiter said, "Dessert?," in that conspiratorial, perky way they have, I said . . . nothing. And then the next night, at another place, I did it again.

The usual reasons that move men and women as they age moved me: I was self-conscious about gaining weight, crossing into the world where you slowly become doughier and wake up as a middle-aged man with a paunch. ("I looked in the mirror," a woman novelist-friend said not long ago, "and saw that I was . . . *stout*. Like a character in Trollope: 'She was a stout, upright lady in the prime of life. . . . ' ") It is true, of course, that the paunch was once a hard-sought ornament of abundance, rather than a flying buttress of overindulgence—the stout lady or gentleman was once the only *steady* lady or gentleman—but though that time might be one to envy, still we live in *this* time and not some other. So I decided to stop eating desserts, to see if that would help. Like all diets, both the reducing kind and the religious kind, mine had an element of logic (lose those calories neatly, and at once!) and an element of magic, too (give up the thing you like best and you will appease the gods of aging).

I love desserts. I think of my mother and I taste desserts. My mother, though a scientist with an academic career, made her own desserts every night of my childhood: lemon tart, chocolate cake, wonderful coffee custard with bittersweet chocolate hardened like a winter lake on top, and hot apple pie with light custard sauce. I am aware that pies and cakes and cupcakes are the more usual thing to love from Mom's kitchen. But she was a Francophile, and made soufflés, and those I loved best of all. Yet they were the one dessert of hers that I couldn't make for my own children. When I left home, she gave me a self-published recipe book that included her formula for apricot and Grand-Marnier soufflés. I had followed it dutifully over the years, and never gotten it quite right. There was a moment when you were supposed to know that the egg whites were beaten—a zone with danger and failure on either side. "DO NOT OVERBEAT / DO NOT UNDERBEAT!" she had written in the recipe, and once again the written orders hurt as much as helped. Although I had seen the proper moment, the true loft, countless times, the presence of the words somehow froze the operation, made the right state of beaten egg whites an unobtainable condition. I could never find the zone.

Sugar flows through every modern life, and body, with a fluidity that would have shocked our sugar-starved ancestors, and so we withdraw from it with the same difficulty that we withdraw from the other shapers of our senses, alcohol and caffeine. For the first time in my life I knew what a craving was, understood the otherwise puzzling condition of friends who had passed through AA or through crack addiction, and whose frailties I respected but whose needs I could never before quite conceptualize, internalize: what was it that could lead people to act in a way so plainly not in their own self-interest? Having seen what the bottle or the pipe does to you, why not just give up the bottle or the pipe? The answer, I now saw, is that the craving isn't a war inside you, as in those old quarrels between the devil and the angel, the kind that used to perch on Sylvester's shoulders as he decided whether it was wrong or right to try to eat Tweetie.

No, it was more of an urge to surrender to some other self-willed person who lives inside you, controls your steps, and just *wants* in the worst way. I would wake up at night and, unself-willed, wander toward the freezer and the ice cream—the state of hunger for something isn't the state of deciding to have, but lies outside decision, lies outside your self, even, exists as a kind of magnetic impulse to which one need only surrender. Hunger is a field that draws you forward and that you enter simply by choosing not to resist. If it were up to me, the addict says, I'd stop. And we shake our head at his rationalization—but it isn't up to him. A habit is not a gleeful preference of something bad for you to something good for you; it is an attraction that draws you toward something that feels neither good nor bad, but only necessary. (Which is why, I suppose, addicts only get better in the company of others. They bond together to try to build a passive force field greater than that other force field, which brought them there.)

The curious thing was that, while it was hard to do without sweets at home, it wasn't nearly as hard when we went out to eat, and especially not when we went out to eat fancy food. It was as if the dessert chefs had given up on dessert, too, and produced something else in its place. At even a moderately upscale establishment, you would invariably get what I had come to think of as the Portman Plaza plate, since it so closely resembled the model that a developer would have proposed for the center of a crime-racked mid-sized city in the seventies: three upright cylinders—small towers of something wrapped in something—with the tops sliced at an angle; a crumbly landscape of some kind; and a reflecting pool running around the edge. The plate would be advertised as, let's say, a chocolate-peanut-butter mousse cake with walnut-balsamic crumble and a sesame sorbet with Concord-grape foam. But the effect was always the same: not enough of a cakey cylindrical thing, too much of a crumbly thing, far too much of a gelatinous thing, and an irrelevance of an off-key runny thing. Without surrendering sugar, dessert had surrendered all its familiar forms—the cake, the soufflé, the pudding—as the avant-garde novel had surrendered narrative, character, and moral. Losing our faith in art is, in a secular culture, what losing our faith in God was to a religious one; God only knows what losing our faith in desserts must be.

Leafing through books at the neighborhood cookbook store, I slowly became aware that our dessert modernism sprang from somewhere else, and had a more revolutionary purpose than I knew—that the Portman plates were to a European movement what the Portman Towers had been to the Bauhaus, the American domestication of something austere and rigorous. Here in New York, the true, uncompromised revolution was limited to a handful of places, and I went to one of them, Wylie Dufresne's wd-50. I broke my sweet fast, and had a full roster of the pastry chef's delicious devisings: cheesecake with dried pineapple, pineapple purée, and pineapple *tuiles;* lemongrass mousse with lemongrass foam. The chef, Alex Stupak, turned out to be an intense intellectual, clear and dry in his judgments.

"I happen not to like sweets," he said as we sat down after dinner and he began to explain his work. "It's an idiosyncrasy of mine. I decided to become a pastry chef because it gave me autonomy. Whether you think your desserts are manipulated or not, they are! When you're conceptualizing an entrée, a protein, you generally expect to get a piece of that thing intact. In pastry, it doesn't occur. Pastry is the closest that a human being can get to creating a new food. A savory chef will look at puff pastry not as a combination of ingredients but as an ingredient in itself. Pastry is infinitely exciting, because it's less about showing the greatness of nature, and more about transmitting taste and flavor. Desserts are naturally denatured food." He looked at me sternly. "Birthday cake is the most denatured thing on earth."

When I asked him who had influenced him, his eyes, which had been narrow slits of purpose, suddenly shone bright. "I admire Albert Adrià more than any other cook in the world," he said.

Everywhere I went, I heard similar talk of Albert, his brother Ferran, and other Catalan dessert wizards. Dan Barber, of the restaurant Blue Hill, spoke reverently of Jordi Roca, whose restaurant, run with his two brothers and situated not far from the Adriàs' elBulli, had recently been voted one of the five best in the world; on a visit to New York, René Redzepi, whose restaurant, Noma, in Copenhagen, had in the same poll been named the best restaurant in the world, spoke of both Adrià and Roca with the same quiet awe.

In search of the truth about the new sweets, I even went to the White House, whose pastry chef, Bill Yosses, I had been made to understand, was the Great Still Center of the American dessert. Yosses turned out to be a smiling, vaguely seraphic presence—at one point, he neatly, calmly distinguished caramel, mere burnt sugar, from butterscotch, brown sugar mixed with butter, for the benefit of his sous-chefs.

"Dessert is aspirational," Yosses said, laying out his philosophy. "It's the one part of the meal you don't have to eat. It's the purest part of the meal: the art part. But it's also the greediest part, the eat-it-in-a-closet part. We don't have to have it, and we do. When I was a kid, I would stuff my face with éclairs. I still would, I guess . . ." His voice trailed off. "The real question is this," he said. "How did this thing, this spice, sugar, become a staple? How did something that ought to be like saffron, a rare thing to add, become the thing we build on? How did a whole way of cooking creep up from sweetness? Why do we use it to end the meal? Those are the big questions." I asked if I should go to Spain. He gave a Yoda-ish smile, and said, "Oh, yes. That's a trip you ought to take." When I consulted Dan Barber again, he was still more emphatic. "Go there!" he said. "That's where it's all happening. Go!" And so I went.

On the plane over, I felt like Alec Guinness or Michael Caine in a Cold War spy movie of the somber, le Carré or Len Deighton kind: a black-and-white film, with a jazz score and a grimly ambiguous ending. I was crossing the salt-caramel curtain, and no turning back.

When I got to Barcelona, there was, just as there ought to be in such a movie, a cool, efficient beauty, in a black frock and a sports car, waiting for me. This was Lisa Abend, an American writer who lives in Spain, and who was to be my companion in Barcelona. She had spent the past season observing the innards at elBulli, while writing a book about the Oompa-Loompas of the operation.

It was twilight, and we sped through the dark, narrow streets of the Old City on the way to our first stop, the Espai Sucre. This "Sweet Space" was, Lisa explained, a working research laboratory and school, where new desserts are regularly conceived and experiments made, with the results exhibited, and eaten, at a nearby restaurant. As we drove, the almost kinetic energy of the Catalan capital was evident, as it had been the last time I was there, twenty years before. At the time, the only dessert seemed to be flan, with a distinct salty taste that I associated with the local *café con leche*. I asked what had happened in the twenty years since.

"I've been doing a lot of research, and it really seems to be the case that the legend is the truth," Lisa said. "Twenty years ago, the Adrià brothers took over a struggling French restaurant up in Roses, and in the nineties they began to collaborate with a chemist here at the university. And, being isolated and inexperienced, they began to do new things. It really did come from two intense brothers who didn't care what the rules were supposed to be."

We pulled up in the darkness to a modern glass storefront amid the medieval buildings and parked on the sidewalk. Inside, Jordi Butrón, the chief scientist-cook of the research center, greeted us solemnly and led us into his classroom. On the blackboard behind his head was a series of abstruse-looking diagrams.

With a close-shaved beard and mustache, he had more the look of a severe French sociologist than of a happy Spanish cook. I explained that I was on a quest to find out what desserts really were and where they were going. He held up a hand and began to speak, in rapid, accented French.

"In retrospect, they're disgusting, many of the things we used to do—too much fat and too much sugar, and a series of clichés taught while being rationalized," he said. "The key thing now for a cook is to develop a library of flavors that you can recall. If I say to you, 'Apple and cinnamon,' you would click in immediately. 'Yes, apple! Yes, cinnamon!' The library of your mind contains that. But what if I say 'Apple, asafetida'? Nothing! You have nothing stored there." He added slyly, "Now, this is a benefit to the chef, because if I do apple and cinnamon and you don't like it you think there's something wrong with me, but if I do apple and asafetida and you don't like it there's something wrong with you." He laughed briefly, professionally. "The development of a pastry chef is not the development of techniques. It is the slow, careful development of a catalogue of savors and flavors, which you can develop the way you develop muscles. There is a logic in every dessert worth eating. Consider the logic of white peach and rich cheese. We must be conditioned not by sight but only by flavor, the tongue, the nose, and the feel in the mouth." He went on placidly, "It is to avoid these errors that we do so much of our teaching and learning blindfolded."

"Blindfolded!" I said, wondering if I had misunderstood. We had been struggling with each other's French.

"Yes, blindfolded," he repeated. He went to a drawer and took out a handful of silken eye masks, which he threw on the desk. "It is important to be able to work with the sensations of the nose and mouth alone, so we spend hours in the dark, tasting. Of course, appearance matters, but it is the last part of the equation. Taste, taste, taste—that is what matters. So I keep people blindfolded for much of the work, which is devoted to the marriages of taste."

Then he opened the door to an immense, pristine kitchen, dominated by a great length of polished black stone. Here, he said, "as many as fourteen young chefs can work, blindfolded, to discover the taste and enlarge their flavor libraries."

I noticed various pieces of space-age-looking machinery littering the beautiful, dark kitchen, and I asked how the new technology contributed to his work.

"It is useful as tools," he said crisply. "If I want to capture the flavor of a raspberry meringue, I use a powdered egg white, and then I have a true raspberry in the form of a meringue, instead of a super-sweet meringue overwhelming raspberries." He shrugged. "Nothing we do with new equipment does more than allow us to reinsert flavors."

We sat down for dinner in the nearby restaurant, and had a meal of five courses, all sweet, or at least sweetish, yet all beginning with a savory theme. First, there was cucumber-ginger-pineapple-tarragon sherbet, then olive-oil cake with San Simón cheese and a perfect white-peach sorbet. "The combination is a classic conception of the savory kitchen: cheese and olive oil," Jordi observed. Then came a cake made with stout, beets, cherries, and Idiazábal cheese, too various to make much sense. Then a green-apple granita with bay leaf, as fresh and acid as a winter morning, and, finally, truffle-hazelnut-toast cream pudding. The genius showed in the details: a curry-and-salt cookie, thrown in as an extra but a study in itself. There was something perfectly modulated in the transition from savory herbs (tarragon and bay) and savory tastes (salt and curry, particularly) into sweet dishes.

"This is kind of amazing," I said to Lisa, as I scraped the plate of truffle-toast pudding and grabbed another curry-and-salt biscuit. Lisa gave me a seraphic, you-ain't-seen-nothing-yet smile, and said, "You'll meet Albert tomorrow."

I sat in my little hotel room in Barcelona, jet-lagged and sugar-satiated, and read about the history of sugar. Primates, I learned, love sweets for reasons that are simple enough to explain: sweetness is the natural sign of ripeness, and the best assurance, especially when balanced with just enough acids, that the thing you're eating is good to eat.

Yet the picture is more complex. The primate's instinct for sugar is particular, adjustable, and sometimes seasonal. The lesser mouse lemur of Madagascar, a gourmand among monkeys, raises its threshold during the rainy season so that, when sugars are less abundant, it requires less sweetness. Yet this may be why the lesser mouse lemur has always remained so deeply lesser. Our nearest relations among the primates, particularly chimps, have a "supra threshold": they love sweets and will practically die to get them—and this, the theory goes, is one of the things that make them forage over extremely large territories, outside the forest. They strolled on all fours, then walked, then ran, just to have dessert.

As both the anthropologist Sidney Mintz and the historian Jean-Louis Flandrin have documented, it was only recently that the instinct for devouring sweets met the availability of abundant sugar. In pre-Crusades medieval European diets, only honey and fruit and other "natural" sweeteners were available, and they were mostly used in savory dishes. For centuries, sugar was a spice as rare as myrrh and as precious as saffron: an expensive extra used to give food taste and color. Or, rather, to take away color. The whiteness of refined sugar, as of salt, was very much part of its mystique, and one of the things that led people to think it must be a medicine. Combinations of white foods, before the days of scientific medicine, were always seen as curative (As indeed they remain—consider the futile ingestion of milk as a cure for ulcers, a sitcom staple even of my childhood.)

Only in the Renaissance did sugar slowly, through the New World, become widely current. "Sweet" became one of Shakespeare's favorite adjectives: it appears seventy-two times in the sonnets alone, and the first writer who mentions them refers to his "sugar'd sonnets." Sweet for Shakespeare means neither sexy nor virtuous but some new thing in between: irresistible, enticing, dear, tender. When Touchstone, in *As You Like It,* says that pairing beauty with honesty is as foolish as making honey a sauce to sugar, he is making more than just a joke. Styles of sweetness are being distinguished even as virtues are, and they are in sufficient abundance to make available a joke on doubling them. A mouth taste was quickly becoming a moral taste. Just as the inner life is being sorted out in Shakespeare's time, so is the sweet life. Fine distinctions between similar states of burnt sugar, between caramel and butterscotch, had just opened up. (A feeling surrounds a flavor when it becomes widespread enough. No one yet quite talks about the umami of a marriage, or the hint of soy when we see our in-laws—but we all talk easily about our saccharine sisters and our vinegary in-laws and our hot-pepper neighbors, even about Nabokov's garlicky puns.)

Then, in the late seventeenth century, the price of sugar plummeted, never to recover, largely as a consequence of that hideous invention the West Indies sugar plantation. "I do not know if coffee and sugar are essential to the happiness of Europe, but I know well that these two products have accounted for the unhappiness of two great regions of the world," a solitary and bitter French humanitarian wrote in 1773: Africa and America are, of course, those two regions, the one where the slaves came from, the other where the slaves were brought. It was the growth of the plantation system in the West Indies that turned sugar from a spice into a table commonplace. Sugar would help fuel the Industrial Revolution—and the irony is that the sugar plantations were the place where something like the first "factory" system was put to work. Because sugarcane rots so quickly, the sugar farm had to become one of the first models of "industrial" production: cutting, curing, and refining all had to take place within a single space, organized as a single brutally efficient system, a kind of Black Mass anticipation of the assembly line.

The cheap-sugar revolution took different paths in different places. In England, sugar combined with tea became the staple drink of the masses. In France, though, the sudden plantation-driven dive in the price of sugar produced something else quite new: it marked the birth of the pastry chef, the coming of dessert-as-we-know-it, the opening path toward the patisserie. It was as though the whole of the table had been tipped, and sugar and sweetness ran out of the meal and down into its ending. Medieval cookery burnt down, and what rose in the ashes was a piecrust.

The French food historian Jean-Louis Flandrin shows, with a care for detail that borders on the obsessive, how the percentages of sugar used in the courses of the ordinary French meal, as recorded in recipe books and food guides, changed in every decade of the seventeenth century and then got fixed at the end. Between the fourteenth and eighteenth centuries, while the use of sweetened dishes of meat and fruit radically declined—by more than eighty percent in the fifteenth century alone—egg and dairy products married to sugar more than tripled. "The eighteenth century menus no longer show *any* sweet or sugared dishes except as entremets and desserts," Flandrin writes. The "caramel curtain," with some dishes seasoned by salt and others by sugar, had descended. In France, a full-blown dessert cuisine emerged, with the pastry chef as its hero. Soufflés rose; egg whites lifted up; aerated egg yolks combined; chocolate was blended with butter and sugar to make buttercream; and egg yolks were kept from cooking while allowed to thicken.

So dessert as we know it is a modern invention, about as old as the steam engine and the telegraph. The surest sign of something truly new is the instant amnesia it creates about the old. French travelers, beginning in the late seventeenth century, were now puzzled and bewildered by the presence of sweet fruits with savory courses in "southern" countries, though all the evidence suggests that it had not been long since they had had them, too. Even Montaigne in the late sixteenth century, traveling south, was puzzled to find fruits always served with roasts—though Montaigne's mom (or, okay, Montaigne's mom's cook) in Bordeaux must have served little else.

Why a true pastry dessert cuisine happened in France in a way that it did not happen elsewhere is a bit of a puzzle. Certainly, the prominence of French pastry was so great that, by the end of the nineteenth century, even the most mundane mid-American city prided itself on having a patisserie in the French style—in Sinclair Lewis's *Babbitt,* for instance, the middle-American Realtor hero makes a trip to the one French bakery in the town of Zenith to marvel at the "refinement that inheres in whites of eggs." But why did it only happen there? There is a first-mover cycle, of course. France having one pastry chef soon had more of them for the same reason that Facebook flourished while Campusbook did not; a network makes its own nodes, and one great baker trains fifty more. Climate has something to do with it. Anyone who has lived through a damp English winter will know that tea is indispensable, while anyone who has lived through a keen but not humid French one will know that chocolate and cake are welcome.

But some of it had to do, surely, with the social organization of French life. One need not be too stern-minded a believer in a single national character to spy in sweets a pattern typical of the French Enlightenment: not so much the English urge to explanation and empirical instance but the French urge to divide, analyze, separate, articulate. The same process that divvied up good old curiosity into separate new "disciplines" divvied up dinner— psychology here and philosophy there and physiology down the hall, where once there was only natural philosophy sitting on the buffet, saying, Help yourself! Take the honey entirely away from the braised lamb and relocate it completely in the newly baked cake. Now you got your sugar hit only when dinner ended, with alcohol and then tobacco smoke to wreathe it round.

Reading the primatologists and the anthropologists, I got

the sense that the double life of sweets ever since the sugar revolution—as a thing we universally crave, and as a highly specific, French-derived cooking culture—has led to a strange fight between disciplines. The primatologists insist that we eat sugar because our genes scream for it, while their humanist colleagues insist that sugar is above all a cultural symbol—we eat as many sweets as we can in order to emulate the rich, who usually get to eat more. This is, of course, a little like the argument that the average man wants to make love to supermodels in order to be like rock stars and quarterbacks. (We *do* want to be like rock stars and quarterbacks, but this is because we envy them their girlfriends.) A power relationship and a primate past are both alive in us at once; the symbolic power relationships are an intrinsic *part* of the primate past. (Something can express a biological imperative and still be a symbolic ornament; the ruffle that your aunt puts on the toilet base is there to decorate, not disable, the toilet.)

Once again, an artifact and an appetite are not opposites to be reconciled but the same drive seen at different moments in its history. The lesser mouse lemur would doubtless devour a crème caramel and a butterscotch pudding indifferently; it takes a pastry chef trained in France to state the difference. The artifact gives the appetite shape; the appetite makes the artifact shine.

The next morning, I met Albert Adrià at the workshop that the Adrià brothers keep in the old quarter of Barcelona. In jeans and a work shirt, Albert had the stocky, proletarian look of a young Braque or Léger. He is a classic younger brother—earnest, hardworking, self-critical—and he explained the rise of the Barcelona dessert as a series of accidents disciplined by labor.

"*Postres?*" he asked. "Why me for *postres*? First, because the pastry chef left. I had just finished moving through all the other stations, and I was due to be at the dessert. And I also have a severe allergy to shellfish, which limits my movement. But the real reason was that pastry seemed much more interesting—a world without limits. Meat cook? Fish cook? What are you going to do with it? And also there was a lot more to learn in pastry—just the techniques! My question was, Why can't you serve main dishes that are sweet, and why can't you have savory tastes during the dessert time period?"

I asked when the new style had first appeared. He furrowed his brow, trying to recollect something that had clearly not been the result of a deliberate plan. "It was an accident of the kitchen, really. I suppose we first made an ice cream with saffron in 1985. My first step is, I have to draw it. I have to sketch it, get it down on paper, and then do the explanatory texts." He began to draw on paper. "This one I wanted to take up, this dirt—one of my most famous desserts involved dirt. A sweetened illusion. The idea came when it was winter at elBulli and I was going up the hill to get my car, and stuff was falling down, and I thought, Shit, that's good! I can use that! It's a dirt road, and, in the course of the fall, I noticed not only how the leaves changed color but also how they changed the color of the ground." The dessert, as it was eventually plated, included cherry sorbet, salted honey yogurt, frozen chocolate powder, and spice bread, all evoking one fall moment: a dessert of frozen time.

Struggling to find words for his inventions, he began to speak about his most recent work: two desserts for the 2010 Cook It Raw conference, in Lapland, which would emphasize low-energy techniques, uncooked food. "Elemental, elemental," he said. "That's what I want. The really new idea I have for Lapland is—you see, I was thinking, if you were thirsty there you would eat the snow or the ice, and if you're hungry you're going to kill the reindeer. So: blood! The most basic thing is to drink the reindeer's blood and eat the snow. So we made sweet snow and sweet blood. The key for the blood is your belief that it is. It looks like real blood only at a temperature of forty degrees—it's a beet-and-orange reduction, and the texture, I promise, is exactly the same as blood. So we're not telling people that it's not real blood. It's meant to be provocative. But it's very delicious."

"Is there anything that didn't work out?" I asked. "Something that you tried and failed at?"

"A lot," he said. "One of the first things that Ferran asked me to do was create hot ice cream."

Hot ice cream! He nodded gloomily. "You would look at it—ice cream—and then you would taste it, and it would be hot. Every year I thought I had it! But I never had it. What we discovered was to use an ice-cream machine but invert it, so that it was pumping in hot air, and to use gelatin to get the form. That was as close as we could get. It's still this idea that we have." He shook his head. "A sort of dream. I have a lot of them."

By now, the story of elBulli has become part of modern cooking lore: how the combination of science and culinary curiosity created a real revolution in cooking, with high-tech equipment borrowed from the mass-produced-food industry for the purpose of wild, semisurrealist picture-making. And how, at the height of this fame, Ferran announced that he would close the restaurant in 2012 and devote himself to "a foundation for pure research in cooking." (What admirers of elBulli often forget to tell you is that it is a very hard place to get to. You weave your way there on narrow, winding cliff roads along the Spanish coast. The terror of the ascent surely adds to the delight of the arrival.)

If Albert is a Braque—a stolid man with a poetic imagination—Ferran is very much a Picasso, a grand maître who knows it. Like every first-rate artist, he has the kind of immense egomania that is oddly impersonal: his greatness is so uncontroversial to him that it is an act of generosity to try to limit it in words and dates. There is a certain kind of artistic egotism that is enveloping rather than narrowing: less "All I care about is my work" than "If you only cared about my work as much as I do, you would be as routinely elated as I am."

I asked dutiful questions about the history, and the future, of desserts, and Ferran responded instantly, in Spanish, not with the guarded caution of his younger brother or the academic certainty of Jordi Butrón but with eager, nodding, flowing eloquence. His guttural, consonant-driven Catalan accent made everything he said sound as though he were murmuring a list of Jewish holidays. "Let us go all the way back to Carême and then come forward to us! Hmm. The problem! The problem! The phrase 'molecular gastronomy' I don't like. 'Techno-emotional'? I'm not crazy about it, but let's use it. Now let's look at the history of desserts."

He called for paper and pen from one of his countless earnest, eager apprentices, and began to draw floridly and actively, making swooping charts of the history of cuisine, filled with Venn-diagram-like circles enclosing famous names and long arcs and arrows connecting one significant moment with the next. He drew as he talked—I realized that he was the inventor of the Barcelona diagram—and soon turned to sketching boxes and vectors on a large sheet of white paper.

"Carême, you see, was a pastry chef," he said. "Everybody thinks of him as a cook, but he was actually a pastry chef. Sugar?" He took two for his coffee. "He was the best pastry chef in France. Now, come to our own time, who's the great innovator?" Dramatic pause. "Michel Guérard!" He trumped with the name of the chef best known as a father of nouvelle cuisine, in the 1970s. "And he was a pastry chef, too. Very interesting that two revolutionaries have been pastry chefs. Whatever they've tried to do, they've tried this symbiosis of the savory world and the sweet. Escoffier, more than being a cook, was a codifier. I don't know why it played out this way, but it did. Since then, Gaston Lenôtre and Pierre Hermé. And, after that, nothing, really. It's been consolidated, but nothing very new came out of it in France. Why did Michel Guérard begin this revolution? Because he was a pastry chef, and the pastry chef was the second-class citizen of the kitchen. He did it to show 'I am a cook.' It's the thinking of a pastry chef that initiated the revolution of nouvelle cuisine!" He looked at me keenly, to see if I was following.

He was, in truth, speaking so quickly, and mentioning so many names and concepts, that I was a bit confused by the argument—until I looked down at the paper where he had been drawing the complex flowchart of French dessert-making. The point it conveyed was simple: there had really been just two hinge points in French cooking—Carême's early-nineteenth-century revolution, and Michel Guérard's twentieth-century one—and both had come from pastry cooks escaping the limits of pastry. Pastry-makers were natural magicians, and magic in cooking would always come from them.

"So, now, here's elBulli!" He drew some more. Then he called for one of the many illustrated books that document the ascension of elBulli, and flipped through its pages for examples. "We started taking things from the sweet world and moving them to the savory: a sorbet, or a savory ice cream," he said. "One early savory ice cream was a Parmesan ice cream, in 1994. It extends an incredible dialogue between me and Albert. One of the important themes for us was about construction: how do you construct a dessert? This opened us up to the whole question of tiramisu—opened an incredible world to us. Deconstruction began here. Black Forest cake. This is mythical."

He also had a trait I'd noticed in other big artists, and that was the urge to emphasize, a little perversely, the mere pragmatic, working logic of what he'd done. (Back in the seventies in SoHo, Donald Judd and Carl Andre would always shrug and talk about materials found on Canal Street, as though you, too, would have thought of minimalism, given their circumstances and rent.)

"Certain things that we've been using that came from the world of magic—anybody could use these and take them," he said expansively. "What distinguishes us from nouvelle cuisine is that we're deliberately provocative. For a while we were play-ing with this idea of provoking 'outside the plate.' Cuisine is this multisensual experience—so we made a balloon, and put in the balloon the scent of an orange, broke it, and you would have this dish of orange underneath. We had a plate of mushrooms, and they would spray a pint of forest scent on it! We did a lot like this. Liquid nitrogen in the dining room so you'd see the smoke. And for a while this theatricality was getting away from us. It was driving the customers crazy! Doing it is easy—whether you do it well or not. Or we'd blindfold you. We have fifty thousand of these kinds of ideas. But we just thought, No, this isn't your path."

Turning the pages of the book while drawing rapid diagrams and speaking in even more rapid Spanish, Ferran went on to explain that the true point of the deconstructed dessert was to create a kind of analytic Cubism of the pastry plate. It wasn't an intrinsic part of Black Forest cake's nature that made you want to break it down into bits but that, if you're possessed by the urge to break things down into bits, it's more obvious that you're doing it when you do it to a Black Forest cake. The Cubists used guitars and tables, ordinary still-life objects, for the same reason: you knew what a guitar or a table looked like, and so could see when it didn't look that way. Once the fracture was achieved and accepted, you could move on to your own mythology. "If we make a curry ice cream, and you put mushrooms there, and eel—strange!" he said. "But if you put chicken stock, and coconut, then it's curry."

Were we, I asked, on the verge of entirely breaking down the line between sweet and savory?

He looked at me with delighted triumph. "It can't be that an American is asking me that!" he said. "A hamburger with ketchup and Coca-Cola? That's the most intense symbiosis of sweet and savory imaginable. It's your cultural theme."

As Lisa and I approached the door, Ferran grabbed the pages of diagrams and handed them to me for further study. He continued brooding on the subject of dessert, explaining that for him the big question was not that of sweet and savory but that of sequence. "What matters is how we end the meal. With a surprise? A flourish? Reassurance? That's the big question about dessert: how do we close out dinner? How do we finish the meal?"

He had a pensive look, and I couldn't help asking him about Albert's unmade dream. His face came alive again. "You mean hot ice cream? Yes. Yes! But . . . it's hard! Ice cream is ice cream because it's cold. But gelatin is the same way: gelatin used to be both gelatin and cold. There must be some way. We'll solve it. We will." Then he signed the historical diagrams in caps, FERRAN ADRIÀ.

Dinner at elBulli that night surpassed expectations, and really did earn for Adrià the role or title of artist: craft can make the difficult seem easy, but art alone makes the excessive seem elemental. What sounds crazily complex and over the top on paper—say, goat-brain tartar with eel—seems delicious and even obvious on the plate. Instead of the sudden drop-off between the savories and the sweets, there was a slowly shading spectrum, over twenty-five or thirty small dishes, from savory to sweet, with the two intermingled. Carême's great artificial act, the one with which French cuisine began—the grassy herbs to one side for the meats; the piquant spices off to the other for the sweets—was broken, and everything was mixed again. There was flash-fried shrimp with cayenne pepper infused and a spun-sugar design above; Iberian smoked ham with a ginger-caramel reduction—and then that Parmesan ice cream with chervil and freeze-dried wild strawberries.

Two dishes stood out as models of sweet and savory so simply mixed they became a new kind of cooking: a dish of wild strawberries presented in a bouillon of wild hare—the joke, of course, as the server explained, is that the hares in the wild eat wild strawberries (though not, he hastened to add, these particular ones), so we taste them twice—and a plate of scampi infused with sweet ginger with sesame seeds beneath. Where dinner at, say, Thomas Keller's Per Se can be like a day at the library under the supervision of a monk, dinner at elBulli really is like a visit to Willy Wonka's candy factory. A sense of fun pervades the place. It is *happy* food—the one true "dessert" is a "frozen pond," which is simply a sheet of hyper-hard ice infused with mint. The "molecular" label doesn't capture the sense of play, extended into the sober domain of fancy food, that gives the place its savor. The illustrated recipe books, no matter how lavishly published, reveal little, because, as with all magicians, the "gimmicks" are cheap and readily available, and break down into foams and powders and frozen shells. Guile and mischief, more than molecular logic, is the guiding principle.

The test of a meal is the talk it makes, hot air rising from the diners, and the room mostly hummed. It was sad to think that there would be only another few hundred days of this, but wise in another way: Alain Senderens, Alain Dutournier, both of them provocateurs and originators in their day, declined into gentle excellence. Now, no one will be able to shake his head and say, elBulli isn't what it used to be—which means that it will become, in memory, by a fixed rule of recall even better than it was.

And at the elBulli table, I began to see at last *why* the slow-food movement and techno-emotional cooking, though seemingly based on different premises—one reactionary and anti-technology, the other all technology and naïve futurism—have lived together at our mental table, as a combined part of the moral taste of our time, so easily. The Hestias of the Hearth, following Alice Waters, and the Willy Wonkas of the Chemistry Set, following the Adriàs, were really united in another way, both allied as makers of true slow food. In a world given over to all forms of speed—speed-of-light communication in every sphere, where anything you write electronically is available everywhere on the planet immediately—the commitment to taking time is itself a commitment to a coherent set of values. You could go to Per Se, or you could eat at Chez Panisse, but in either case what you're doing is going to eat. You're not going to eat on your way somewhere else, or before some other thing, or hoping to get done in time for *Dancing with the Stars*. You're going to eat, in a world where you mostly eat to go.

The common shape of time was the same, and the real end of dinner is to articulate time. (Or, when it's bad, to announce new kinds of tedium.) The point of eating is to slow down life long enough to promote what Brillat-Savarin called, with simple charm, good cheer. It doesn't just take time, but *makes* time—carves out evenings, memories. That's what Darwin meant when he said that we recall good dinners as happy days, wrapped like flies in a spider's web by the silk of memory. Good dinners *become* happy days. Both Willy and the Hestias do that with splendor and certainty, in a time when no one else does it quite so much. They ask for your attention, not just for your appetite.

A meal at elBulli showed that the French line setting off savory from sweet could be entirely bypassed, like other French defensive lines in history, by mechanical ingenuity, speed, and superior strategic thinking. But I was still interested in desserts as such, pure desserts, desserts that always ended sweetly. And so the next morning Lisa and I traveled to meet with the young Mozart of pastry, Jordi Roca, at the restaurant he runs with his brothers, in Girona, in northeast Catalonia, about an hour from elBulli.

Where elBulli is old-fashioned and even a little run-down, as though to frame the hypermodernity of its plates all the more sharply, El Celler de Can Roca, to give the full name of the Roca brothers' three-star place, is of exquisitely contemporary design, with small groves of poplar trees contained within the zigzagged green-glass walls of the restaurant proper. A long, low-lying wine cellar sits just across an allée of trees from the restaurant, and in it the sommelier, Josep Roca, the second brother—the oldest brother, Joan, is in the kitchen—keeps his wines in tenderly nourishing musical environments, playing recorded melodies in the caves: Bach for the champagne, romantic cello music for the Burgundys, and local guitar music for the Spanish wines.

Jordi, the baby brother, is still young-looking—startlingly so—at thirty-two. Dreamy of visage and gentle of voice, he came out of the kitchen before lunch, tentative and eager and even a little wide-eyed in his chef whites, to talk about his dessert work. He had inherited the pastry station, he admitted, because it was the younger brother's station, but he thought that there was room to grow there. "Desserts in Catalonia don't have the weight of the past," he explained, in the French he had learned during several *stages*. "We had *crema Catalana*. A cake or two or three. So we felt free to invent and compete."

After an apprenticeship at elBulli, he realized that his preoccupation was with scent. "That was something that hadn't really been realized enough in desserts, I thought: the power of aromas. We had this new machine that could extract essential oils, and I began to play with it. I began making perfumed desserts." He laughed. "I went to Sephora and found the most wonderful aromas in all the women's perfumes. And I started making desserts built around their smells. Calvin Klein–like aromas. I wanted to make something as wonderful to taste as Chanel perfume was to smell. For me, that's where all that new chemistry and equipment helps. We have the machine to extract essential oils. Another just for smokes. Working with smokes and smells, this has a—fragile aspect? Sense memory extends to the heart of who we are. I think that there's a freedom there, for a certain delicacy." He shrugged. "You'll see," he said.

Did he have a dream dessert that he had tried and failed to perfect? He nodded. "Yes, there's one I'm working on. I haven't really . . . perfected it yet. You see, I'm a big fan of F. C. Barcelona"—the soccer team—"and I wanted to make a dessert that would re-create the emotions Lionel Messi feels when he scores a goal." Messi is the great Argentine striker who stars for Barcelona. "I feel I'm close. Could I try it out on you at the end of lunch?"

The desserts came around. And here was the real thing, here were true desserts: not dancing nimbly on the edge between sweet and salty, like Albert Adrià's, but plain old-fashioned sweets touched by the invention and audacity of a liberated imagination. There was watermelon rind with bitter almonds and tarragon; a hot lemon-mint eucalyptus liquid that, as it was poured, solidified into a small, sweet iceberg. Then lemon custard and granita, with the floral scents in a small cup alongside: you eat and smell by turns. Lemon zest, pure distilled mint flowers. And then an apricot ice-cream bombe with a spun-sugar shell, apricot foam inside, and an apricot sabayon inside that.

Finally, the server arrives with the Messi dessert, as Jordi fusses anxiously in the background. He presents half of a soccer ball, covered with artificial grass; the smell of grass perfumes the air. On the "grass" is a kind of delicately balanced, S-shaped, transparent plastic teeter-totter with three small meringues on it, and a larger white-chocolate soccer ball balancing them on a protruding platform at the very end. A white candy netting lies on the grass near the white-chocolate ball.

Then, with a cat-that-swallowed-the-canary smile, the server puts a small MP3 player with a speaker on the table. He turns it on and nods.

An announcer's voice, excited and frantic, explodes. Messi is on the move. "Messi turns and spins!" the announcer cries, and the roar of the crowd at the Bernabéu Stadium, in Madrid, fills the table. The server nods, eyes intent. At the signal, you eat the first meringue.

"Messi is alone on goal!" the announcer cries. Another nod, you eat the next scented meringue. "Messi shoots!" A third nod, you eat the last meringue, and, as you do, the entire plastic S-curve, now unbalanced, flips up and over, like a spring, and the white-chocolate soccer ball at the end is released and propelled into the air, high above the white candy netting.

"MESSI! GOOOOOAL!" The announcer's voice reaches a hysterical peak and, as it does, the white-chocolate soccer ball drops, strikes, and breaks through the candy netting into the goal beneath it, and, as the ball hits the bottom of a little pit below, a fierce jet of passion-fruit cream and powdered mint leaves is released into your mouth, with a trail of small chocolate pop rocks rising in its wake. Then the passion-fruit cream settles, and you eat it all, with the white-chocolate ball, now broken, in bits within it.

You feel . . . something of what Messi must feel: first, the overwhelming presence of the grass beneath his feet (he's a short player); then the tentative elegance of acquired skill, represented by the stepladder of the perfumed meringues; and, finally, the infantile joy, the childlike release, of scoring, represented by the passion-fruit cream and the candy-store pop rocks. I saw Jordi watching us from the kitchen entrance. He had the anxious-shading-into-delighted look that marks the artist.

In those le Carré and Deighton thrillers, the things the antihero learns on the other side of the curtain tend to be brooded on stoically rather than applied with spirit. What you saw on the other side of the curtain stays there. What I learned in Barcelona was that genius can produce what it chooses—but not much of it was really applicable to the table I sit at or the kitchen I cook in. It wasn't just that you can't do this at home; it's that home is the last place you were ever meant to do this. The earlier great changes in cooking were a kind of baroque template, suitable for simplification—you made haute cuisine with cream and butter, nouvelle cuisine by leaving them out—but "techno-emotional" cooking was created only for the three-star stage. It was pure performance, cabaret cooking, the table as stadium show. As often happens with the avant-gardists, by advancing the form they had only deepened the crisis. There was nothing that you could do with what I had learned, other than serve cake and ice cream while the soccer game was on, which we knew how to do already.

And yet something, at least, came out of the quest. I invited Bill Yosses, the White House chef, over for dinner, and laid a small trap for him: I was going to make my mother's apricot soufflé, and see if I could achieve the zone. Over dinner, we talked desserts some more: the mysteries of plating, the needs of family life.

Then I led him into the kitchen, showed him the apricot-purée base, the transparent egg whites in the unlined copper bowl, the five soufflé dishes waiting to be buttered. He murmured instruction. "Butter around the outer edge, too," he urged. "All the way around the outer rim like this. Make a small space—climb up to grow up. And then put the dishes in water: not a bain-marie or anything deep, just a shallow tray of water. You don't want to lower the temperature too much."

He watched as I beat the egg whites and they thickened and turned opaque. "Do you know why you use unlined copper?" he asked. "It's for the static electricity. A small electrical storm going off in the bowl." An act of God, making clouds of white.

We approached the zone, the perfect moment of stiff-but-not-too-stiff peaks. ("DO NOT UNDERBEAT / DO NOT OVER-BEAT!") I beat. He waited. I beat some more. He nodded—go on. I went on, far longer than I usually would, and then he tapped my shoulder. There! That was it. The zone was there: not the gauzy, moist shiny area where I used to stop but a step above.

"I remember how there was one kid at Le Cirque back when who just did this," Yosses said. "Starting around five-thirty, he had the *bouilli* or the soufflé base, and he beat egg whites all night."

As we put the soufflés in the oven, he said, "Fifteen minutes," and when fifteen minutes had passed he held his hand above them, to measure the heat rising, as much as the texture firming, and nodded one last time.

They were perfect. The apricot intensity shone; the egg

whites' neutrality and airiness softened and lifted it; the hotness gave an edge of taste delight that is always allied to danger, even tiny danger. A thousand small adjustments turn rules into skills, and then three smaller ones turn real skills into art. With Yosses's help, I had taken something elaborate and made it something that seemed elemental. The primate instinct—get sweets at any price—had been turned into this polished performance. The virginal egg whites, the electric storm that whitened them and made them stiff: the perfect zone was drier and older than I had imagined. You could beat them more and they would be better.

The quest I had undertaken showed, at least, that whatever makes us age, it is not the sugar that we eat. It is the years that are passing. The older we get, the harder we work at everything, even our pleasures. We have to follow the recipes more precisely, put in a sixteenth of an inch of water, if only because we notice our failures more. And yet in return we can sense at last what the pleasures truly are, and where they come from. The fictions that force the feelings become ever dearer to our lives the more fictional we know them to be. Dessert is completely inessential to life; we can do without it; sugar blew in on a bad wind from the Caribbean not so long ago, and we can do without *it*. And yet it is completely at the center of life, complex and rich enough to make something that touches the edge of art, or at least of stage magic. You never need to eat it; you never miss a chance. It sits as a joke on a primate trait—the chimps that kept after sweetness all the time, like the ones that hungered for sex all the time, ended up making more of themselves than the next bunch of apes—and yet it makes this apricot soufflé, smelling like the kitchen you grew up in. It is the most particular thing; it is the most abstract and conceptual thing. A line of verse enters your head: "Though life is fading / love resists / though sweets are ending / sweet persists." Sweetness exists outside its objects, as Shakespeare's favorite adjective, as an idea of the best thing on the table, which, to fully get, we have first to give up.

Ferran's question is still the one that counts: how do we finish the meal? But then, how do we finish anything? At least I know now that if we beat hard enough, and long enough, and do both more than we ever thought we would have to, we might yet arrive at a lighter end.

18

LAST E-MAIL TO ELIZABETH PENNELL

Dear E.P.:

I want to tell you, finally, about something that happened last summer. Yes, I have gone back to writing to you, my imaginary confidante, whatever you may have thought of Russian Jews on Locust Street in Philadelphia. You were wrong about them, but you were right to be a feminist food critic at a time when no other existed, and to demand that our ancestors be right about everything in advance is as mad as hoping that our descendants will think us right about everything in retrospect. Life is too short, and the room too empty, if we fail to forgive our predecessors everything short of the unforgivable. (What is unforgivable? Ah! That I shall save for another book.) There's no winning. But there *is* trying.

And there is dining. I had been haunted enough by Jacques Decour and his last letter, that the obvious thought occurred even to me. We were going back to Paris for a July visit, and I wondered if perhaps the auberge that he mentioned—the Auberge des IV Pavés du Roy, whose menu he wanted to leave for his girlfriend—might have left a trace, however remote, on the world's store of information. There must be somewhere in some obscure corner of the scholarly Web a reference to the auberge, I thought. After all, I had found traces of the Omelet King—even the Omelet King's royal omelet pan!

Well, the Auberge des IV Pavés du Roy turns out to have a whole Web page, a menu, a brief history—the works. You can read the menu, the dishes, and see pictures of the place! It turned out to still exist at 55 Avenue du Manet, in Montigny-le-Bretonneux, a small town about an hour outside Paris, not too far from Versailles. Not a well-known small town, or a picturesque one, just a small suburban town. It *must* be the place—how many Auberges des IV Pavés du Roy could there be? So we made a date to go out on a beautiful July Thursday; I discouraged the kids, but they wanted to get out of Paris and the heat, or wanted to be near us, or maybe they were actually interested.

It was a nice place, a very nice place, in that half-in-the-country, half-not-in-the-country way of French inns. It was an old-fashioned stuccoed auberge, with a cast-iron sign hanging out front and a pretty garden in the back, and a children's play set near the garden. The cook was the husband, and the very harried but trying-hard hostess was his wife. There was some kind of local event going on when we arrived, and, puzzled to have taken a reservation all the way from Paris—we had called the day before to confirm and ask the way—Madame had a table for us in the garden. We sat and waited, at first a bit awkwardly—what *were* we doing here, after all?—and then comfortably, as the *commis,* right out of Marcel Pagnol, brought us bread, which reassured the children, and then Sancerre rouge, nicely cold, which reassured the parents. Then the menus came, and *you* know how it is when menus come, Elizabeth, it is hard to stay awkward—the act of ordering, choosing, is itself so touched by hope. I doubt that anyone can completely despair when menus appear. (In movies and television shows, when they want to create a mood of absolute alienation they always set the thing in a cafeteria.)

So we ordered and then we talked, naturally enough, about the Resistance. Luke, now sixteen, asked me if "in the big picture" the Resistance had made any difference. I tried to explain that it all depends what you mean by difference. No, they hadn't really done much, spending a lot of time on guard against one another's betrayals and fighting among themselves, socialists against Christian Gaullists and communists, who were courageous but committed to Stalin, against everyone else. And they were the victims of horrible retaliation by the Germans, satanic cruelty even in a relatively placid occupation zone like France. So, no, they hadn't really made much of a difference to the outcome of the war.

But in another way they had made all the difference. They had saved the honor of France, which was not just an abstraction but a living reality; you could hold your head up after the war and say, Some people didn't submit, and that was true, too. They had acted with so much courage—courage for its own sake, courage because you could be courageous and couldn't live with yourself without it—that they had supplied a kind of moral pattern for the rest of the century. Their fiction had become a feeling. Any country that could produce men and women as brave as Jacques Decour didn't have to feel lost, or ashamed of itself. So it depends what you mean by difference, I said, and then I realized that it didn't depend on what you meant by difference so much as on what you thought the big picture was.

Then, at Olivia's insistence, I narrated, rather lamely, a history of the French Revolution, getting half of it wrong, but the essential point—that what started in glory ended in chaos, and what began in a declaration of all the rights of man ended in a denial of every one; but that the articulation of what was right was either no help at all or a constant source of hope—was there. It depends on how you see it. Brillat-Savarin's eternal point was that at some level it didn't matter, that the hub-bub of the Palais Royal created a series of values—of which the restaurant we were sitting in now was a modest but real microcosm—that endured whatever squalid mess the politicians made of things, and that that was the right point to make.

How was the food? The food was fine. Sixty years ago it would have seemed *very* good. Seventy years ago, Decour's time, it would have seemed like the best food in the world. We had filets of beef with green peppercorn sauce, and sautéed potatoes—they used to do *pommes soufflées* at these places, but no more, *I* know why—and green beans. The desserts were *really* good: Luke said that the profiteroles were the best he had ever had, and he is one who has eaten many profiteroles. I had an old classic, apple sorbet doused with Calvados, the kind of thing that is so hard to find these days. It was the kind of lunch Liebling writes about longingly from his New York of Schrafft's and Longchamps and chicken à la king and pot pie (not that these are not good things in their way), and with the tastes of Barcelona still sharp on my lips—gingered scampi and smoked eel and brains—I knew that it was old-fashioned. Still, it was the fashion that I, too, had loved of old.

When lunch was ending with those good profiter-oles and an extra glass of Calvados—Martha gave me the are-you-really-*sure*-about-that? look that I think they hand out, secretly, on the wedding day, to big eaters' spouses—we explained why we had come, and Madame explained that yes, it was the same place, and yet it wasn't the same place. That is, it *was* the same place—it had been the Auberge des IV Pavés du Roy for a half century, one could see the photographs of the old place inside—but when they had expanded the highway back in the early seventies, they had had to move it back some ways from the road. So though the same it *was* different and (one hoped) even better. They did have beautiful black-and-white photographs up inside, of the place as it had been back in the thirties. It had been very chic then for people to come out from Paris. Madame shrugged. (Here is one of those photographs, the auberge just as it was when Jacques Decour came here.)

In a way it was truer to the spirit of the adventure—righter— that it be the same and different, too. Food, after all, can't be held in place. But the front is the same, and the place is, more or less, the same, and the town is the same, and the arrangement, tables inside, tables out in the garden, is the same.

Then Madame said, with real eagerness, "Did you find us on the Internet?" I could see that she hoped we did, with visions of Americans surfing the Web to this spot and crowding in for lunch. Martha told her the long story, eagerly—about Jacques Decour and the last letter and our search for him. It was well told, as by one oiled—not indecorously, just a little productively—by more red Sancerre than she is used to.

"Ah. So you didn't find us on the Internet," Madame said at last, disappointed a little. A lot. But then, being polite, she said she'd like a copy of whatever it is I was writing, which she shall have, whether she really wanted it or not.

I reread Decour's last letter when we got home to Paris, and realized then that I had missed something essential. In a way, as Huck Finn would say, I missed the whole blame point, missed it a thousand miles. Decour was a communist, a Marxist, and buried in the letter is the clear cool claim that he is talking about food because he refuses to talk about God. *Vous savez que je m'attendais depuis deux mois à ce qui m'arrive ce matin, aussi ai-je eu le temps de m'y préparer, mais comme je n'ai pas de religion, je n'ai pas sombré dans la méditation de la mort; je me considère un peu comme une feuille qui tombe de l'arbre pour faire du terreau. La qualité du terreau dépendra de celle des feuilles.* "You know that I've been waiting for two months for what's going to happen to me this morning, and that I have had time to prepare myself, but, as I have no religion, I have not fallen into a meditation on death; I consider myself a little as a leaf who falls from the tree to make the soil. The quality of the soil depends on that of the leaves." It is a nonbeliever's claim, quietly defiant. *As I have no religion, I don't think of death.* The questions of food rise from that context.

Faith in history, not to mention in the Utopian state, has vanished, in various ways, noisy and silent, but the relation between the end of faith in Heaven and the assertion of faith in something else has not. The continuity of life is won in the face of time and tragedy, and the rituals of an inn in the country is one of the places that we locate it. We find it here. I don't believe in a good God, and I don't believe, as Decour must have, in History. But I believe in the inn of the four seasons: that Decour went there with the girl he loved, that he left her the menu when he knew the Nazis were going to kill him, that it has moved, and not moved, been rebuilt and is still the same, so that we can eat there now. They could walk in now, and be happy again in the garden. It would all be different but they would still be at home. We walked under the sign, and contemplated the connections. He had thought about *that* in his last moments. That the table came last to mind is another way in which the table always comes first.

Did I tell you that I found a photograph of him? Here he is. He looks terrifically elegant, doesn't he? Oddly humorous, and he seems to be making a joke with his fork above those two bowls. What's he doing, exactly? I think he may have a little bit of pasta in one bowl, and the sauce in the other—a French manner of eating pasta that I've often noticed, more controlled and precise than the Italian way. He's certainly engaged in a small, sweet joke about eating, whatever the joke may be. I look at the picture often, and wonder. In his three-piece suit and neat parted hair, who could imagine that he would choose the fate he chose, and try to keep the pleasures of the table present in his mind even as he did? In any case there he is, and there we are, and whatever connection there may be, straight or crooked, occult or true, it passed across and around a table. For people who believe in this life alone, trying to decide how best to live, questions of food will always be of great importance.

That night, back in Paris, none of us were really hungry—I can't eat more than one real French meal a day, who can?—but by ten-thirty or so, still bright in the Palais Royal, where we were, luckily, blessedly, staying in a friend's beautiful apartment, I did a quick dish of spicy rice and beans, a dish that the children love, and that Martha and I associate with one of the worst nights of our life, and then with its happy ending—a night when Luke was desperately sick with what turned out to be

salmonella, food poisoning, and we had carried him to Necker, the children's hospital, and they had made the diagnosis and had prescribed drugs for it. We had gotten him home—I had raced to an all-night pharmacy on Montparnasse, I think it was, and then given it to him and—miracle!—he seemed almost instantly better. We tucked him in, and, after a day's pain, we realized suddenly that we were hungry. And I made rice and spicy beans, and we were happy.

I looked out on the beautiful placid gardens, where the great comic adventure of the restaurant had begun two centuries before, when Chantoiseau had opened his little bouillon parlor and Brillat-Savarin had praised it, and where so many pilgrims had come since to have dinner and find love, or something.

What is it that we want from eating? Comfort? Absolutely. A symbol of love shared? For sure. But above all, food matters for us as a daily symbol of the sacred, which means for secular people that it is a kind of sacred-in-itself. Questions of food are all just questions of living refracted outward, like the imaginary mountains explorers see in the Arctic, projections forward of their own ice-breaking boats. The plate of rice and beans, the dumbest thing I do, is also the most blessed, since it sums up in a single spicy point a whole story of our lives, and the intersection of others. We can have our cake and eat it, too, if we are willing to see that the point of having cake is to eat it and accept that then it will be gone. The secret of life is detachment and attachment in equal measure, the cake devoured but still held in our mind.

We are, after all, animals who experience our lives as if we were gods. We eat, burp, grow, shit. And yet we construct from the brutal sensory necessities a shape and a history and a purpose to life; we sit down and choose from the menu. The truth is that we have a hard time treating cooking as an art because it is so easy for us to experience it as a miracle. Dinner is often our brush with Olympus. The gods sat down to dinner twice a day, even though they would live forever if they never ate again.

We eat like animals and dine like . . . well, like demigods at least, minor local deities of minor local shrines. And we have a tragic dimension dignified enough for deities, too, since our animal nature assures that we will not be animals forever. Our knowledge of mortality is the overwhelming fact of our life. We seek for some kind of comfort and escape from that terror, and none is better than the apparent continuities and the small miracle of eating: you *always* do this. You were starving, and now you're not. In the most beautiful of psalms, the shadow of death, whose valley we all walk through, is met by a spread table. It isn't an accident that Jesus' most original act was at a table, too, which seemed so shocking to a peasant honor society, where values depended on clean and unclean. Jesus would eat with *anybody,* whores and tax collectors, Gentiles and tribesmen. What did he eat? We can't be sure, but we know he liked wine enough to make a lot. He ate what he liked where he liked with whom he liked, at a table open to all.

That was what Decour had *really* meant, I think, by "ques-

tions of food" in his letter, and that was why he thought of
them at the very end: it was the closest he could come, as close
as he needed to come, to an idea of the sacred. We have trouble
thinking that food is art, but no trouble at all imagining that
it might be divine. We doubt that Ferran Adrià is as good as
Picasso, but accept that wine might be made the blood of God.
Our difficulty with the idea of food as a fine art is not that we
have trouble elevating it that high; it is that we have difficulty
in making it descend that low. We may not share the particular
sacredness of the particular table—but no one has any difficulty
with the concept: water into wine and wine into blood? Oh, yes,
I get that. Saffron rice and honey and you become a man? How
else? What you eat is how you please omniscient power? It's
obvious, isn't it? There are many metaphysical ideas that bewil-
der even the metaphysicians; the idea that food is the material of
faith is not one of them.

Cooking is the faith that raw ingredients can be conjured
into a nightly miracle. The oldest of all recorded stories is the
story of Enkidu from the epic of Gilgamesh, and it is a story of
the divine power of food and sex and wine to make us human.
Enkidu, a kind of wild, uncivilized ape-man, is saved by a pros-
titute, a member of the oldest profession, or priesthood. "Nothing does Enkidu know of eating bread / and to drink strong
drink he has not been taught," she says. And then "the whore
opened her mouth, saying to Enkidu, 'Eat the bread, O Enkidu,
it is the staff of life; drink the strong drink, it is the custom of
the land.' Enkidu ate bread until he was sated: Of the strong
drink he drank seven goblets. His soul felt free and happy, his
heart rejoiced, and his face shone . . . he anointed himself with
oil and at that moment became a human being."

Eat the bread, O Enkidu, drink the strong drink. Without fixed
faith, we still take hold of food, but we take it where we find
it. Where other times and other tribes have leaped from wine
to God, those of us who no longer have a credible idea of the
sacred reach to the thing itself; the pleasure alone becomes the

point, and its accompaniments—family, an idea of France or Italy, the table of life—become too big to lose. It is not that God is in the details, but that our ability to grasp and discriminate the details gives us something to put in place of God; not that this dish is sacred, but that an idea of the sacred remains somehow residual in the dish.

And so, a short cooking credo, in honor of Enkidu and the whore:

> The four essential savory secrets: anchovies, bacon, cinnamon, saffron. (Add a can of tomatoes, a humble chunk of protein, a neutral starch, and there isn't much else you need.)
> The five humble helpers: frozen peas, canned beans, Karo syrup, packaged gelatin, powdered cornstarch.
> The three miraculous drugs: sugar, caffeine, and spirits.
> The three basic principles. First, the rule of triple action: take something to eat, do something to it, do something else to it, but for God's sake don't do something *else* after that, or if you do, it had better be really worth doing. Then, the rule of four and three: almost everything (salmon, chicken breasts, fish steaks, beef steaks, mushrooms, grilled bread) tastes best if it is sautéed for four hot minutes on one side and then three slightly cooler on the other. Third, the truth of oven extremes: there is no golden mean behind the oven door: let your oven be very hot or rather cool, but never in between.
> And, finally, the truth of taste: taste is a fiction, shaped by a time. But the fiction is not the barrier to the feeling. It's what gives the feeling force. We make up our tastes as we make up our pesto, and it is the making-it-up that makes it matter.

.   .   .

I get blue sometimes, Elizabeth, when I think of the people I've loved who are gone—it gets me blue to think that *you* are dead now. I always get impatient, despairing, when people say that the dead are alive in spirit, or are alive in us. They aren't. The best I can do is to think that they are sleeping off their jet lag in the next bedroom, like furious children giving in at last, but they don't *want* to be in that room. They're angry as hell, because they want to be sitting right here at this table with the rest of us and the best we can do is to have the grace to be furious on their behalf. I am furious on yours. Because I think you would like this rice, these beans, these spices, and see the joke of having them—you a Francophone and English aesthete both—having this dinner at the end of this day, marked by a lunch in the country.

How did I make them? Well, you take onion and turmeric and mix them . . . oh, it's too long to tell, and right in the middle of the recipe is a can of beans, which you open—a tin, as you would have said, which you open with a tin-opener—and while one of the smaller secrets of cooking is that canned beans, drained and salted, are really indistinguishable from slow-cooked beans you do yourself (you know my quixotic views on shell beans), still, do we really want a can of beans being opened and drained in this last, ever-more-elegiac paragraph? Besides, spicy rice and beans is one of those things you have to do mostly by feel and look. More by the spirit than the letter, God knows. I'll show you when I see you.

Reading on the Way Home

Though this book isn't meant to be a scholarly history of the subject, it does draw on scholarly histories, and on the amazing renaissance of academic studies of cooking, culinary, agricultural, and all-around eating history that has appeared in the past quarter-century. This literature hasn't always been neatly integrated into what amateur diners say about food or think they know about it—bringing the two together is one of the purposes of this book. Some of these new studies were books I was asked to review; more often, they were books I found I had to draw on to make sense of my own senses and appetites.

In places, of course, what the scholars know is less profound than what the eaters already experience. The search for the "ideological" or intellectual basis of how we eat and why we eat what we eat can seem remote, since after all, we eat all the time. But we could say the same about breathing, and it is worth knowing something about how our lungs work, and what kind of air is good for them, even while we go on breathing; we don't breathe better, but we might breathe easier. The things we do without thinking are often the things most worth thinking about. If we don't think about them, then the thoughts we have are just the thinking that others have done for us. Good history, even when it's wrongheaded in parts, always clears away myths and puts better stories in their place; every myth cleared away is a spot where common sense can blossom.

Most of the key books receive shout-outs as called for in this book's chapters, but, without even remotely pretending to list all of the books that, passing under my eyes in the past quarter-century, entered my mind and thus these pages, let me try to name some of the most obvious and, mostly, scholarly ones, particularly for those who might want to read more.

On restaurants, their invention and meaning, and the life of Paris around the time of their first appearance, Rebecca Spang's excellent, mind-changing history, *The Invention of the Restaurant: Paris and Modern Gastronomic Culture* (Cambridge: Harvard University Press, 2001), is essential. So is Amy B. Trubek's *Haute Cuisine: How the French Invented the Culinary Profession* (Philadelphia: University of Pennsylvania Press, 2000). The writings of Priscilla Parkhurst Ferguson on the birth of the French food "field" (or scene) are indispensable, particularly her *Accounting for Taste: The Triumph of French Cuisine* (Chicago: University of Chicago Press, 2004). W. Scott Haine's *The World of the Paris Café: Sociability Among the French Working Class, 1789–1914* (Baltimore: Johns Hopkins University Press, 1996) is a mine of information (though he draws the lines between café, bistro, and brasserie too tightly). In French on the same subject, and just as helpful, is *Des Tavernes aux Bistrots* by Luc Bihl-Willette (Lausanne: Editions L'Age d'Hommes, 1997). I also relied on Andrew P. Haley's *Turning the Tables: Restaurants and the Rise of the Middle Class, 1880–1920* (Chapel Hill, NC: University of North Carolina Press, 2011).

Giles MacDonogh has taken the two great gastronomes, and inventors of food writing and brought them out of legend into history in his *Brillat-Savarin: The Judge and His Stomach* (London: J. Murray, 1992) and *A Palate in Revolution: Grimod de La Reynière and the Almanach des Gourmands* (London and New York: Robin Clark, 1987). The best version of Brillat-Savarin's book for those who read French is the 1975 edition (Paris: Hermann) with a "reading" by Roland Barthes, by far the best thing ever written about Brillat or the birth of gastronomy; in English, the best edition is still M.F.K. Fisher's translation (New York: Harcourt Brace Jovanovich, 1978). In French, Francois-Regis Gaudry's *Mémoires du restaurant: histoire illustrée d'une invention française* (Geneva: Aubanel, 2006); Alain Huetz de Lemps and Jean-Robert Pitte, *Les Restaurants dans le Monde et a travers les ages* (Grenoble: Editions Glenat, 1990); and Philippe Alexandre and Beatrix De L'Aulnoit, *Le Roi Carême* (Paris: Albin Michel, 2003) are all very fine. About Carême, the first great cook, one should also read Ian Kelly's *Cooking for Kings: The Life of Antonin Carême, the First Celebrity Chef* (New York: Walker and Company, 2003). And I should add that the very first book I ever published, in collaboration with the artist (and best high-school friend) Jack Huberman was a cartoon life of Carême, *Voilà, Carême! The Gastronomic Adventures of History's Greatest Chef* (New York: St. Martin's, 1980)—let me know if you can find a copy! It was while researching that book that I first encountered so many others.

The great Robert Courtine of *Le Monde* had tragically ugly politics when it counted, but his books on the history of French cooking are indispensable, particularly his *Le Ventre De Paris: de la Bastille à l'étoile—des siècles d'appétit* (Paris: Perrin, 1985), and his *Anthologie De La Littérature Gastronomique: Les Ecrivans à Table* (Paris: Editions de Trevise, 1970). The last is one of my favorite books; the opening epigraph to this book, from Léon Abric, comes from there.

About the history of recipes, I recommend the chewy *The Recipe Reader: Narratives, Contexts, Traditions,* edited by Janet Floyd and Laurel Foster (Aldershot: Ashgate Publishing Limited, 2003), which includes, among other good things, a Talia Schaffer essay on Elizabeth Pennell that first made me aware of her. See also Sandra Sherman's *The Invention of the Modern Cookbook* (Santa Barbara, CA: Greenwood Press, 2010).

On France, its cuisine and its crisis, see Michael Steinberger,

Au Revoir to All That: Food, Wine, and the End of France (New York: Bloomsbury, 2009), as well as Patric Kuh's *The Last Days of Haute Cuisine* (New York: Viking, 2001). For a sort of defense of the state of the art there's Hervé This and Pierre Gagnaire, *Cooking: The Quintessential Art* (Berkeley and Los Angeles: University of California Press, 2008). My friend Benedict Beauge's *Le Gourmand des Quatre Saisons* and his wonderful *Aventures de la cuisine française* (both Paris: Nil editions, 1999) are a defense of French traditions and a critique of them, often on the same page.

On questions of wine, in addition to the historical books mentioned in the text, I turn to Rachel Herz's *The Scent of Desire* (New York: Harper Perennial, 2008) and to Lawrence Osborne's *The Accidental Connoisseur* (New York: North Point Press, 2004). Maynard A. Amerine and Edward B. Roessler's *Wines: Their Sensory Evaluation* (San Francisco: Freeman & Company, 1976) is also a lot of fun. On spices, including sugar, and their history, there is Wendy Woloson's *Refined Tastes: Sugar, Confectionery and Consumers in Nineteenth-Century America* (Baltimore: Johns Hopkins University Press, 2002), and Nicholas Whittaker's *Sweet Talk: The Secret History of Confectionery* (London: Gollancz, 1998) and, more far reaching, Andrew Dalby's *Dangerous Tastes: The Story of Spices* (Berkeley and Los Angeles: University of California Press, 2000) and, most stimulating of all, Wolfgang Schivelbusch's *Tastes of Paradise: A Social History of Spices, Stimulants and Intoxicants* (New York: Vintage, 1993).

On larger, more ultimate if moony questions of What It All Means for Man, I learned from James E. McWilliams's *A Revolution in Eating: How the Quest for Food Shaped America* (New York: Columbia University Press, 2005), Richard Wrangham's *Catching Fire: How Cooking Made Us Human* (New York: Basic Books, 2009), and Tom Standage's *An Edible History of Humanity* (New York: Walker, 2009). The great Canadian scholar Margaret Visser's many writings on the rituals of eating are essential, too, though for some reason I haven't found the occasion to quote them nearly as often as I read them. Inspiring studies in the anthropology of the table, I'd be glad if some subtle shared Canadian hue colors every one of these pages. I'd particularly single out her *The Rituals of Dinner: The Origins, Evolution, Eccentricities, and Meaning of Table Manners* (New York: Penguin, 1992). A. J. Liebling's *Between Meals* remains the model. It seems only right, and fit, that I first encountered Jacques Decour, and his last letter, in Liebling's great, now overlooked anthology of French Resistance writing, *The Republic of Silence* (New York: Harcourt Brace and Company, 1947).

Darra Goldstein's extraordinary journal *Gastronomica* has become a constant resource for anyone concerned with the higher history of the higher (and lower) cooking; I'm happy and proud to say that the chapter on the problem of taste, and its history, in this book began life as the keynote lecture at a symposium at Williams College on the occasion of *Gastronomica*'s tenth birthday.

And in addition to the dedicatees, especial thanks to the cooks who have illuminated my life, and made me always aware that beneath all conversation and arguments are the plain facts of the kitchen, and among them most of all Peter Hoffman, Dan Barber, and Ruthie Rogers. My thanks to my first family, the original table, Mom Myrna, Dad Irwin, Alison, Morgan, Blake, Hilary, Melissa; I still set a table for eight in my mind. (In memoriam: Eugenio Donato.) And to George Andreou, who composed the menu, and Henry Finder, who tasted all the plats. And thanks, too, to Lydia Buechler at Knopf, and to my indispensable and alarmingly brilliant trio of assistant- apprentices who have occupied the lion's chair in the hallway while this book was being written—who dug out books, made lists, and read chapters and, for this one, actually tested recipes: Rebecca Cooper, Madeline Schwartz, and, especially, Ariel Knutson.

Permissions and Credits

ALSO BY ADAM GOPNIK

ANGELS AND AGES

A Short Book about Lincoln, Darwin, and the Birth of the Modern Age

In this captivating double life, Adam Gopnik searches for the men behind the icons of emancipation and evolution. Born by cosmic coincidence on the same day in 1809 and separated by an ocean, Lincoln and Darwin coauthored our sense of history and our understanding of man's place in the world. Here Gopnik reveals these two men as they really were: family men and social climbers, ambitious manipulators and courageous adventurers, grieving parents and brilliant scholars. Above all, we see them as thinkers and writers, making and witnessing the great changes in thought that mark truly modern times.

History/Biography

THROUGH THE CHILDREN'S GATE

A Home in New York

Not long after Adam Gopnik returned to New York at the end of 2000 with his wife and two small children, they witnessed one of the great and tragic events of the city's history. In his sketches and glimpses of people and places, Gopnik builds a portrait of our altered New York: the changes in manners, the way children are raised, our plans for and accounts of ourselves, and how life moves forward after tragedy. Rich with Gopnik's signature charm, wit, and joie de vivre, here is the most underexamined corner of the romance of New York: our struggle to turn the glamorous metropolis that seduces us into the home we cannot imagine leaving.

Memoir/Essays

VINTAGE BOOKS
Available wherever books are sold.
www.randomhouse.com